MACMILLAN
MUSIC and YOU

Cover Design and Illustration
Heather Cooper

Illustration Credits
Deborah Barnett-Brandt
Karen Bauman
Christian Beauregard
Jerry Dadds
Eldon Doty
Julek Heller
Mangal
Fred Marvin
Bob Masheris
Barbara Maslin
Michael McNelly
Richard Osaka
Deborah Pinkney
Jan Pyk
Doug Rosenthal
Gregg Russitano
Joel Snyder
Cameron Wasson
Larry Winborg
Fred Winkowski
Joe Veno

MACMILLAN
MUSIC and YOU

Barbara Staton, Senior Author
Merrill Staton, Senior Author
Marilyn Davidson
Ann Davis
Nancy Ferguson

Macmillan Publishing Company
New York

Collier Macmillan Publishers
London

ACKNOWLEDGMENTS

Grateful acknowledgment is given to the following authors and publishers. In the case of songs and poems for which acknowledgment is not given, we have earnestly endeavored to find the original source and to procure permission for their use, but without success. Extensive research failed to locate the author and/or copyright holder.

Atheneum for *Music* by Mary O'Neill, from WHAT IS THAT SOUND! Copyright © 1966 Mary O'Neill. Reprinted with permission of Atheneum Publishers, a division of Macmillan, Inc.

Belwin-Mills for *Tzena, Tzena*, music by Issachar Miron and Julius Grossman, lyrics by Mitchell Parish. Copyright © 1950 by Mills Music, Inc. Copyright renewed. Used by permission. All rights reserved. *Scarborough Fair* (as excerpted from SINGING ISLAND by Seeger and MacColl). Copyright © 1968, 1970, Belwin Mills Publishing Corp. Arrangement used by permission.

Bulls-Eye Music Inc. for *Mule Train* by Johnny Lange, Hy Heath, Fred Glickman, from GREAT GOLDEN FOLK SONG SING ALONG. Copyright © 1949, Copyright renewed 1977 by Bulls-Eye Music Inc.

Chappell/Intersong Music Group for the words to *Tumbling Tumbleweeds* by Bob Nolan. Copyright © 1934 by Sunset Music Publishing Corp. Copyright renewed and assigned to Williamson Music Co. All rights administered by CHAPPELL & CO., INC. International Copyright Secured. All rights reserved. Used by permission.

Cherry Lane Music for *Take Me Home, Country Roads* by Bill Danoff, John Denver, Taffy Nivert. Copyright © 1971 Cherry Lane Music Publishing Co., Inc. *Follow Me* by John Denver. Copyright 1969, 1971 Cherry Lane Music Publishing Co., Inc. All rights reserved. Used by permission.

Clara Music Publishing for *Island in the Sun* by Harry Belafonte. Copyright © 1956, 1957 (renewed) by Clara Music Publishing Corp. All rights reserved. Used by permission.

Columbia Pictures Publications for *One Brick at a Time* by Cy Coleman and Michael Stewart. Copyright © 1980 Notable Music Co., Inc. *Threnody for the Victims of Hiroshima* by Krzysztof Penderecki. Copyright © 1961 by DESHON MUSIC, INC. and PWM EDITIONS. All rights reserved. Printed in the U.S.A. Used by permission. *Carol of the Drum* by Katherine K. Davis. © 1941, 1969 MILLS MUSIC, INC.

Marilyn Davidson for the music to *The Horseman*, lyrics by Walter de la Mare. Copyright © 1987 Marilyn C. Davidson.

Erica Whitman Davis for *Time for Acceptance and Love*. Copyright © 1985 by Erica Whitman Davis.

Sean Deibler for *Autumn Canon*. Reprinted by permission of Sean Deibler, the author. Copyright © 1980. All rights reserved.

Randy DeLelles for the musical *Why the Sun and the Moon Live in the Sky* by Randy DeLelles and Jeff Kriske. Library of Congress copyright—registration #PAU 888 256.

Dovan Music for *I Can See Clearly Now* by Johnny Nash. Copyright © 1972 Dovan Music.

Carl Fischer, Inc. for *Let Love Come Near* by Ed Robertson. Copyright © 1975 by Carl Fischer, Inc., New York. International Copyright Secured. Used by permission.

Harper & Row for the text of *Enter This Deserted House* from WHERE THE SIDEWALK ENDS by Shel Silverstein. Copyright © 1974 by Snake Eye Music, Inc. Reprinted by permission of Harper & Row, Publishers, Inc.

Hinshaw Music, Inc. for *The Lion and the Unicorn* by Ed Harris. Copyright © 1982 by Hinshaw Music, Inc. Reprinted by permission.

House of Bryant Publications for *Rocky Top* by Boudleaux Bryant and Felice Bryant. Copyright © 1967 by House of Bryant Publications, P.O. Box 570, Gatlinburg, Tennessee, 37738.

Jeff Kriske for the musical *Why the Sun and the Moon Live in the Sky* by Randy DeLelles and Jeff Kriske. Library of Congress copyright—registration #PAU 888 256.

Lorenz Corporation for the words and arrangement for *Song of Peace* by Jean Sibelius and Leland Issac. Copyright © 1934, stanzas 1 and 2 renewed 1962 by Lorenz Pub. Co.; Copyright © 1968, stanza 3 by Lorenz Pub. Co. Used by permission.

MMB Music Inc. for *Harvest Time* by Tossi Aaron from IN CANON by Erling Bisgaard. Copyright © 1978 Magnamusic/Edition Wilhelm Hansen, St. Louis. Used by permission.

Macmillan for *Night* by Sara Teasdale. Reprinted by permission of Macmillan Publishing Company from COLLECTED POEMS by Sara Teasdale. Copyright © 1930 by Sara Teasdale, renewed 1958 by Morgan Guaranty Trust Co. of N.Y.

Mark Foster Music Co. for *Cotton Eye Joe*, verses 3–6 used by permission of Mark Foster Music Company. *Hanerot Halalu*, arranged by Blanche Chass. Used by permission of Mark Foster Music Company, Box 4012, Champaign, IL 61802.

Copyright © 1991 Macmillan Publishing Company, a division of Macmillan, Inc.
All rights reserved. No part of this book may be reproduced or transmitted in any form or by any means, electronic or mechanical, including photocopying, recording, or by any information storage and retrieval system, without permission in writing from the Publisher.

Macmillan Publishing Company
866 Third Avenue
New York, N.Y. 10022
Collier Macmillan Canada, Inc.

Printed in the United States of America

ISBN: 0-02-295005-2   9 8 7 6 5 4 3 2 1

Edward B. Marks for *Lift Ev'ry Voice and Sing* by J. Rosamond Johnson and J. W. Johnson. Used by permission of Edward B. Marks Music Company.

Marvin Music Co. for *Catch a Falling Star* by Paul Vance and Lee Pockriss. Copyright © 1957 by Marvin Music Company. All rights reserved. International Copyright Secured.

Noteman Press for *A Round Round* from THE HARMONIOUS RECORDER (Soprano Book, Alto Book, and Teacher Edition) by Dorothy Gail Elliott. Used by permission of copyright owner Noteman Press, 2603 Andrea Lane, Dallas, TX 75228.

Prentice-Hall for *Perry Merry Dictum Dominee* from THE KODALY METHOD by Lois Choksy. Copyright © 1974, page 172. Reprinted by permission of Prentice-Hall, Inc., Englewood Cliffs, N.J.

Regent Music Corp. for *Do You Hear What I Hear?* by Noel Regney and Gloria Shayne. Copyright © 1962 by Regent Music Corporation. Reprinted by permission. All rights reserved.

Rockhaven Music for *Sing It All Together*. Copyright © 1987.

The Sacred Music Press for *Promised Land* by Natalie Sleeth. Copyright © 1979, The Sacred Music Press, 501 E. Third Street, P.O. Box 802, Dayton, OH. Used by permission.

St. Nicholas Music Inc. for *Rockin' Around the Christmas Tree* by Johnny Marks. Copyright © 1958 St. Nicholas Music Inc. All rights reserved. Used by permission. This arrangement copyright © 1986 St. Nicholas Music Inc.

Sammy Smile Music for the musical *Song Sleuth* by Harvey Edelman and Neil Fishman. Copyright © 1987 Sammy Smile Music.

Schirmer Music for the melody of *Song of Peace* by Jean Sibelius and Leland Isaac. Used by arrangement with Associated Music Publishers. *We Gather Together* by T. Baker, used by arrangement with G. Schirmer, Inc.

Shawnee Press, Inc. for *Deck the Halls*, arranged by Carl E. Licht. Copyright © 1959, Harold Flammer, Inc. All rights reserved. Used by permission.

Shearer & Rudich for *Sing a Rainbow* by Arthur Hamilton. Copyright © 1955; 1983; MARK VII MUSIC.

Jerry Silverman for *The City Blues* from FOLK BLUES by Jerry Silverman. Copyright © 1983 by Saw Mill Music Corp., 160 High Street, Hastings-on-Hudson, N.Y. International Copyright Secured. Made in U.S.A. All rights reserved.

The Society of Authors for *The Horseman* by Walter de la Mare. The Literary Trustees of Walter de la Mare and The Society of Authors as their representative.

Up With People for *Earthsounds* by Jane Allen, arranged by Carroll Rinehart and Herbert Allen from MAGIC IN THE AIR SONGBOOK. Copyright © 1979 by Up With People. (Registered as an unpublished work, 1976.)

Warner Brothers for *I Shall Sing*, words and music by Van Morrison. Copyright © 1970 WB MUSIC CORP. & CALEDONIA SOUL MUSIC. All rights reserved. Used by permission. *Lean on Me* by Bill Withers. Copyright © 1972 & 1973 INTERIOR MUSIC CORPORATION. All rights reserved. Used by permission. *You've Got a Friend*, words and music by Carole King. Copyright © 1971 by COLGEMS-EMI MUSIC INC., Hollywood, CA. All rights reserved. Used by permission. *That's What Friends Are For* by Carole B. Sager and Burt Bacharach. Copyright © 1982, 1985, WB MUSIC CORP., WARNER-TAMERLANE PUBLISHING CORP., NEW HIDDEN VALLEY MUSIC & CAROLE BAYER SAGER MUSIC. All rights administered jointly by WB MUSIC CORP. & WARNER-TAMERLANE PUBLISHING CORP. All rights reserved. Used by permission. *We Are Family* by Nile Rodgers & Bernard Edwards. Copyright © 1979 CHIC MUSIC, INC. All rights administered by WARNER-TAMERLANE PUBLISHING CORP. All rights reserved. Used by permission.

James Zimmerman for *Orion*. Copyright © 1972 by James Zimmerman. All rights reserved.

LISTENING MAPS: The authors and publisher thank the following for creating these Listening Maps: Marilyn Buckner, pages 65, 138; Dr. Thomas Ashbaugh, page 229.

PHOTOGRAPHY

AFTER IMAGE: © Albert Moldvay, 233R; © Rick Rusing, 233L. © CLARA AICH: 14, 175LC, 216, 297–9 all. ART RESOURCE: Giraudon, 32, 133B, Giraudon/ARS/SPADEM, 135; Scala, 13, 61; Scala/ARS/SPADEM, 219; Estate of Ben Shahn/V.A.G.A., NY, 147. ATLANTA SYMPHONY: 52, 53. THE BETTMANN ARCHIVE, INC.: 69, 82, 156. BLACK STAR: © Ted Spiegel, 202–3B. THE BRITISH LIBRARY: MS Harley (978, f.11,v), 180. CLICK/CHICAGO: © Jim Pickerell, 71B; © Marc Segal, 148–9B; © Bruno Widen, 71 inset. BRUCE COLEMAN: © Nicholas DeVore III, 72; © G.D. Dodge & D.R. Thompson, 108TL; © Frank W. Lane, 198; © John Shaw, 132. CULVER PICTURES, INC.: 60, 139T, 192, LEO DeWYS: © F. Damm, 152–3; © J. Everts, 64; © Everett Johnson, 190R; © Michael Tamborrino, 25B. DOT: © Enrico Ferorelli, 73R; © Dan Nerney, 153. © MARJORY DRESSLER: 19TL,TR, 83 all, 101 all. © SAM EMERSON: 213. © DEBORAH FEINGOLD: 17. FOLIO, INC.: © Peter Garfield, 109LC. FPG: © Farrell Grehan, 88; © E. Nagele, 23T; © R. Thomas, x–1TC. f/STOP PICTURES, INC.: © Clyde Smith, 36 all. DAVID GAHR: 27 both. GAMMA-LIAISON: © Peter Jordan, 4 both. © H.D. HACKETT: 158 both, 161. © RICHARD HAYNES: 19B, 84, 93, courtesy, Parparim Ensemble. © JAMES HEFFERNAN STUDIOS: 122BL, 122–3BC. GRANT HEILMAN: 31TR. IMAGE BANK: © H.J. Anders, 208–9B; © Arthur d'Arazien, 78–9B; © H.W. Hesselmann, 143TR; © Robert Kristofik, 191; © Eric Meola, 78–9TC; © Peter Miller, 78TL; © Paul Slaughter, 221; © John Lewis Stage, 100; © Alvis Upitis, 54–5B. JET PROPULSION LABORATORY: 108–9, 112 inset, 113 all. © WOLFGANG KAEHLER: 223. © BARBARA KIRK: 2. KURZWEIL MUSIC SYSTEMS: 25T. MAGNUM: Dennis Stock, 30–1TC. MANHATTAN VIEWS: © Melabee Miller, 149TR. © 1968 METRO-GOLDWYN-MAYER INC.: 212. THE METROPOLITAN MUSEUM OF ART: Bequest of Mary Stillman Harkness, 1950 (50.145.74, view #2), ITR; Gift of Madame Lilliana Teruzzi, 1971 (1971.4.1–.2), 23C. © LAWRENCE MIGDALE: 142–3TC, 208–9TC, 209R. (Photo credits continued on page 310)

AUTHORS

Barbara Staton has taught music at all levels, kindergarten through college, and for eight years was music television teacher for the State of Georgia. She is author of a four-volume series of books and records designed to teach music concepts through movement. She holds a B.S. degree in Music Education and an M.A. in Dance and Related Arts. Mrs. Staton has written numerous songs for television and recordings and is a composer member of ASCAP.

Dr. Merrill Staton earned his M.A. and Ed.D. degrees from Teachers College, Columbia University, and is nationally known as a music educator, choral conductor, singer, ASCAP composer, and record producer. He has been music director of and has conducted the Merrill Staton Voices on many network TV series and recordings. Dr. Staton has been a leader in the field of music education for over thirty years, and pioneered the use of children's voices on recordings for education.

Marilyn Copeland Davidson has taught music for over thirty years at all levels and is presently teaching elementary general music in Pequannock, New Jersey. She also teaches graduate music education courses. She holds a B.S. degree from Ball State University in Muncie, Indiana, a diploma from the Juilliard School of Music, and has completed the Master Class level of Orff-Schulwerk. She has served as national vice-president and president of the American Orff-Schulwerk Association.

Ann B. Davis has been a music educator for over thirty years. She graduated from Wilson College in Chambersburg, Pennsylvania, with a B.A. degree in English Literature, and did graduate work in Music Education at Teachers College, Columbia University. Mrs. Davis currently teaches general music in the Norwood, New Jersey, public schools, where she conducts children's choruses, chamber and show choirs, string and recorder ensembles, and where she directs ahd produces musicals.

Nancy Ferguson holds a Master of Arts degree from Memphis State University, a B.S. degree in Music Education from Murray State University, and teacher certification in Orff music from the Royal Conservatory of Music in Toronto. Ms. Ferguson has taught music at all levels and has published numerous articles and books on music and music education. She was supervisor of music for the Memphis City Schools for 19 years before assuming her current position as Associate Professor of Music at the University of Arizona, Tucson, Arizona.

SPECIAL CONTRIBUTORS

Dr. Betty Atterbury
Mainstreaming

Marshia Beck
Movement

Mary Frances Early
African American Music

Joan Gregoryk
Vocal Development

János Horváth
Kodály

Virginia Mead
Dalcroze

Mollie Tower
Listening Selections

CONSULTANTS AND CONTRIBUTING WRITERS

Dr. Betty Atterbury
University of Southern Maine
Gorham, Maine

Marshia Beck
Holy Names College
Oakland, California

Diane Bennette
Bergenfield Public Schools
Bergenfield, New Jersey

Teri Burdette
Barnsley Elementary
Rockville, Maryland

Dr. Robert A. Duke
University of Texas
Austin, Texas

Mary Frances Early
Atlanta Public Schools
Atlanta, Georgia

Nancy Ferguson
University of Arizona
Tucson, Arizona

Diane Fogler
Rockaway Township Public Schools
Rockaway, New Jersey

Joan Gregoryk
Chevy Chase Elementary
Chevy Chase, Maryland

János Horváth
University of Calgary
Calgary, Alberta, Canada

Dr. Judith A. Jellison
University of Texas
Austin, Texas

Dr. JaFran Jones
Bowling Green State University
Bowling Green, Ohio

James Kenward
Howe Avenue Elementary
Sacramento, California

Tom Kosmala
Pittsburgh Public Schools
Pittsburgh, Pennsylvania

Virginia Mead
Kent State University
Kent, Ohio

Jane Pippart
Lancaster Public Schools
Lancaster, Pennsylvania

Belle San Miguel-Ortiz
San Antonio Independent School District, San Antonio, Texas

Dr. Susan Snyder
Hamilton Avenue Elementary
Greenwich, Connecticut

Mollie Tower
Austin Independent School District
Austin, Texas

contents

UNIT 1 What Is Music? 1
Musical Elements 2
Music Has Texture 8
Music Has Rhythm and Dynamics 10
Music Has Pitch and Duration 12
Music Has Form 14
Music Has Tone Color 15
The Shape of a Melody 16
Changing Texture 20
Instruments of Yesterday 22
Using Yesterday's Instruments Today . 26
Review 28

UNIT 2 Start with a Motif 30
Rhythm Patterns 32
Contrast 36
A Humorous Song 38
Syncopation Adds Excitement 40
Motif 42
Motifs Identify Characters 48
Review 50

Focus On
Robert Shaw 52

UNIT 3 How About Style? 54
The Piano 56
Steps and Skips 62
Form Through Movement 66
Melodic Sequences 68
Repeated Rhythm 70
A Folk Tune from the Netherlands 75
Review 76

UNIT 4 Style and Performance 78

Choral Singing 80
Rhythm Patterns 84
Listening for Musical Texture 86
Rondo Form 91
Categories of Voices 94
Chorales and Chorale Preludes 100
Review 102

Musical
Why the Sun and Moon Live in the Sky . . 104

UNIT 5 Scales 108

Inspiration 110
A Scale-wise Melody 114
Melodies Built on a Major Scale 120
Steps and Skips 124
A Melody Built on the F Major Scale 126
A Melody Built on the D Minor Scale . . . 128
Melodies Built on a Chromatic Scale 130
A Melody Built on a Whole-Tone Scale . . . 134
Something Different 136
A Master Composer Uses Musical Accents 138
Review 140

UNIT 6 America's Own Sound 142

Spirituals 144
Singing the Blues 146
Singing in Harmony 150
Singing in Unison and in Parts 154
From Ragtime to Jazz 156
A Composer's Choice 160
Review 162

Musical
Song Sleuth 164

UNIT 7 Check the Meter 174
Listening for Beat 176
Notation Then and Now 180
Getting Started......................184
Major or Minor?.....................186
The Musical Theater 190
Steady Beat 194
Tarantella 198
Rhythm Practice 200
Stay with the Beat 202
Creating a Short Melody 204
Review 206

UNIT 8 Sounds and Styles 208
Listening for Electronic Instruments 210
Bluegrass and Country Music 214
Sounds of Other Lands 218
Unusual Rhythm Effects 220
Calypso and Salsa 222
The Four Families of the Orchestra 226
Chordal Movement 228
A Variety of Tone Colors 230
Choosing Appropriate Tone Colors 234
Making a Music Video................236
Review 238

Songbook 240

More Choral Music 279

Playing the Recorder 297

Glossary of Terms 301
Classified Index 306
Listening Selections 307
Alphabetical Song Index 309

UNIT 1
WHAT IS MUSIC?

P'i P'a (four-stringed lute), Chinese, Ming Dynasty, THE METROPOLITAN MUSEUM OF ART, NY

MUSICAL ELEMENTS

- What musical elements do you hear in this song?

That's What Friends Are For

*Words and music by
Carole Bayer Sager and Burt Bacharach*

And I ne-ver thought I'd feel this way
1. And as far as I'm con-cerned
2. Well you came and o-pen-ed me.

I'm glad I got the chance to say that I do be-lieve I
And now there's so much more I see And so by the way I

love you. And if you should ev-er go a-way
thank you. And then for the times when we're a-part

well then close your eyes and try to feel the way we do to-day
well then close your eyes and know these words are com-ing from my heart

And then if you can re-mem-ber

2

𝄋 **Refrain**

Keep smil - ing keep shin - ing know - ing you _ can al - ways count on me for sure _ that's what friends _ are for.

1.&2. For good _ times and bad _ times I'll be on _ your side for - ev - er
3. In good _ times and bad _ times

more. That's what friends _ are

|1. for. |2. for. *D.S.* 𝄋 |3. for. _

THAT'S WHAT FRIENDS ARE FOR

- What *is* music?

> **mu·sic** (myōō′zik), *n.* the art or science of producing and arranging combinations of sound

Peter Gabriel working in a recording studio

● What is in every sound?

"Rock-a-My-Soul" is a **folk song.** No one person composed the song. It emerged from the culture of a group of people with shared experiences and was passed along from generation to generation.

- Listen for the way pitch, duration, and tone color are organized in this song.

Rock-a-My-Soul

African American Spiritual
Arranged by Mary Val Marsh

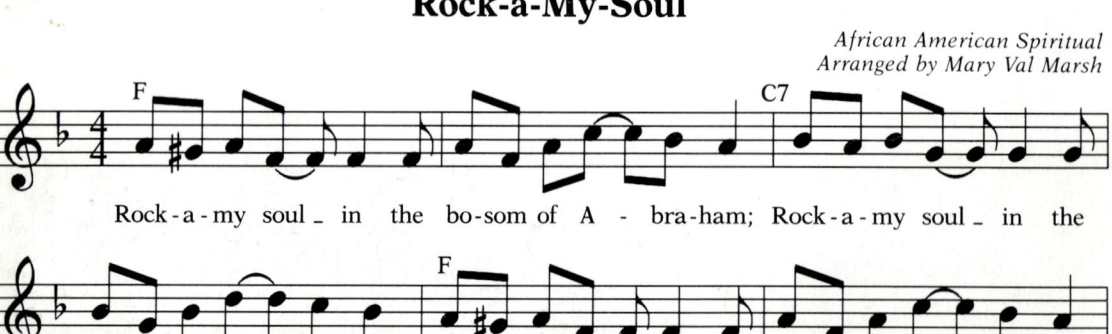

Rock-a-my soul in the bo-som of A-bra-ham; Rock-a-my soul in the bo-som of A-bra-ham; Rock-a-my soul in the bo-som of A-bra-ham;

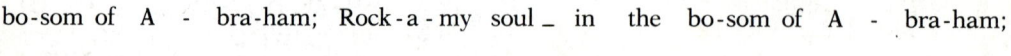

Descant
Oh, rock-a-my soul ⎯⎯⎯ So high,

Melody

Oh, rock-a-my - soul. { 1. My Lord is so high, you can't get o-ver Him;
2. His love is so high, you can't get o-ver it.

- How are the musical elements of "Rock-a-My-Soul" different from those of "That's What Friends Are For"?

MUSIC HAS TEXTURE

All music has **texture** (layers of sound). Musicians create texture with voices and instruments.

Detail of *The Nativity* by Piero Della Francesca, showing Renaissance musicians with lutes

The Doobie Brothers in concert

• How many layers of sound do you hear in this popular song of the sixteenth century, "Greensleeves"? Is the texture thick or thin?

Greensleeves

16th-Century English Song

A - las, my love, ___ you do me wrong ___ to cast me off ___ dis-cour - teous - ly; And I have loved ___ you so long, ___ De - light - ing in ___ your com - pa - ny. Green - sleeves ___ was all my joy, ___ Green - sleeves ___ was my de - light. Green - sleeves was my heart of gold, ___ And who, but my la - dy Green - sleeves.

MUSIC HAS RHYTHM AND DYNAMICS

- Do you think the long sounds in "Lonesome Valley" add to the lonely feeling of the words?

Lonesome Valley

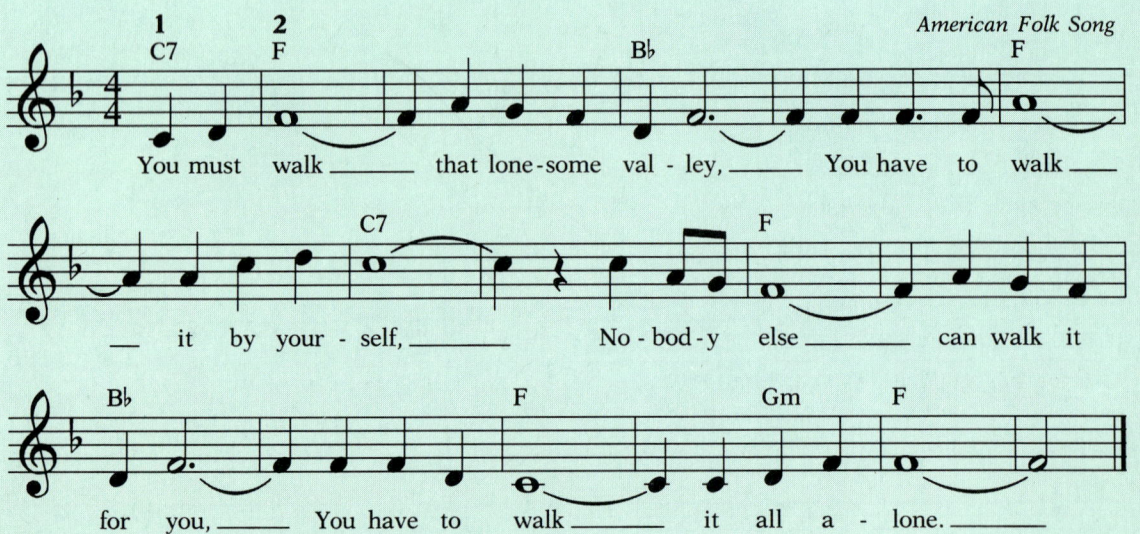

American Folk Song

These notes are used in "Lonesome Valley."

A **tie** is a curved line that combines the duration of the connected notes.

- Find the longest sound in "Lonesome Valley."

- Read "Slow Down" using your normal speaking voice.

- Speak "Slow Down" as a four-part round using the **dynamic markings** shown.

  p *(piano)* means soft
  mf *(mezzo forte)* means medium loud
  f *(forte)* means loud
  mp *(mezzo piano)* means medium soft

MUSIC HAS PITCH AND DURATION

A musical note represents a sound. It shows the **duration** (how long it sounds).

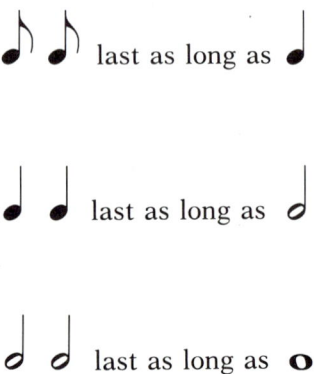

When a note is placed on the **staff** (a set of five lines and four spaces) it shows the **pitch** (how high or low it is). Each pitch has a letter name.

Ledger lines are used to show pitches that are higher or lower than those on the staff.

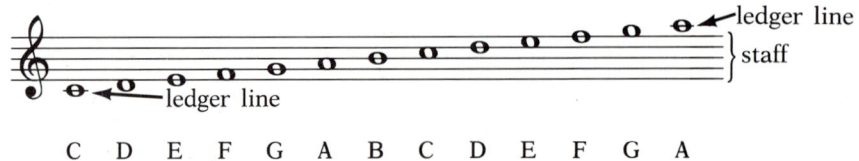

The history of **musical notation** goes back to the Middle Ages. In the tenth century, only one line was used to show an exact pitch. Other pitches were represented by symbols arranged around that line.

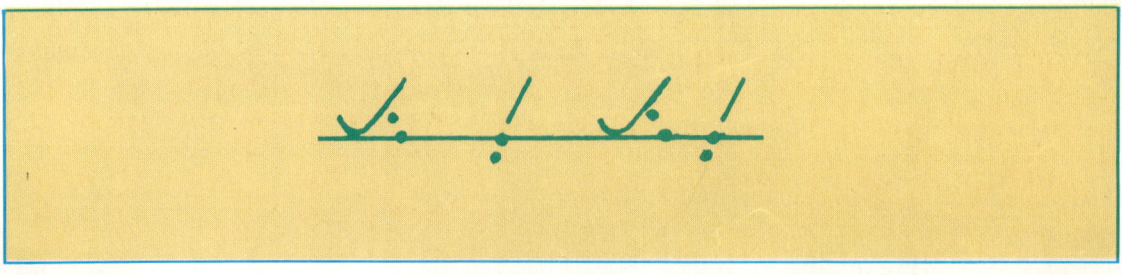

Later, a second line was added to the staff. By the thirteenth century, more lines had been added, and square-shaped notes were being used.

It was not until the seventeenth century that musical notation began to look like the notation used today.

- Name the first pitch in "Viva, Viva La Musica." Then follow the melody as you listen to the song.

Early music using square notation

Viva, Viva La Musica

Words and music by Michael Praetorius

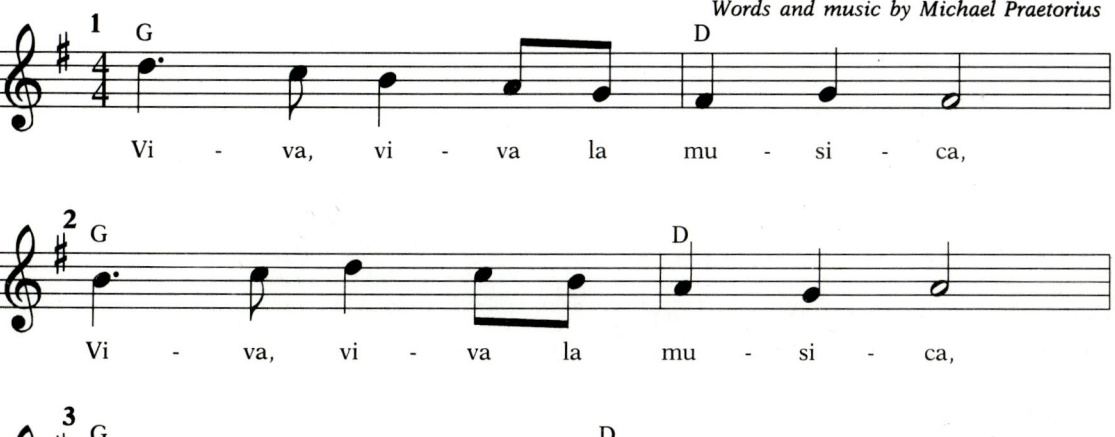

MUSIC HAS FORM

British composer Ralph Vaughan Williams (1872–1958) used two folk songs from the sixteenth century to shape the form of the orchestral arrangement *Fantasia on "Greensleeves."*

- Sing "Greensleeves" on page 9.
- Follow the melody of "Lovely Joan" as it is played on a recorder.

"Lovely Joan"

Lovely Joan

English Folk Song

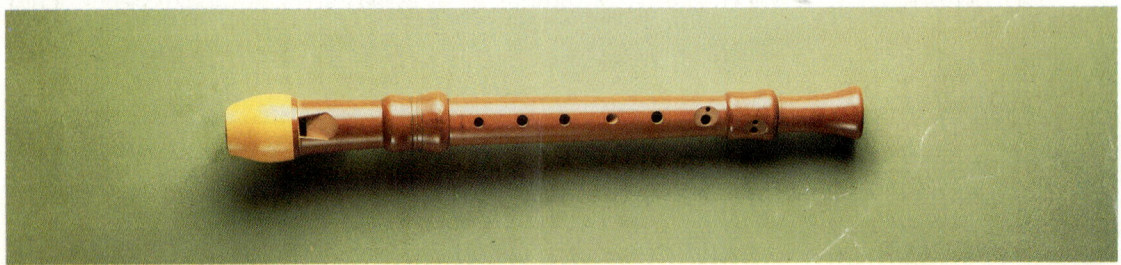

A recorder

- Listen for the order of these two melodies in *Fantasia on "Greensleeves."* Do you hear ABA form?

Fantasia on "Greensleeves" by Ralph Vaughan Williams

MUSIC HAS TONE COLOR

Tone color is the unique sound of each instrument or voice. During the **baroque** (bə-rōk′) **period** (1600–1750), composers began to combine voices and instruments in different ways to produce new tone color in music.

- Look at this painting of a musical group of the baroque period. Do any of the instruments in the painting look familiar?

Musicians Society by Jan Miese Molenaer

At the end of the seventeenth century, the **concerto grosso** (kən-chert′ō grō′sō) form was developed. Two groups of musicians were used, one small, the **concertino** (kän-chər-tē′nō), and one large, the **ripieno** (ri-pyā′nō), to alternate the tone colors in a kind of echo effect.

- Listen for the echo effect in this *concerto grosso* by Johann Sebastian Bach (yō′hən se-bäs′tyän bäKH).

 Brandenburg Concerto No. 2, Third Movement, by Johann Sebastian Bach

THE SHAPE OF A MELODY

The thirteenth-century round "Come, Follow" uses all the pitches in the C major scale.

- Follow the melody of "Come, Follow."

Come, Follow

English Folk Song

Come, fol - low, fol - low, fol - low, Fol - low, fol - low, fol - low me! Whith - er shall I fol - low, fol - low, fol - low, Whith - er shall I fol - low, fol - low thee? To the green - wood, to the green - wood, To the green - wood, green - wood tree.

- Which line of "Come, Follow" moves down the scale?

John Denver is a modern-day troubadour. His song "Follow Me" has the same message as "Come, Follow."

- Follow the melody of this song. Find places where the melody moves down the scale for four or more pitches.

John Denver

Follow Me

Words and music by John Denver

Fol-low me where I go, what I do and who I know,
Make it part of you to be a part of me.
Fol-low me up and down, all the way and all a-round,
Take my hand and say you'll fol-low me.

"Tzena, Tzena" is a composed song based on the sounds of Israeli folk music.

● Learn the melody of the verse and of the refrain.

In the round "Come, Follow," the same melody enters at different times.

In "Tzena, Tzena," different melodies enter at the same time.

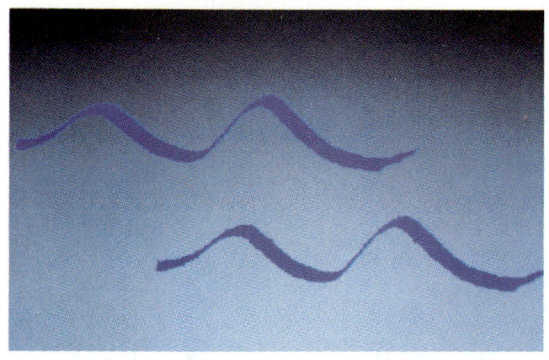

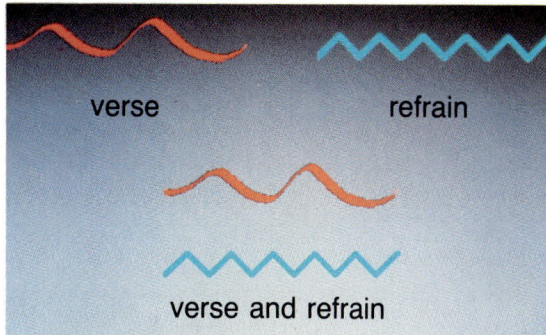

- Sing the verse of "Tzena, Tzena." The verse and the refrain may be sung together. Create harmony by combining the two sections.
- Play these rhythm patterns on the tambourine to accompany "Tzena, Tzena."

CHANGING TEXTURE

A **fugue** (fyoog) is like a game of tag. One **voice** (vocal or instrumental part) chases another. Usually there are three or more voices. The first voice introduces the **subject** (the main melody). The other voices enter at different times, and each imitates the subject in a different way. **Episodes** are sections in which the subject is not heard at all. All the voices catch up with each other in the **coda** (ending section).

Bach and His Family by Toby Edward Rosenthal

Johann Sebastian Bach is considered the master of the fugue form. The melody below is the subject of Bach's Fugue in G Minor ("The Little").

- Follow the melody of the first two measures of the subject played on a synthesizer (sin′thə-sī-zər).

This diagram shows the general outline of the first four entrances of the subject in the Fugue in G Minor.

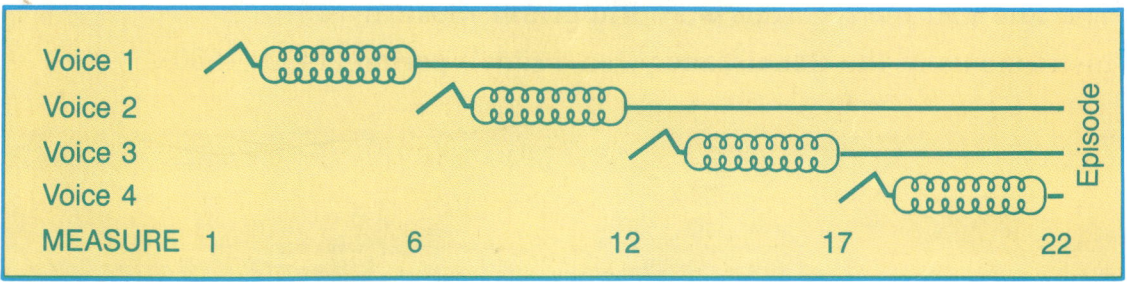

- Listen for the many entrances of the subject.

 Fugue in G Minor ("The Little") by Johann Sebastian Bach

JOHANN SEBASTIAN BACH

Johann Sebastian Bach

Johann Sebastian Bach was born in Germany in 1685. His family had been known for 200 years as professional musicians. Johann Sebastian grew up learning the violin, viola, organ, and harpsichord.

Bach became a church organist and choirmaster. Part of his job was to compose music for the Sunday services. Bach was fascinated with how the pipe organ worked, and he was always finding ways to improve its tone. Later, the influence of Italian music led him to compose concertos for violin and orchestra.

It was not until many years after his death (1750) that Bach's music was recognized for its greatness. A very important work by Bach is the *Well-Tempered Clavier*. Its 48 preludes and fugues demonstrate a new and better way of writing music for keyboard instruments that is still being used today.

INSTRUMENTS OF YESTERDAY

The lute and the recorder were important musical instruments of the **Renaissance** (ren-ə-säns′) **period** (1430–1600).

A group of musicians playing a lute, a recorder, a bass viol, and a type of portable harpsichord, by an unknown painter of the sixteenth century.

The **lute** (lo̅o̅t) was a quiet and expressive instrument with a hollow, pear-shaped body. There were lutes of many different sizes, and most had eleven strings. During the sixteenth century the lute was the instrument most often played at home.

The **Renaissance recorder** (whistle flute) was made of wood and usually had eight holes. The mouthpiece was at one end. After 1750, the recorder gradually became less popular. However, there are many recorder performing groups today. You may learn to play the recorder in school because it is easy to produce a good sound.

 Description and sounds of Renaissance instruments, prepared by Laurence E. Libin, Curator of Musical Instruments, Metropolitan Museum of Art, New York City

The organ and harpsichord were important musical instruments of the baroque period (1600–1750).

The **baroque organ** had a wide range of notes that were played by using many keyboards and pedals. Both hands and feet were used to play it. The baroque organ had many pipes, which determined the tone color by their shape and size. Some pipes were as long as 64 feet. Rows of knobs, known as stops, controlled the flow of air through the pipes and created a great variety of sound. The baroque organ could be made to sound like other instruments or even a human voice.

The **harpsichord** (härp′si-kôrd) was the most important keyboard instrument of the baroque period. When a key was pressed, a small quill plucked a string. This produced a tone that sounded for as long as the string vibrated. The harpsichord was able to produce **chords** (several tones produced at the same time), making it perfect for accompaniment.

Top, baroque organ in a church, Rothenbach, Germany; *bottom*, a harpsichord from the late seventeenth century

- Listen to the sound of the harpsichord.

 "Greensleeves" performed on harpsichord by Igor Kipnis

INSTRUMENTS OF TODAY

Renaissance and baroque instruments have their modern-day counterparts.

Today's **guitar** is related to the lute. The guitar has a body with a flat back and sides that curve inward. The modern guitar has six or twelve strings. Some guitars produce sound electronically.

Today's **flute** is related to the recorder. Both the flute and the recorder are woodwind instruments; however, today's flute is usually made of metal. Its tone is similar to that of the recorder but not so soft nor so gentle. At least two flutes are usually found in a full-sized modern orchestra.

The **synthesizer** is a major contribution of the twentieth century to the music world. Most synthesizers are played from a keyboard. The synthesizer uses a computer to imitate instruments, voices, and other sounds. It not only produces sounds but can also change them. Synthesizers have become very popular in rock music and for movie and television scores.

USING YESTERDAY'S INSTRUMENTS TODAY

Traditional instruments such as those shown here have been used to accompany American music throughout its history. The same instruments accompany the folk and country music of today.

• What instruments can you identify in the photographs?

Wilma Lee Cooper

Jean Ritchie

Grandpa Jones

Frank Wakefield

John Hartford

Mike Cross blends the sounds of instruments of yesterday with the sounds of modern instruments to create a unique style.

"Bonnie Prince Charlie/Road to Lisdunvarna/Lark in the Morning" is a traditional song.

- As you listen, try to name the instruments you hear.

 "Bonnie Prince Charlie/Road to Lisdunvarna/Lark in the Morning" by Mike Cross

- Describe the texture of the song.

Mike Cross

TAKE ANOTHER LOOK

Music is a song to sing.

- Sing your favorites of these songs.

That's What Friends Are For
Lonesome Valley
Rock-a-My-Soul
Follow Me
Come, Follow
Tzena, Tzena
Greensleeves

Music is for listening.

- Listen to Fugue in G Minor ("The Little").
- Remember. Music has . . .

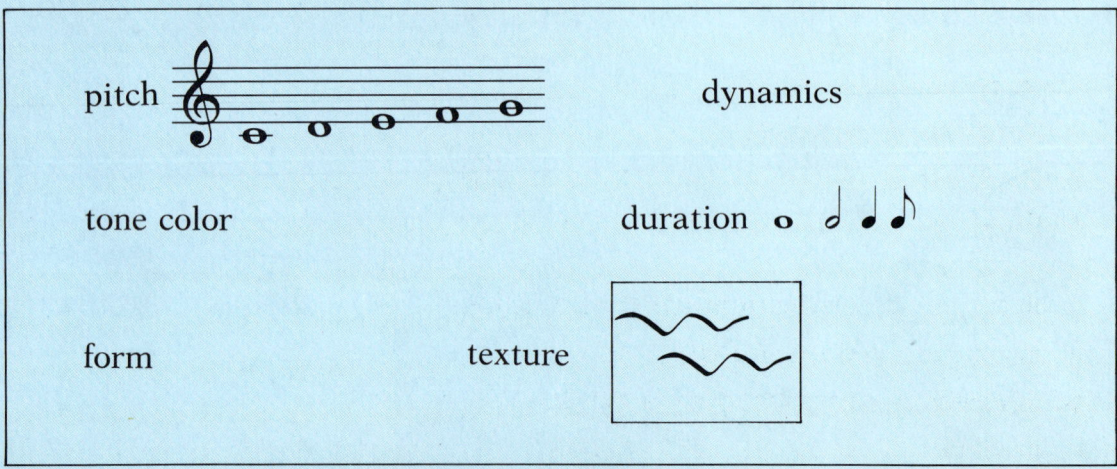

JUST CHECKING

• How much do you remember? Choose the best answer for each question.

Use this song segment with questions 1 and 2.

1. Which group of letters names the pitches?
   a. C' E E E C' B A
   b. E G G G E D C'
   c. A C' C' C' A G F

2. How many eighth notes are there in the song segment?
   a. none   b. 2   c. 4

3. Which sounds for the same length of time as ♩ ?
   a. ♪ ♪   b. ♪♩   c. ♩ ♩

4. Which shows the notes in order from longest to shortest duration?
   a. ♪ o ♩ ♩   b. o ♩ ♪♪   c. o ♩ ♪ ♪

5. Texture in music is ___.
   a. loudness or softness
   b. the melody
   c. layers of sound

6. Which best describes texture that is thick?
   a. a song played on a lute
   b. a singer accompanied by a guitar
   c. a fugue

UNIT 2
START WITH A MOTIF

RHYTHM PATTERNS

The famous Symphony No. 5 by Ludwig van Beethoven (lood'vig vän bā'tō-vən) begins with this simple **motif** (mō-tēf'), or short musical idea.

The eighth rest (𝄾) is a silence that lasts as long as an eighth note.

• Tap the rhythm of the motif.

Beethoven extended the motif by repeating the rhythm pattern.

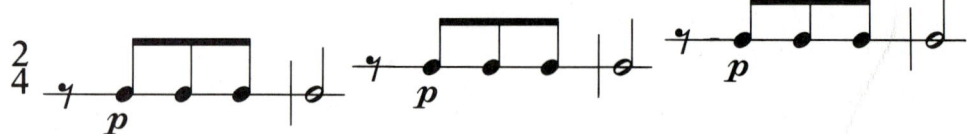

• As you listen to the recording, raise your hand briefly whenever you hear the motif.

 Symphony No. 5, First Movement, by Ludwig van Beethoven

The Electric Light Orchestra, an orchestral rock group, used an early rock-and-roll song by Chuck Berry and combined it with the motif from Beethoven's Symphony No. 5 to create "Roll Over Beethoven."

- Listen for the motif.

 "Roll Over Beethoven" by the Electric Light Orchestra

LUDWIG VAN BEETHOVEN

Ludwig van Beethoven was born in 1770 in Bonn, Germany. Beethoven's father was determined that his son would be a great pianist and started teaching young Beethoven when he was five years old. Until he was eleven, Beethoven was made to practice scales. He then began to study the preludes and fugues of Johann Sebastian Bach. He got his first paying job as a court organist at the age of 14.

While still a teenager, Beethoven began to compose music. At 17, he visited the music "capital" of Europe, Vienna, and played for Mozart. Later, Beethoven studied with the famous composer Franz Joseph Haydn.

When Beethoven was about 30, he began to lose his hearing and could no longer give public performances. However, he could still "hear" the music in his head and continued to compose. Beethoven died in 1827. He is best known for his nine symphonies.

Wolfgang Amadeus Mozart (1756–1791), another famous composer, wrote "Kanon." This song is a four-part **canon.** In canon form, the melody is introduced and then imitated one or more times.

- Follow the notation as you listen. Focus on the rhythm patterns that are similar to the motif in Beethoven's Symphony No. 5.

The pattern may also be written like this.

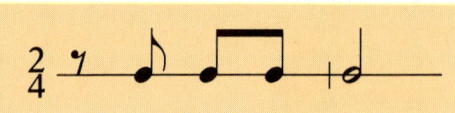

Kanon

*Words and music by
Wolfgang A. Mozart*

Friends, for-get the cares that bore us, Come and join the jol-ly cho-rus! A song of praise, to hap-py days! Let us be mer-ry one and all! You sit so i-dly in your plac-es With gloom-y looks up-on your fac-es. Come on, re-joice And raise your voice To hap-py days—A song of praise, a song of praise! Are you like don-keys, far too old to bray? Are you like

Notes represent sound and rests represent silence.

- Read the pattern below using different body percussion for each kind of note.

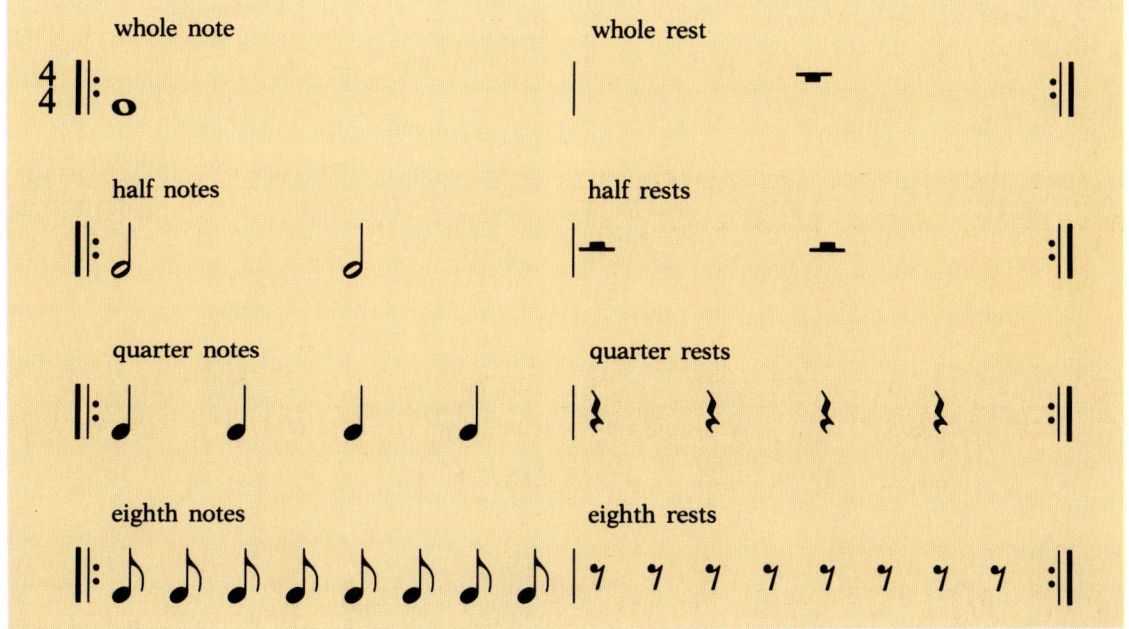

- Feel the duration of the rests in "Kanon."

CONTRAST

Contrasts in music, like the differences among the seasons, help provide interest.

36

A **descant** (des′kant) is a different melody, higher in pitch, sung with the main melody.

- Listen to the melody and the descant of "Autumn." How does the descant contrast with the melody?

In "Autumn," the rhythm remains smooth and sustained. **Legato** (li-gät′ō) describes a smoothly connected style. A contrasting style is **staccato** (stə-kät′ō), or detached.

- Sing the song *legato* and then sing it *staccato*. Decide which style is more appropriate for "Autumn."

A HUMOROUS SONG

Pitches in a melody may be repeated, may move by **step** (to the next note higher or lower), or may move by **skip** (to a note farther away than a step).

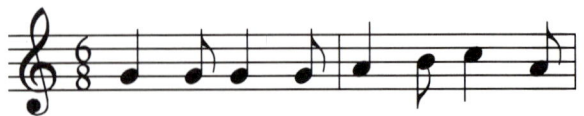

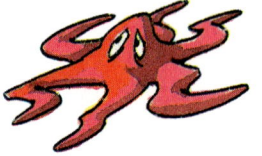

- Follow the notation as you listen. Find some steps, skips, and repeated pitches.

The Thing

Words and music by Charles R. Grean

Moderately bright

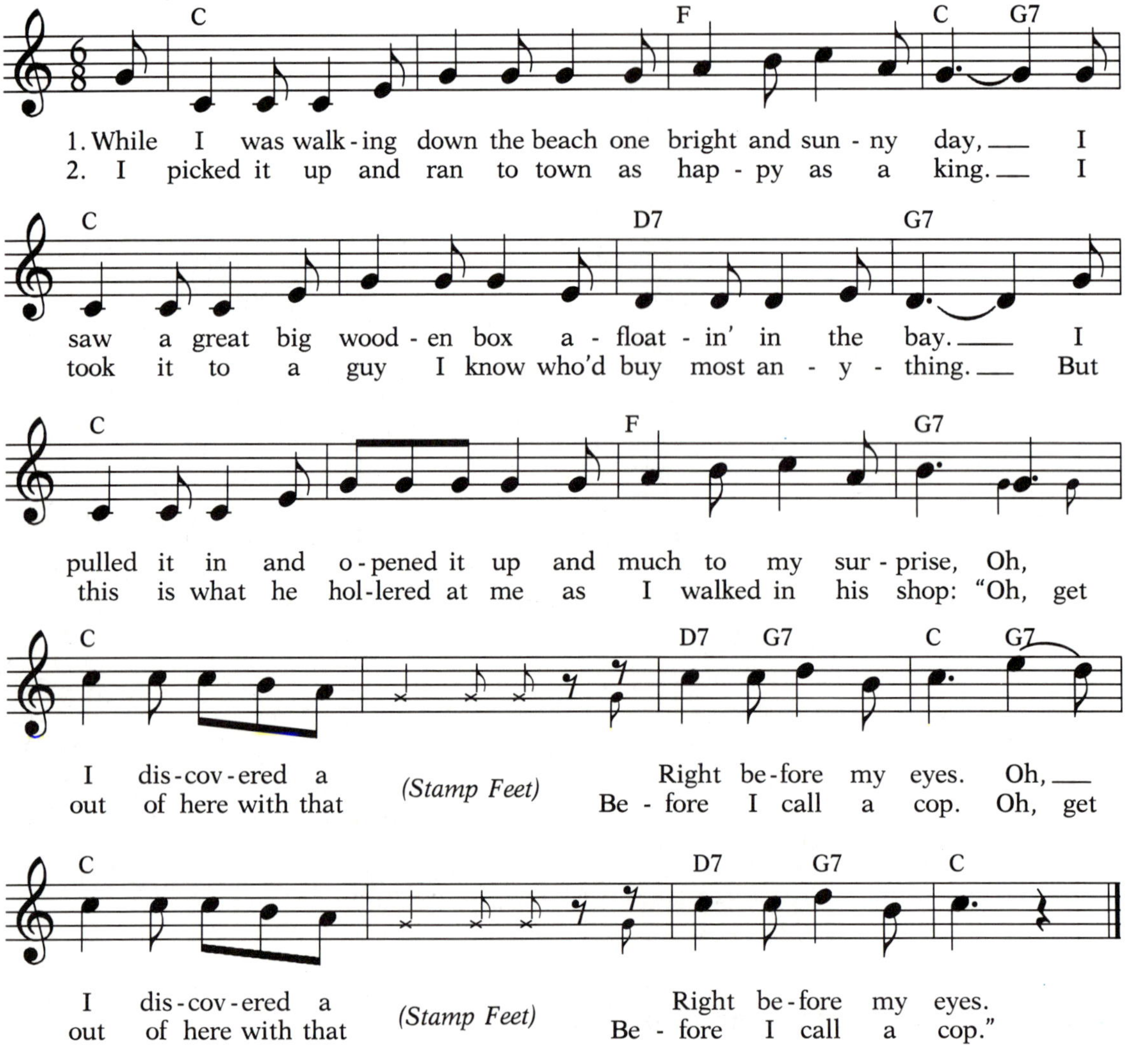
C F C G7
1. While I was walk-ing down the beach one bright and sun-ny day, I
2. I picked it up and ran to town as hap-py as a king. I
C D7 G7
saw a great big wood-en box a-float-in' in the bay. I
took it to a guy I know who'd buy most an-y-thing. But
C F G7
pulled it in and o-pened it up and much to my sur-prise, Oh,
this is what he hol-lered at me as I walked in his shop: "Oh, get
C D7 G7 C G7
I dis-cov-ered a (Stamp Feet) Right be-fore my eyes. Oh,
out of here with that (Stamp Feet) Be-fore I call a cop. Oh, get
C D7 G7 C
I dis-cov-ered a (Stamp Feet) Right be-fore my eyes.
out of here with that (Stamp Feet) Be-fore I call a cop."

3. I turned around and got right out a-runnin' for my life,
   And then I took it home with me to give it to my wife.
   But this is what she hollered at me as I walked in the door:
   "Oh, get out of here with that xxx and don't come back no more.
   Oh, get out of here with that xxx and don't come back no more."

4. I wandered all around the town until I chanced to meet
   A hobo who was looking for a handout on the street.
   He said he'd take most any old thing, he was a desperate man.
   But when I showed him the xxx, he turned around and ran.
   Oh, when I showed him the xxx, he turned around and ran.

5. I wandered on for many years, a victim of my fate,
   Until one day I came upon Saint Peter at the gate.
   And when I tried to take it inside he told me where to go:
   "Get out of here with that xxx and take it down below.
   Oh, get out of here with that xxx and take it down below."

6. The moral of the story is if you're out on the beach
   And you should see a great big box and it's within your reach,
   Don't ever stop and open it up, that's my advice to you,
   'Cause you'll never get rid of the xxx, no matter what you do.
   Oh, you'll never get rid of the xxx, no matter what you do.

The Thing
Words and Music by Charles R. Grean.
TRO—Copyright © 1950 and renewed
1978 Hollis Music, Inc., New York, N.Y.
Used by permission.

- What do you think "The Thing" is?

SYNCOPATION ADDS EXCITEMENT

- Follow the notation as you listen to "Dry Bones." Why do you think the melody gradually moves upward in the B section?

Dry Bones

African American Spiritual

E-ze-kiel cried, "Them dry bones!" E-ze-kiel cried, "Them dry bones!"

E-ze-kiel cried, "Them dry bones!" Now hear the word of the Lord.

gradually getting faster

The foot bone con-nect-ed to the leg bone,

The leg bone con-nect-ed to the knee bone,

The knee bone con-nect-ed to the hip bone,

The hip bone con-nect-ed to the back bone,

The back bone con-nect-ed to the shoul-der bone,

The shoul-der bone con-nect-ed to the neck bone,

The neck bone con-nect-ed to the jaw bone,

The jaw bone con-nect-ed to the head bone,

Now hear the word of the Lord.

C *fast*

Them bones, them bones gon-na walk a-round, Them bones, them bones gon-na walk a-round, Them bones, them bones gon-na walk a-round,

gradually slower last time

Now hear the word of the Lord.

Syncopation (sing-kə-pā′shən) is rhythm that has sounds and silences where you do not normally expect to hear them. One way to create this effect is to place a rest after the **bar line,** where the strong beat usually occurs. Not hearing the expected sound adds a feeling of excitement to the music.

- Find this syncopated pattern in "Dry Bones."

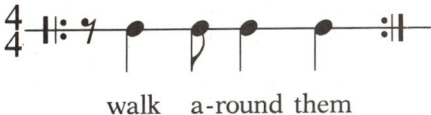

walk a-round them

- Speak these words as an **ostinato** (äs-tə-nät′ō), or repeated pattern, for the song. Be sure to feel the eighth rest at the beginning.

gain. _____ And the cold wind blew, _____

and the cold wind blew! _____

and the cold wind blew! _____

From REFLECTIONS OF A LAD AT SEA by Don Besig and Nancy Price. Copyright © 1982, Shawnee Press, Inc.; Delaware Water Gap, PA 18327. All Rights Reserved. Used by permission.

- Play these patterns from "The Ghost Ship" on the bells.

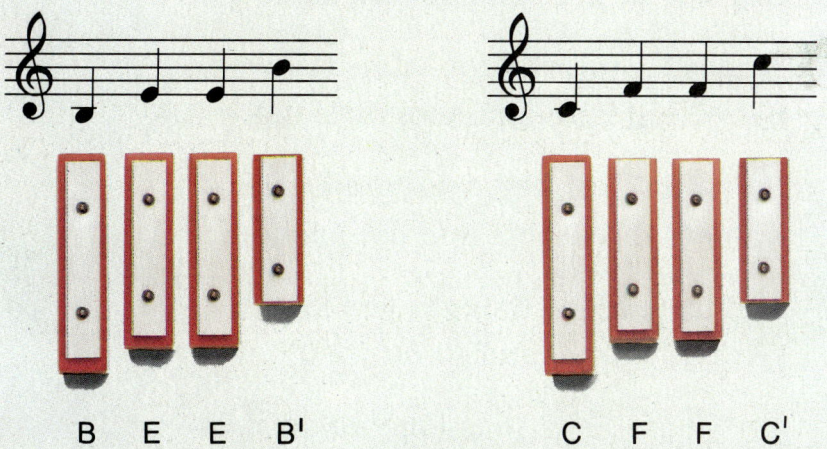

- How are these patterns different?
- How are they similar?

Anyone can write a motif. Start with a poem.

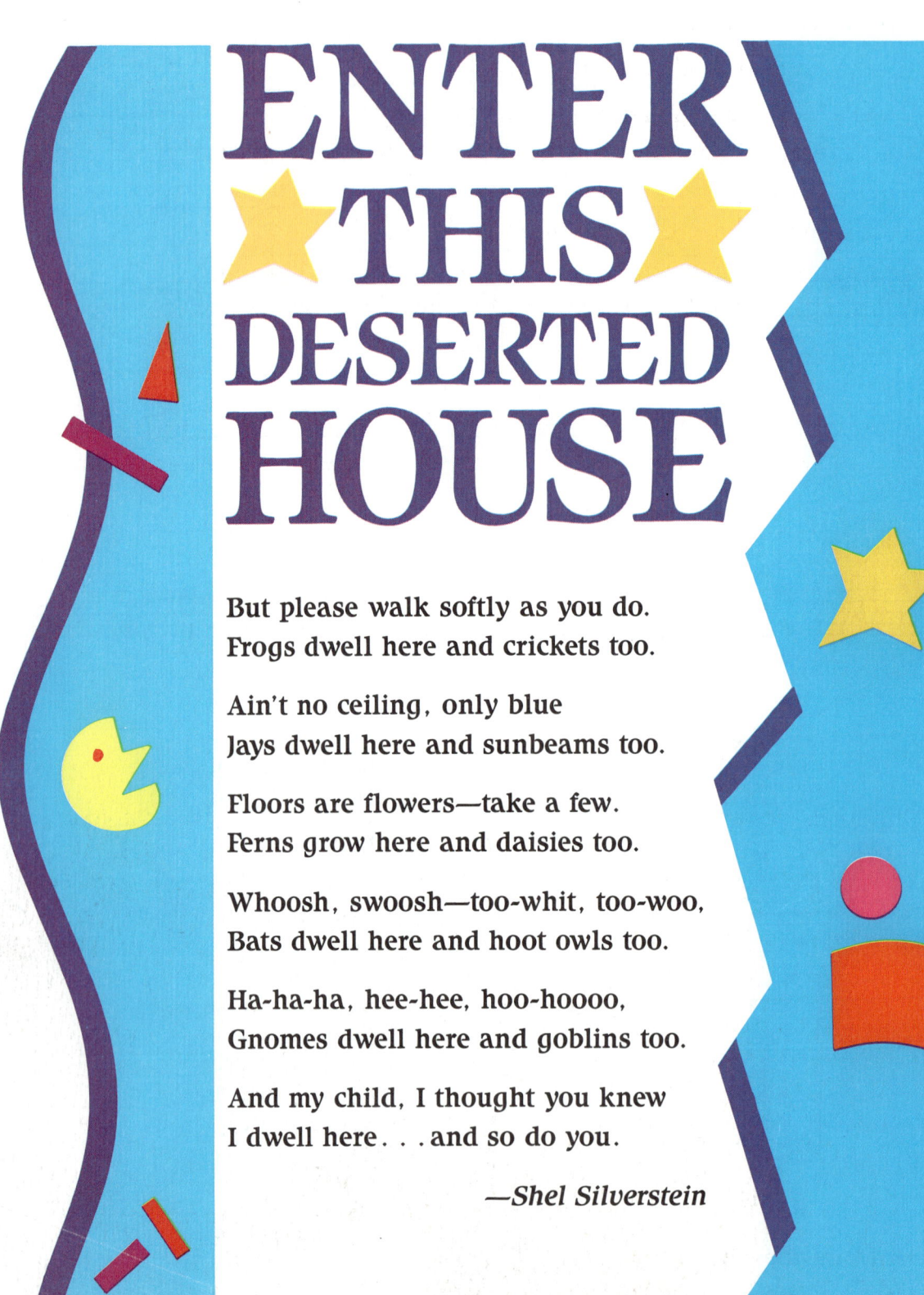

ENTER ★ THIS ★ DESERTED HOUSE

But please walk softly as you do.
Frogs dwell here and crickets too.

Ain't no ceiling, only blue
Jays dwell here and sunbeams too.

Floors are flowers—take a few.
Ferns grow here and daisies too.

Whoosh, swoosh—too-whit, too-woo,
Bats dwell here and hoot owls too.

Ha-ha-ha, hee-hee, hoo-hoooo,
Gnomes dwell here and goblins too.

And my child, I thought you knew
I dwell here... and so do you.

—Shel Silverstein

- Select a short phrase from the poem.

    Enter this deserted house

- Divide the words into syllables.

    En-ter this de-sert-ed house

- Speak this phrase making some syllables long and others short. Using different durations for syllables will give you a rhythmic motif.
- Choose a pitch on the bells for each syllable. Begin on E. Using different pitches for syllables will give you a melodic motif. Remember: pitches in a melody may be repeated, may move by step, or may move by skip.

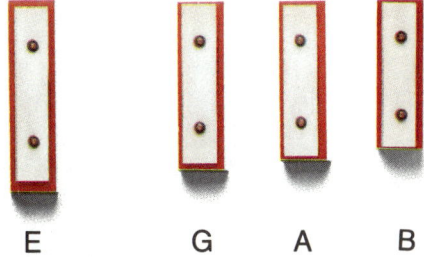

E   G   A   B

- Play these pitches on the bells using your spoken rhythm and you will have a motif!

MOTIFS IDENTIFY CHARACTERS

Detail from *Black Hawk*, Charles Robert Patterson, courtesy of the QUESTER MARITIME COLLECTION, Stonington, CT

Black Hawk by Charles Robert Patterson

The Flying Dutchman is an opera by Richard Wagner (1813–1883). It takes place in an eighteenth-century village on the coast of Norway. The opera is based on a legend of a sailor sentenced for his pride. He must sail forever on a ghost ship unless he can find a woman who will love him. Once every seven years he is allowed to come ashore to look for her.

In Wagner's opera, the ship lands on the coast during a storm. The Dutchman meets a woman named Senta and they fall in love. However, Senta is also loved by a man named Erik. The Dutchman gives up hope and sets sail. Senta jumps into the sea to show her love for the Dutchman. The Dutchman's ship sinks and the two rise to heaven.

In the **overture** (a musical introduction), Wagner uses motifs to represent the characters.

The Dutchman's motif
The Dutchman is condemned to sail forever in a ghost ship through stormy seas.

Senta's motif
Senta loves the Dutchman and she seeks to release him from his curse.

- Identify each motif whenever you hear it.

 The Flying Dutchman Overture by Richard Wagner

REVIEW

TAKE ANOTHER LOOK

- Sing your favorites of these songs.

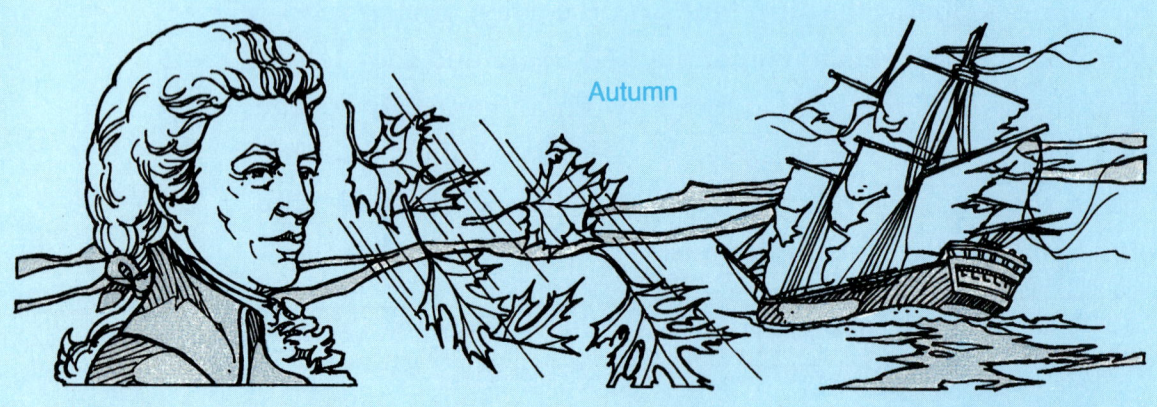

Kanon   Autumn   The Ghost Ship

- Listen again for Beethoven's famous motif.

Symphony No. 5   Roll Over Beethoven

- Clap this rhythm combination.

JUST CHECKING

- How much do you remember? Choose the best answer for each question.

1. Which rest has the same duration as ♩ ?

    a. ▬　　　　b. 𝄽　　　　c. ▬

2. Which note has the same duration as 𝄾 ?

    a. ♪　　　　b. ♩　　　　c. 𝅗𝅥

3. Select the best description of a motif.
    a. a song with a *legato* style
    b. a song about a ghost ship
    c. a short musical idea

4. Which of these rhythm combinations did Beethoven use as a motif in Symphony No. 5 ?

    a.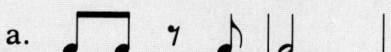

    b.

    c.

5. Which example has a note and rest of the same duration?

    a. 𝅝 ▬

    b. ♩ ▬

    c. 𝅗𝅥 ▬

FOCUS ON
Robert Shaw

Robert Shaw (b. 1916) has earned many honors, including seven Grammy awards. In 1941 he formed the Collegiate Chorale, which later became the Robert Shaw Chorale. The chorale has toured in 47 states and 29 countries. From 1953 to 1957, he was Music Director of the San Diego Symphony. In 1956, he also became Associate Conductor of the Cleveland Orchestra. Shaw became the Music Director of the Atlanta Symphony Orchestra in 1967.

Robert Shaw is highly regarded as a musician and as a spokesman for the arts.

 Robert Shaw speaks

Robert Shaw commissioned the composer Paul Hindemith (1895–1963) to write a modern **requiem** (rek′wē-əm), or musical composition in honor of the dead. Hindemith was a master at composing modern music using forms from earlier periods. The words were taken from the poetry of the American poet Walt Whitman. This performance features Robert Shaw conducting the Atlanta Symphony Orchestra and Chorus.

- Listen for the entrances of the different sections of the orchestra and voices in this fugue.

When Lilacs Last in the Dooryard Bloom'd: Requiem for those we Love, Seventh Movement ("Introduction and Fugue"), by Paul Hindemith

UNIT 3
HOW ABOUT STYLE?

Jean Sibelius Memorial, Helsinki, Finland

THE PIANO

- Listen for the accompaniment to the song. What instrument do you hear?

Let Love Come Near

Words and music by Ed Robertson

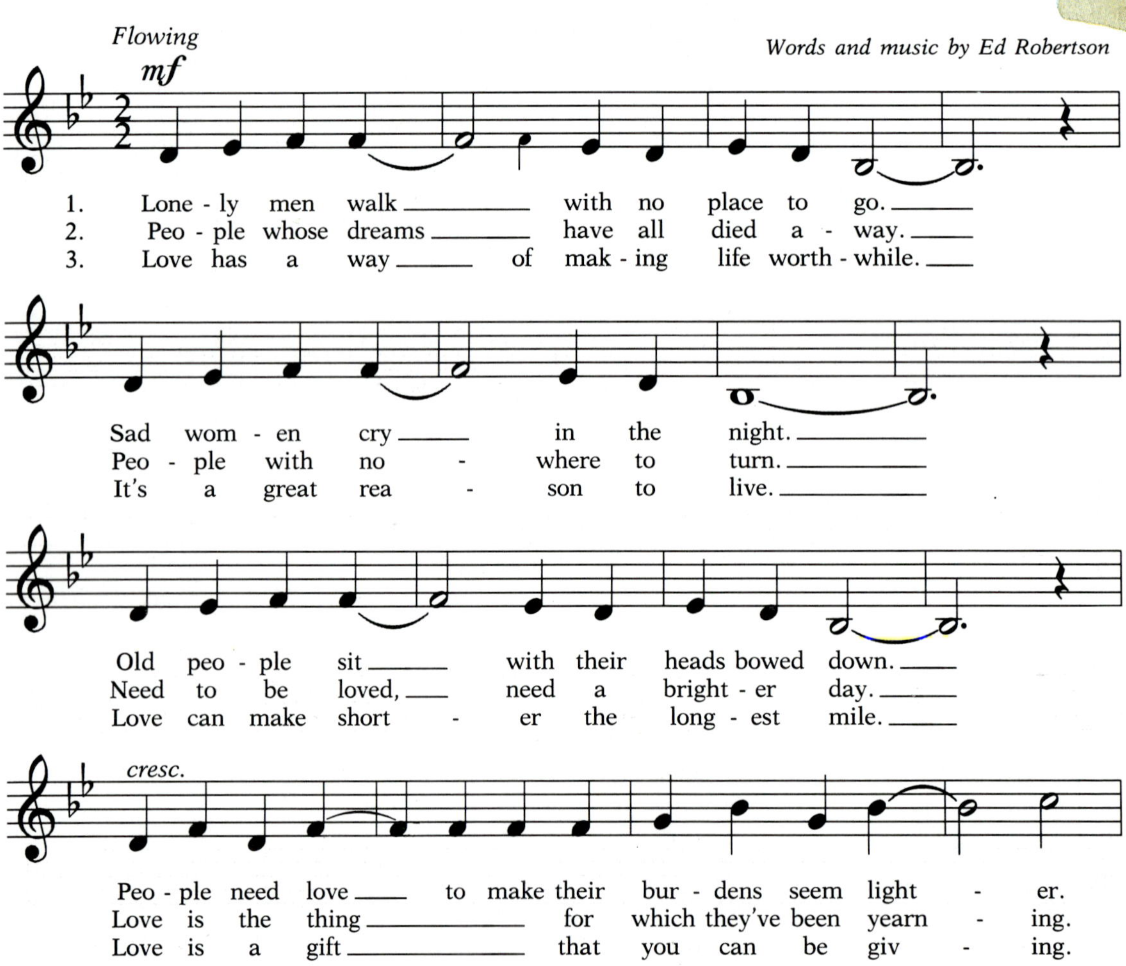

Flowing — **mf**

1. Lone-ly men walk with no place to go.
2. Peo-ple whose dreams have all died a-way.
3. Love has a way of mak-ing life worth-while.

Sad wom-en cry in the night.
Peo-ple with no-where to turn.
It's a great rea-son to live.

Old peo-ple sit with their heads bowed down.
Need to be loved, need a bright-er day.
Love can make short-er the long-est mile.

cresc.

Peo-ple need love to make their bur-dens seem light-er.
Love is the thing for which they've been yearn-ing.
Love is a gift that you can be giv-ing.

The piano is a large stringed instrument played by means of a keyboard. When the keys are pressed down, the strings are struck by felt-covered hammers. This action produces the sound of the piano. It is also the reason the piano is included in the percussion family.

Here are two types of pianos.

spinet piano

The piano keyboard has 88 keys, making the range of pitches (lowest to highest) very wide.

grand piano

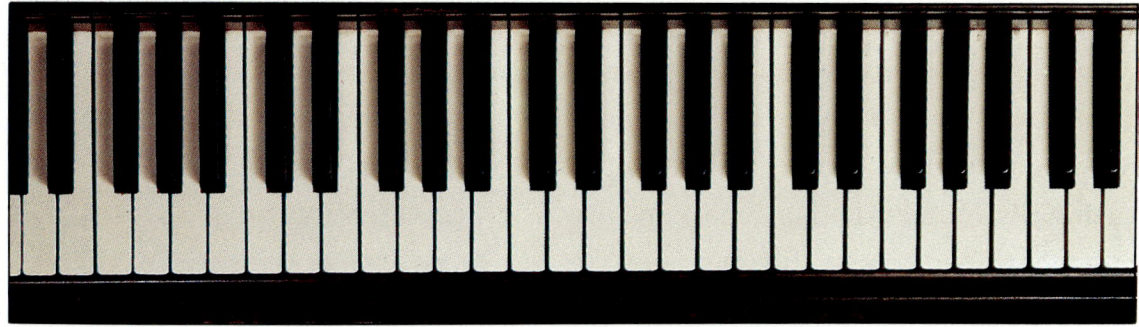

The pedals on a piano make certain effects possible. There are three pedals on most pianos.

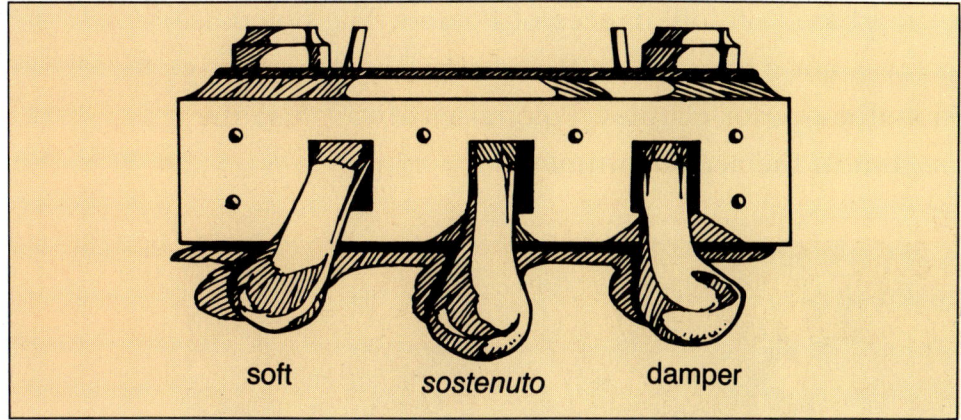

The **soft pedal** moves the hammers sideways so that not all the strings are struck when a key is played. The sound is not as loud.

The ***sostenuto*** (sō-stə-nōōt′ō) **pedal** sustains only the notes that are being played at the moment the pedal is pushed down.

The **damper pedal** holds felt bars (the dampers) away from the strings so that they continue to vibrate. The sound is not deadened immediately.

Another of the special effects possible on the piano is the ***glissando*** (gli-sän′dō), created by sliding the fingers across the keys.

- Look inside a piano to see the mechanism that produces the sound. Try creating a *glissando*. Try the pedals and hear their effects.

Musical **style** is the way a composer combines the elements of music to give it its unique quality. When composers use folk music, typical dance rhythms, or literature of their country to express pride in that country, their music is called **nationalistic** in style. Nationalism in music began during the nineteenth century in Europe.

Frédéric Chopin (frā-dā-rēk′ shō′pan) was the first Polish composer whose music was accepted around the world. He was the master of the **polonaise** (päl-ə-nāz′), a type of composition based on folk dances of Poland. The polonaise, however, was not a folk dance. It developed into a courtly processional dance for couples. Polonaises always use the same rhythm in the accompaniment.

- Feel the strong beat as you listen to this famous polonaise.

 Polonaise in A Flat Major by Frédéric Chopin

FRÉDÉRIC CHOPIN

Frédéric Chopin, Eugène Delacroix, LOUVRE, Paris

Frédéric Chopin was born in 1810 near Warsaw, Poland, and died in 1849. His mother was Polish and his father was French. He began to compose melodies on the piano before he took his first lessons. At age six, he gave his first piano concert. At age seven, he published his first composition.

When he was 17, Chopin became a student at the Warsaw Conservatory. There he developed his own style of composing. After graduating, Chopin visited many foreign cities. In 1831, he moved to Paris, France. Except for occasional travels, he lived in Paris for the rest of his life. Although Chopin never returned home, he remained a Polish nationalist. His many polonaises express the influence of his homeland.

Chopin was a shy man. Rather than giving large public concerts, he preferred playing for small gatherings. He developed the art of piano playing, sometimes fiery, sometimes dreamy. Chopin wrote a few compositions for piano and orchestra, some pieces for small groups of instruments, and some songs. But he wrote most of his music for the solo piano. It seems fitting that Chopin is known as the "Poet of the Piano."

STEPS AND SKIPS

Pitches in a melody may be repeated, may move by **step** (to the very next note higher or lower), or may move by **skip** (to a note farther away than a step).

- Follow the melody of this Hungarian folk song. Listen for steps and skips.

Sing It All Together

Hungarian Canon
Words by B.S. and M.S.

1. If you want to sing a song, join us in our sing - ing.
2. If you do not know the words, just sing la la la la.

Come a - long and sing a song, start the raft - ers ring - ing.
If you want to sing in thirds, then sing la de da da.

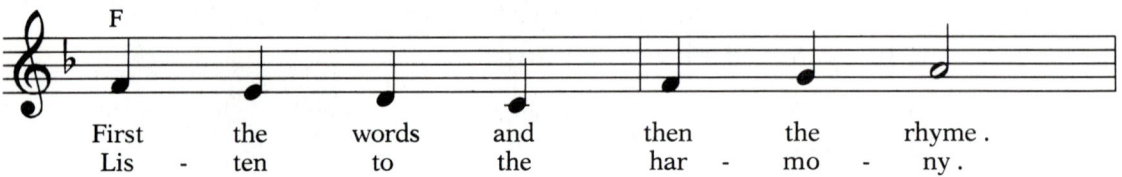
First the words and then the rhyme.
Lis - ten to the har - mo - ny.

Play and sing it one more time, sing it all to - geth - er.
Mu - sic is for you and me, sing it all to - geth - er.

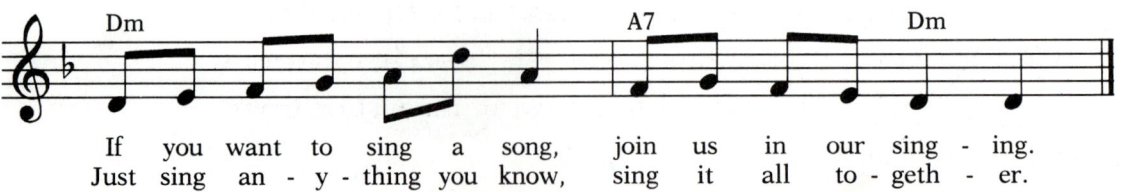
If you want to sing a song, join us in our sing - ing.
Just sing an - y - thing you know, sing it all to - geth - er.

- Look at the first five pitches in "Sing It All Together." These pitches are the first five steps of the D minor scale.
- Play the bells from D to high D. This is the sound of a **minor** scale.

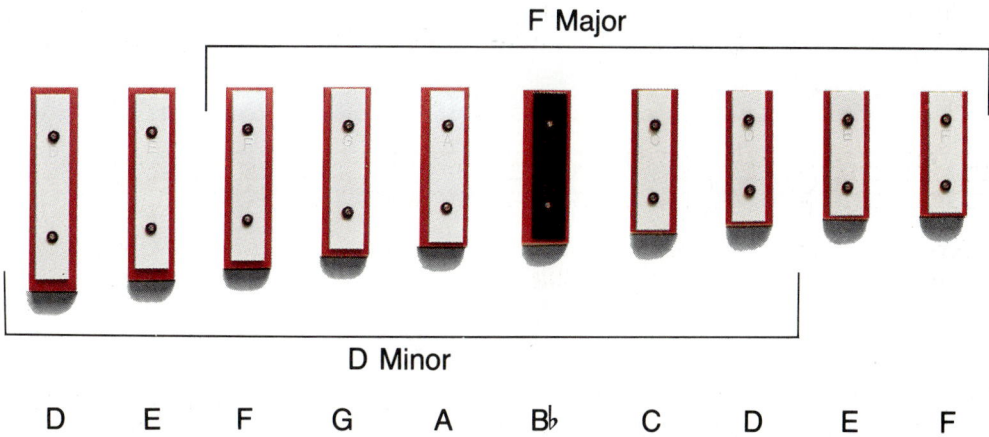

- Now, begin on F and play to high F on the bells. This is the sound of a **major** scale.
- Play both scales upward and downward. Listen for the difference in the sound. Remember that a **scale** is a series of pitches placed in order from lowest to highest or from highest to lowest.

Another nationalistic composer, Bedřich Smetana (bed′ər-zhiKH smet′ən-ə), who lived from 1824 to 1884, was known as the "Father of Czechoslovakian Music." His most famous composition describes the river that runs through his country. It is called *The Moldau*.

- Follow the main theme of *The Moldau*. Does the melody move by steps or skips?

- Follow the listening map on page 65 as you listen to *The Moldau*. Notice when the main theme is in minor and when it changes to major.

The Moldau by Bedřich Smetana

FORM THROUGH MOVEMENT

You can show the form of music when you dance.

- Listen for the phrases in "Sing It All Together" on page 62. Decide what the phrase form is.
- Find ways to show the form through movement. Use the same steps for phrases that are repeated. Use different steps for contrasting phrases.

- Try composing a melody using the same phrase form as "Sing It All Together." Use these pitches.

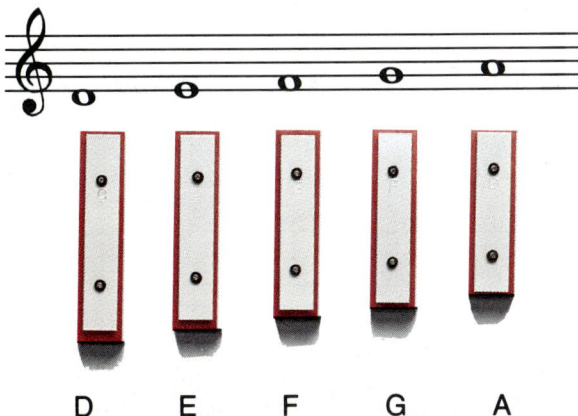

- **Phrase a** Create a melody on the bells that is eight beats long. Start and end on D.
- **Phrase b** Create a different eight-beat melody. Start on F and end on A.
- **Phrase c** Create a melody that is four beats long. Start on D and end on A.
- Now play these phrases together using the phrase form aabbca.

MELODIC SEQUENCES

Patterns within a melody may be repeated on different pitch levels. This is called **melodic sequence.** "Rock-a-My-Soul" uses the melodic sequences below.

- Sing the song and find them.

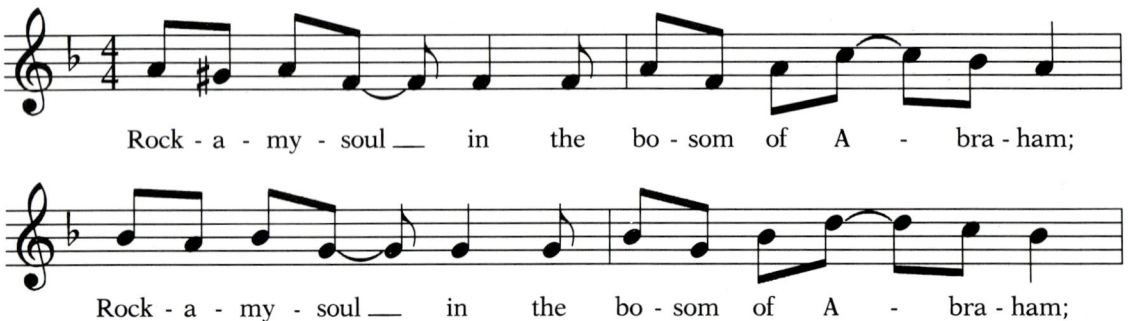

Rock - a - my - soul — in the bo - som of A - bra - ham;

Rock - a - my - soul — in the bo - som of A - bra - ham;

- Play part of "Sing It All Together" on page 62 as a melodic sequence. Using bells, play line three of the song.

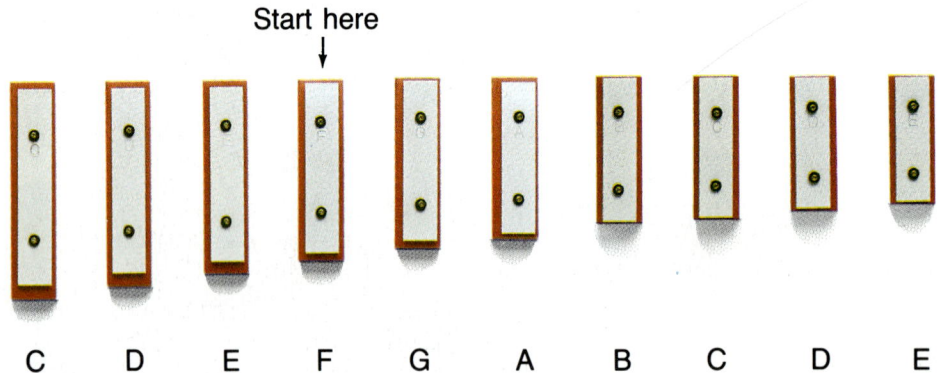

- Now, play this same melody, starting on a higher pitch.

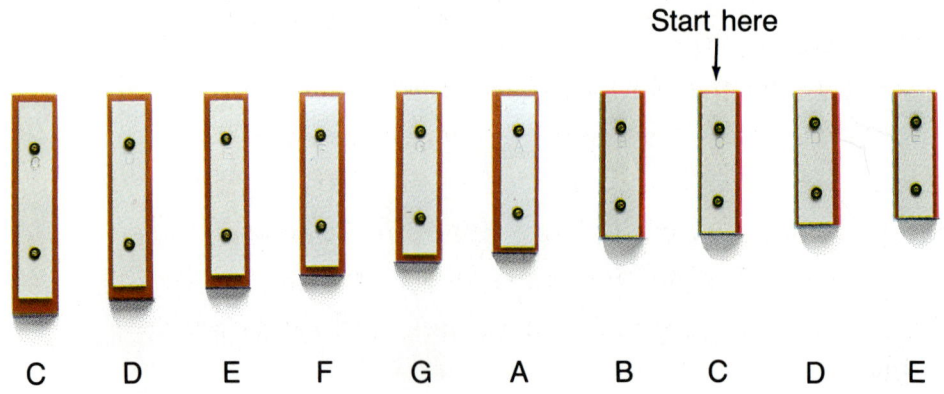

A **concerto** (kən-chert′ō) is a large work for solo instrument and orchestra. It is usually written in three large sections called **movements.**

The Concerto in A Minor by the Norwegian composer Edvard Grieg (ed′värd grēg) is one of the most popular concertos for piano. Grieg was a nationalistic composer. He was very interested in Norwegian folk music and often used it in melodies in his compositions.

- Listen for melodic sequences in the first movement of this concerto.

 Concerto in A Minor, First Movement, by Edvard Grieg

EDVARD GRIEG

Edvard Grieg was a Norwegian composer who lived from 1843 to 1907. Grieg studied in Denmark and Germany, and his early work was greatly influenced by German composers. He returned to Norway to teach and conduct, and his compositions began to reflect the atmosphere and style of Norwegian life. Grieg founded the Norwegian Academy of Music in 1867. At that time Norway was ruled by Sweden. The people of Norway longed for independence. This may have been the reason Grieg collected many Norwegian folk tunes and used them in his compositions. His most famous works include the *Peer Gynt Suites, Holberg Suite* for strings, and the Concerto in A Minor.

REPEATED RHYTHM

The Finnish composer Jean Sibelius (zhän sə-bāl′yəs), who lived from 1865 to 1957, wrote this song as part of his orchestral composition *Finlandia*. The melody has become so popular that people all over the world sing it. Several different sets of words have been written for it, including a Finnish national anthem.

● Find the lines of the song that have the same rhythm.

Song of Peace

Music by Jean Sibelius
Words by Leland Isaac

Finlandia is a nationalistic **symphonic poem** (an orchestral work based on a story or theme). It was written for a performance in support of the fight for freedom of the press in 1899. Finland was a part of Russia at that time. *Finlandia* awoke so much national spirit that no one was allowed to perform it in Finland under its actual title. After Finland became a free country in 1917, this symphonic poem became a symbol of independence for its people.

- Listen for the melody of "Song of Peace" in this composition.

Finlandia by Jean Sibelius

This modern American pop song expresses feelings similar to those of "Song of Peace."

• Listen for repeated rhythms in the melody of the refrain.

We Are Family

Moderately

Words and music by
Nile Rodgers and Bernard Edwards

Refrain

We are fam - i - ly. I got all my fam - i - ly with me.

We are fam - i - ly. Get up, ev - 'ry - bod - y, and sing.

Verse

Ev - 'ry - one can see we're to - geth - er as we walk

on by. ___ And we flock just like birds of a feather. I won't tell a lie. ___ All of the people around us, they say, ___ "Can they be ___ that close?" Just let me state for the record: We're giving love in a fam-

Refrain

-'ly dose. We are fam-i-ly. I got all my fam-i-ly with me. We are fam-i-ly. Get up, ev-'ry-bod-y, and sing.

Verse

Living life is fun, and we've just begun to get our share ___ of this world's de - lights. High hopes we have for the fu - ture. And our goal's in sight. No, we don't get de - pressed. Here's what we call our gold - en rule: Have faith in you and the things you do. You won't go wrong. This is our fam - 'ly jewel.

Refrain
Repeat and fade

We are fam - i - ly. I got all my fam-i-ly with me.

We are fam - i - ly. Get up, ev-'ry-bod-y, and sing.

A FOLK TUNE FROM THE NETHERLANDS

This folk song has become a favorite song in this country for the Thanksgiving holiday.

- Does this song move mostly by steps or by skips?

We Gather Together

Netherlands Folk Song
Translation by T. Baker

1. We gath-er to-geth-er to ask the Lord's bless-ing;
   He chas-tens and has-tens His will to make known;
   The wick-ed op-press-ing now cease from dis-tress-ing,
   Sing prais-es to His name: He for-gets not His own.

2. Be-side us to guide us, our God with us join-ing,
   Or-dain-ing, main-tain-ing His king-dom di-vine;
   So from the be-gin-ning the fight we were win-ning;
   Thou, Lord, wast at our side, All glo-ry be thine!

3. We all do ex-tol thee, thou lead-er tri-um-phant,
   And pray that thou still our de-fend-er will be.
   Let thy con-gre-ga-tion es-cape trib-u-la-tion;
   Thy name be ev-er praised! O Lord, make us free!

- Sing the first verse *legato*. Then sing the first verse *staccato*. Decide which is more appropriate.

TAKE ANOTHER LOOK

Style is the sum of its musical parts.

rhythm + melody + form + tone color + texture = STYLE

- Think of words that describe the style of each of these compositions.

Polonaise in A Flat Major

The Moldau

Finlandia

- Sing your favorites of these songs. Think about what in the music gives each song its style.

Song of Peace

Let Love Come Near

Sing It All Together

We Are Family

JUST CHECKING

- How much do you remember? Choose the best answer for each question.

1. Which statement describes the way sound is produced on a piano?
    a. The strings are plucked by a metal pick.
    b. The strings are struck by a hammer connected to the keys.
    c. The strings are hit by the keys.

2. The damper pedal on the piano:
    a. makes the sound softer.
    b. creates a *glissando* effect.
    c. holds felt bars off the strings so they continue to vibrate.

3. Which phrases refer to nationalistic music?
    a. uses only folk songs and dance rhythms
    b. began during the nineteenth century
    c. reflects national pride
    d. often uses folk melodies and rhythms

4. Which two pitches are a step apart?

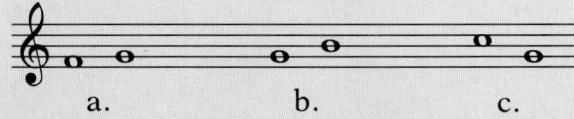

5. This song segment moves:

  a. mostly by steps.   b. mostly by skips.   c. only by skips.

UNIT 4

STYLE AND PERFORMANCE

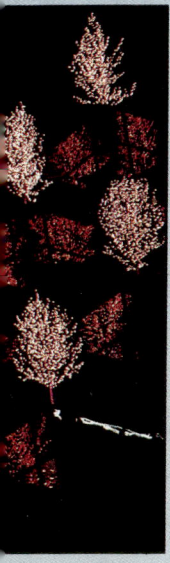

CHORAL SINGING

Think about what makes a good choral performance. Some important goals are: pronounce the words clearly, keep in tune, sing the rhythm correctly, and stay together.

- Think about the qualities of a good choral performance as you listen to this song.

Time for Acceptance and Love

Words and music by Erica Whitman Davis

Refrain *mp*

Descant: No - el, No - el, lots of good cheer,

Melody *mf*: We're all the same in more ways than we know, and we

Ha - nu - kah greet - ings, Hap - py New Year.
all go to - geth - er wher - ev - er we go. We

No - el, No - el, Hap - py New Year, and Sha -
all share the sun and the moon up a - bove, and it's

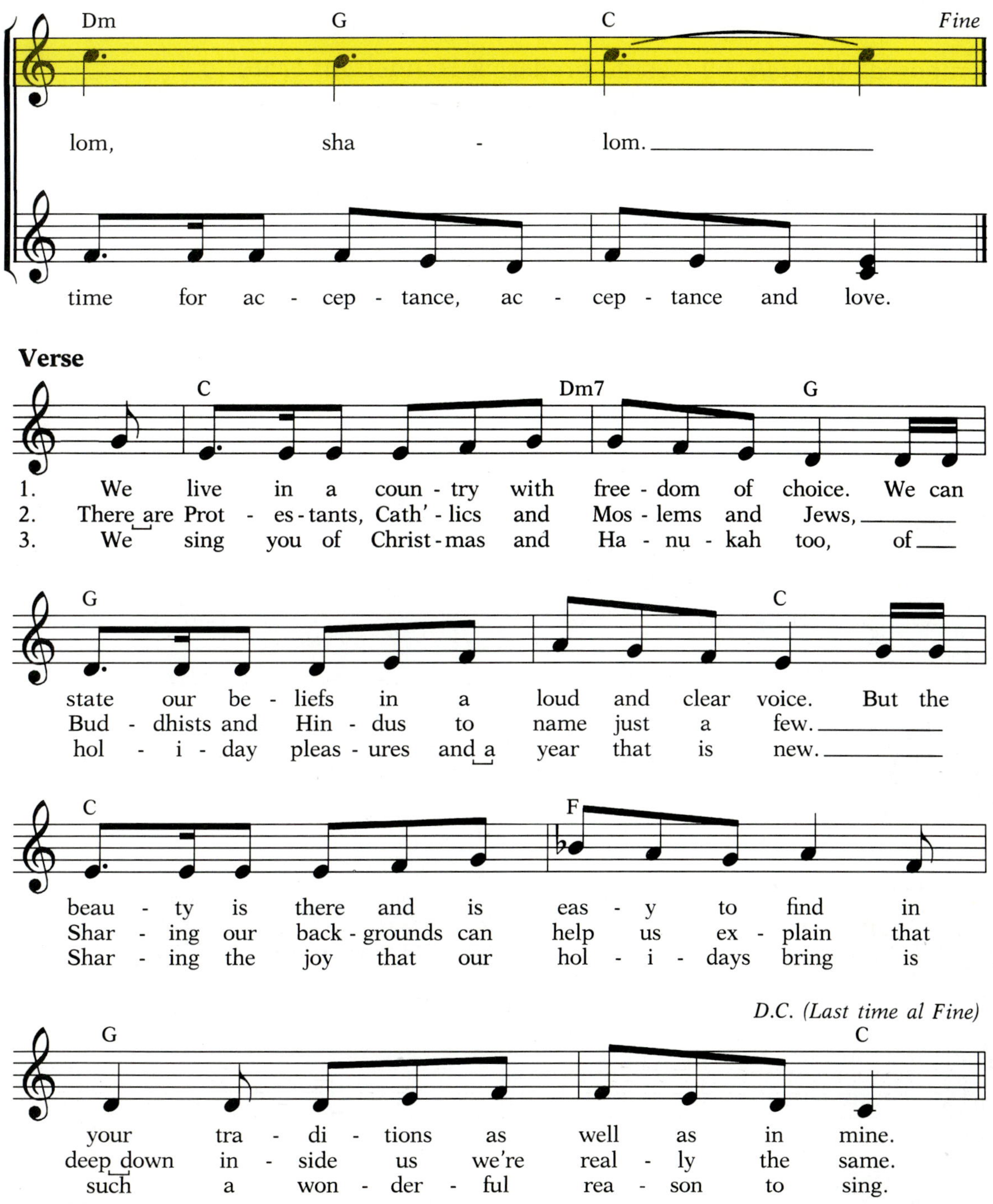

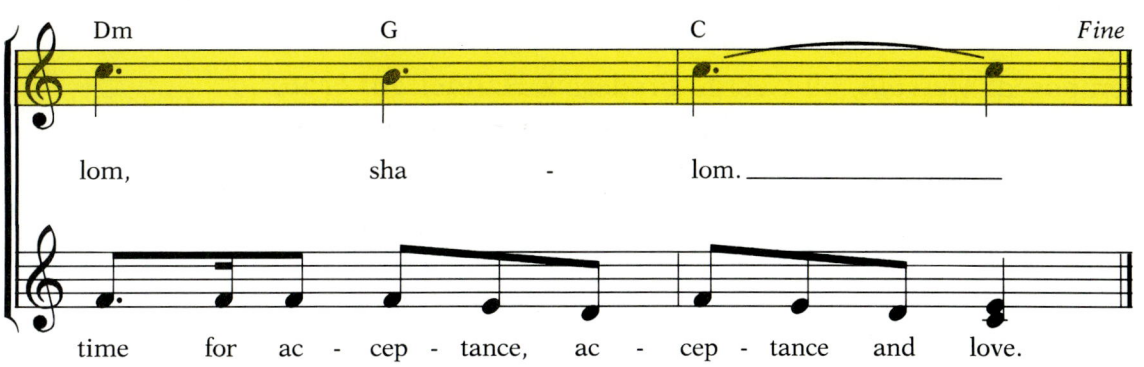

lom, sha - lom. _____
time for ac - cep - tance, ac - cep - tance and love.

Verse

1. We live in a coun - try with free - dom of choice. We can
2. There are Prot - es - tants, Cath' - lics and Mos - lems and Jews, ___
3. We sing you of Christ - mas and Ha - nu - kah too, of ___

state our be - liefs in a loud and clear voice. But the
Bud - dhists and Hin - dus to name just a few. _____
hol - i - day pleas - ures and a year that is new. _____

beau - ty is there and is eas - y to find in
Shar - ing our back - grounds can help us ex - plain that
Shar - ing the joy that our hol - i - days bring is

D.C. (Last time al Fine)

your tra - di - tions as well as in mine.
deep down in - side us we're real - ly the same.
such a won - der - ful rea - son to sing.

81

"Hallelujah" is a chorus from the best-known **oratorio** ever composed, *Messiah*, by George Frederick Handel. An oratorio uses soloists, chorus, and orchestra to tell a religious story, without acting it out on stage.

Messiah was written in 1741. When the king of England heard the "Hallelujah" chorus for the first time, he rose to his feet to honor it. Because the king stood, the entire audience stood also. This has become a tradition that is still in practice when "Hallelujah" is sung. This chorus is often heard during the holiday season.

GEORGE FREDERICK HANDEL

Detail from *George Frederick Handel*, Thomas Hudson

George Frederick Handel was born in 1685 and died in 1759. During his youth in Germany, Handel attracted much attention as a musician. By the time he was 20, Handel had composed and staged two successful operas. He then spent four years in Italy learning about Italian opera. In 1711, Handel visited London. Italian opera was very popular, and Handel met with one success after another. By 1712, he had made London his home.

By 1738, Handel had also composed several popular oratorios. *Messiah* (1741), which he wrote in only three weeks, was an instant success. From then on, Handel wrote mainly oratorios.

Handel's music is known for its drama and impact. He composed numerous oratorios and operas, as well as choral and orchestral music.

Texture was a very important characteristic of baroque music. When you hear "Hallelujah," you will notice that sometimes the singers all sing the words in unison. This is called **monophony** (mə-näf'ə-nē). Sometimes one group sings the melody, while the others sing harmony at the same time. This is called **homophony** (hō-mäf'ə-nē).

Sometimes imitation is used, with each group singing the words at different times. This is called **polyphony** (pə-lif'ə-nē).

- Look at these diagrams. They show you what texture "looks like."

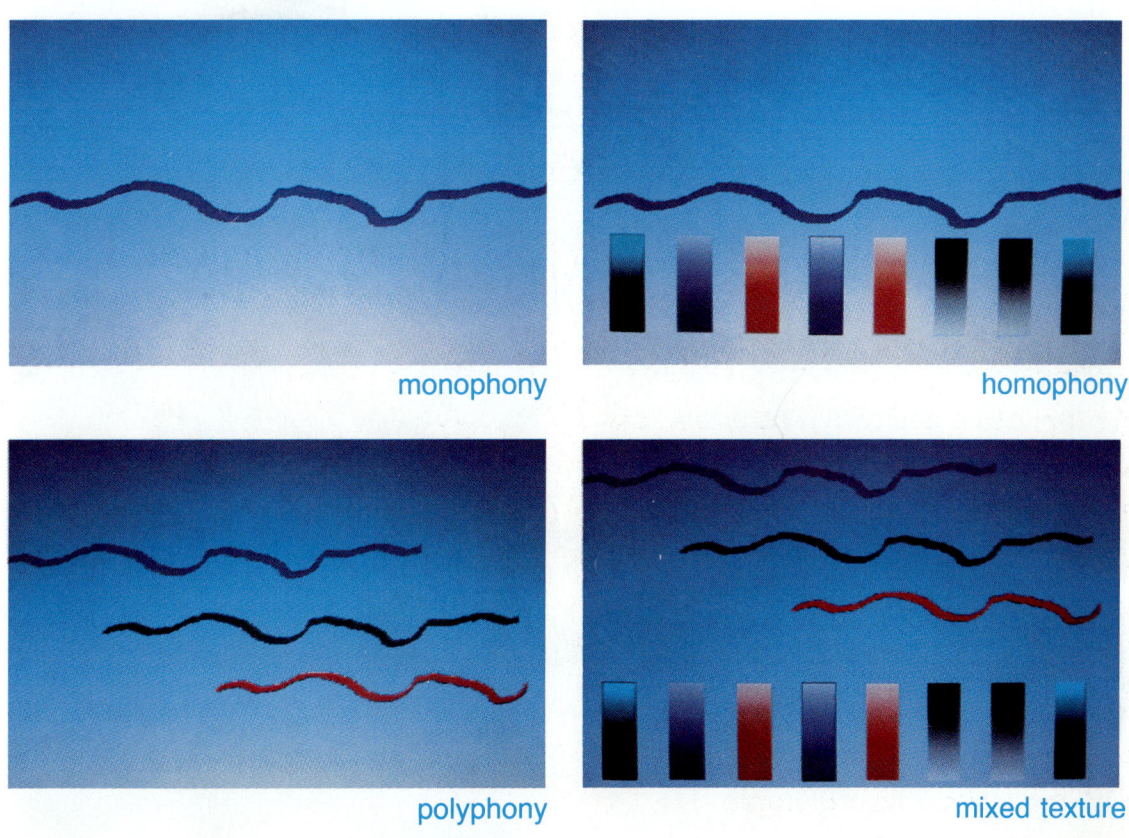

monophony

homophony

polyphony

mixed texture

- Use the diagrams to help you listen to "Hallelujah." Notice when the texture changes. Decide when the texture is monophonic, homophonic, polyphonic, or mixed.

 "Hallelujah" from *Messiah* by George Frederick Handel

RHYTHM PATTERNS

- Tap the strong beat as you listen to this folk song.

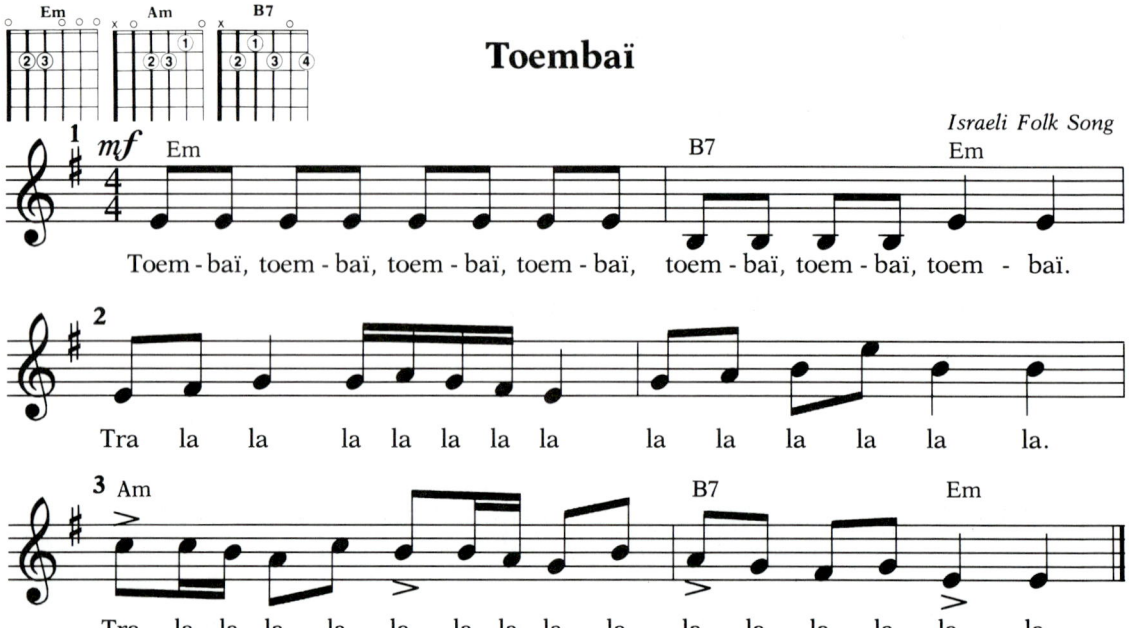

Notice the **meter signature**. 4/4 means there are four beats in each measure (top number) and ♩ is equal to one beat (bottom number).

♫ are called sixteenth notes. Sixteen of them sound as long as four quarter notes. How many sixteenth notes sound as long as ♩ ?

• Clap these rhythm patterns.

• Find these rhythms in "Toembaï." Read the rhythm using the counting system you practiced.

LISTENING FOR MUSICAL TEXTURE

This song was probably sung originally as a single, unaccompanied melody. When sung this way, the song is monophonic in texture.

When an accompaniment is added, the music becomes homophonic.

- Listen for monophonic and homophonic textures in this holiday song.

The Huron Carol

Canadian Carol
English words by J. E. Middleton

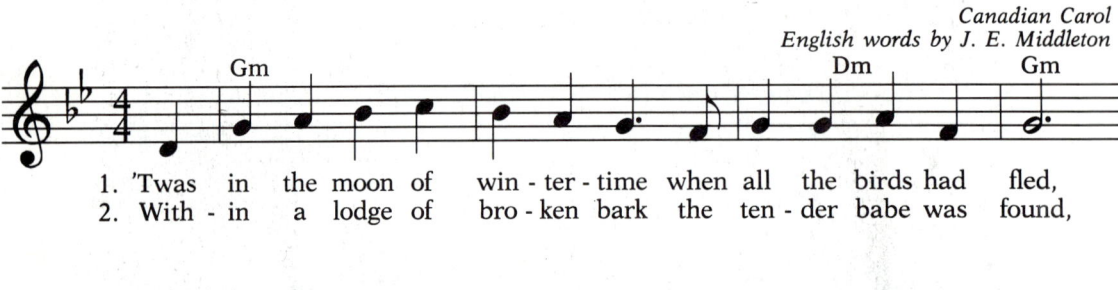

1. 'Twas in the moon of win-ter-time when all the birds had fled,
2. With-in a lodge of bro-ken bark the ten-der babe was found,

That might-y Git-chi Man-i-tou sent an-gel choirs in-stead.
A rag-ged robe of rab-bit skin en-wrapped his beau-ty 'round;

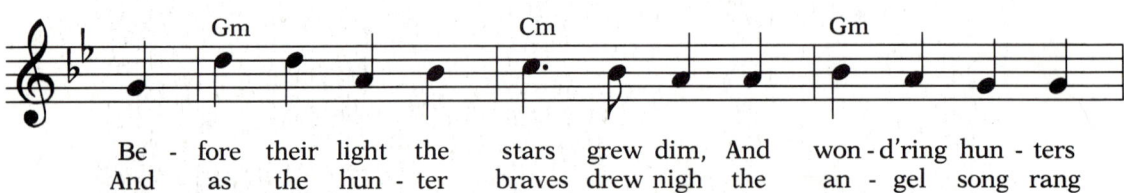

Be-fore their light the stars grew dim, And won-d'ring hun-ters
And as the hun-ter braves drew nigh the an-gel song rang

heard the hymn: }
loud and high: } "Je-sus, your King, is born. Je-sus is

born. In ex-cel-sis glo-ri-a!"

Huron Coat, mid 1800's, PEABODY MUSEUM, HARVARD UNIVERSITY, Cambridge

Above, a Huron coat from the mid-1800s, which appears to be modeled on a European military coat. *Right,* a Huron moccasin from the early 1800s, embroidered with beads and tin jinglers.

Huron Moccasin, early 1800's, PEABODY MUSEUM, HARVARD UNIVERSITY, Cambridge

When this well-known carol is sung with an accompaniment, the texture is homophonic.

- Listen for an echo in this song. How does the echo change the texture?

Do You Hear What I Hear?

*Words and music by
Noel Regney and Gloria Shayne*

1. Said the night wind to the lit-tle lamb,
2. Said the lit-tle lamb to the shep-herd boy,
3. Said the shep-herd boy to the might-y king,

"Do you see what I see? ___ (Do you see what I see?)
"Do you hear what I hear? ___ (Do you hear what I hear?)
"Do you know what I know? ___ (Do you know what I know?)

Way up in the sky, lit-tle lamb.
Ring-ing thru the sky, shep-herd boy.
In your pal-ace warm, might-y king.

Do you see what I see? (Do you see what I see?) A
Do you hear what I hear? (Do you hear what I hear?) A
Do you know what I know? (Do you know what I know?) A

star, a star, danc-ing in the night, With a
song, a song, high a-bove the tree, With a
Child, a Child, shiv-ers in the cold, Let us

tail as big as a kite, ___ With a
voice as big as the sea, ___ With a
bring Him sil-ver and gold, ___ Let us

89

RONDO FORM

A **rondo** is a musical form in which the first section (A) is repeated after each contrasting section.

- Listen for the sections in "Do-Di-Li." Describe the form, using A, B, C, and D.

CATEGORIES OF VOICES

The voice is an instrument. Voice type is determined by how high or low a person can sing. This is called the **voice range.** There are four main categories of adult voices.

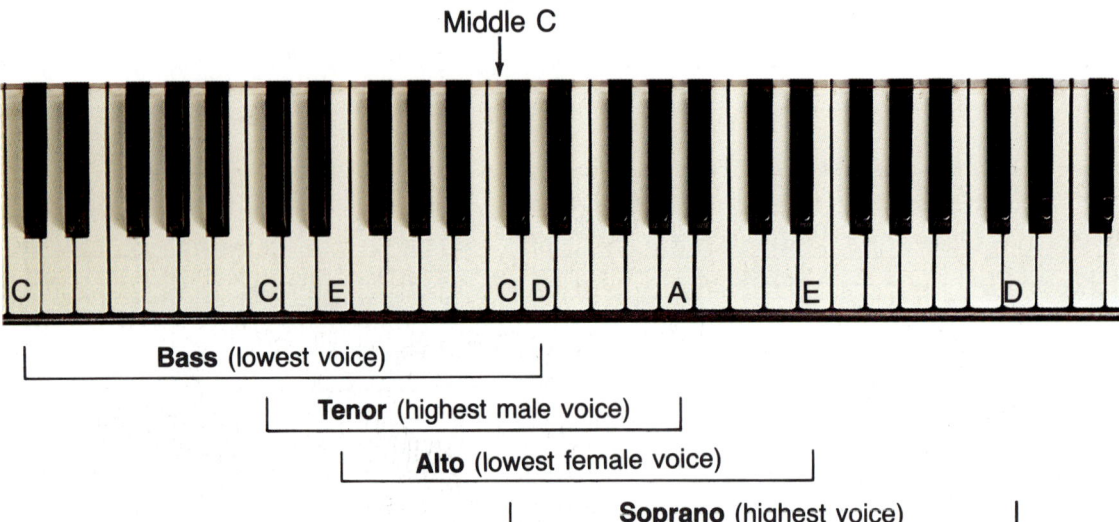

- Look at the notation below from "Hallelujah." How many voice types do you expect to hear? Listen for each part when you hear this chorus.

Most students in the sixth grade have about the same voice range. The range includes these pitches:

When boys' voices first begin to change, they will be able to sing some slightly lower pitches than before. This stage is called **cambiata** (kam-bē-ä′tə). When the changes in boys' voices are complete, boys will usually be tenors or basses. Girls also experience a voice change. Older girls will usually become altos or sopranos.

- What adult voice is most similar in range to the voice range of most sixth-grade students?

Notice the meter signature for "Deck the Halls." **C** (common time) is another way of writing $\frac{4}{4}$ meter.

- Tap the strong beat to show meter in four.

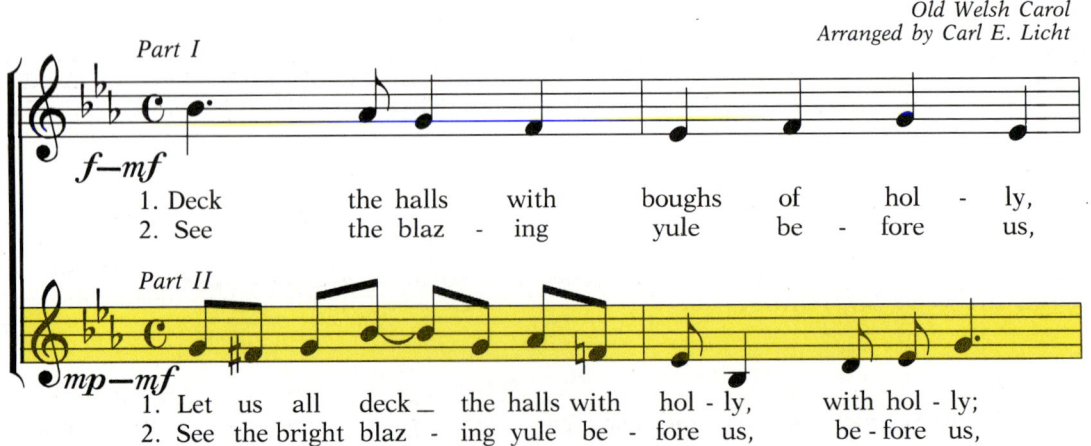

Deck the Halls

Old Welsh Carol
Arranged by Carl E. Licht

Part I

f—mf

1. Deck the halls with boughs of hol - ly,
2. See the blaz - ing yule be - fore us,

Part II

mp—mf

1. Let us all deck the halls with hol - ly, with hol - ly;
2. See the bright blaz - ing yule be - fore us, be - fore us,

- Compare the ranges of Parts I and II. Which is lower?

CHORALES AND CHORALE PRELUDES

A **chorale** is another name for a hymn sung in some Protestant churches. It usually has a simple tune and is easy to sing. Chorales were developed in Germany by Martin Luther (1483–1546), the founder of the Lutheran church. It was a way for the congregation to participate in the music of the service.

One of the best-known compositions in this style is "Jesu, Joy of Man's Desiring," by the German composer Johann Sebastian Bach.

- Listen to the chorale sung by a choir. Decide if it is homophonic or polyphonic.

 "Jesu, Joy of Man's Desiring" (chorale), from Cantata No. 147 by Johann Sebastian Bach

A **chorale prelude** is based on the melody of a chorale and is used as an introduction to the chorale. It is played on the organ just before the chorale is sung.

- Listen to this composition which Bach wrote in the style of a chorale prelude. It features a second melody called a **counter-melody.** Using a counter-melody is another way to create polyphony.

As you listen, follow the listening map below. Identify whether you are hearing the original chorale, the counter-melody, or a combination of both.

 "Jesu, Joy of Man's Desiring" (chorale prelude), from Cantata No. 147 by Johann Sebastian Bach

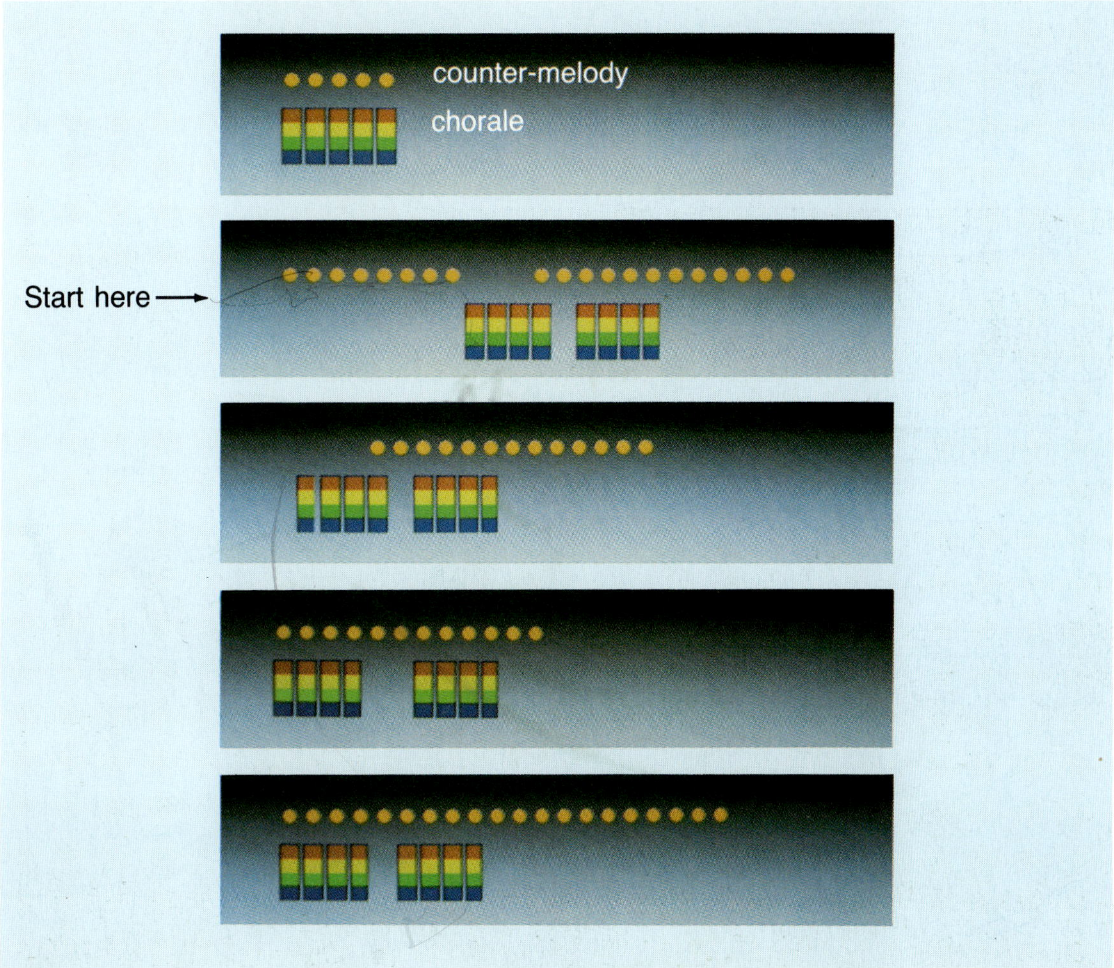

TAKE ANOTHER LOOK

- How will knowing the style of a song affect the way you sing it? Sing each song once more, thinking about the appropriate style.

    Time for Acceptance and Love
    Toembaï
    Deck the Halls

- Listen again for the different textures in "Hallelujah" from *Messiah*.

JUST CHECKING

- How much do you remember? Choose the best answer for each question.

1. Which term describes the highest adult voice?
   a. *cambiata*   b. tenor   c. soprano

2. Which term describes the highest male adult voice?
   a. alto   b. tenor   c. bass

3. Which term describes a boy's changing voice?
   a. *cambiata*   b. tenor   c. soprano

4. What is essential to a good choral performance?
   a. keeping the pitch in tune
   b. pronouncing the words clearly
   c. singing the rhythm correctly
   d. all of the above

5. The group of four sixteenth notes is ____.

6. Which group shows an eighth note followed by two sixteenth notes?

7. Which best describes texture that is monophonic?
   a. two melodies playing at the same time
   b. a melody alone
   c. a melody with accompaniment

WHY THE SUN & MOON LIVE IN THE SKY

A Musical Play Based on
an African Folk Tale
Adapted and arranged by
Randy DeLelles and Jeff Kriske

Cast
Narrator
Sun Children (6–8 boys)
Moon Children (6–8 girls)
Water Children (4)
Shadow Players (4)
Instrument Players

NARRATOR: The story you are about to hear is from a different land. Many years ago, people questioned how things came to be. This is their story of why the Sun and the Moon live in the sky.

Samanfo
African Folk Song

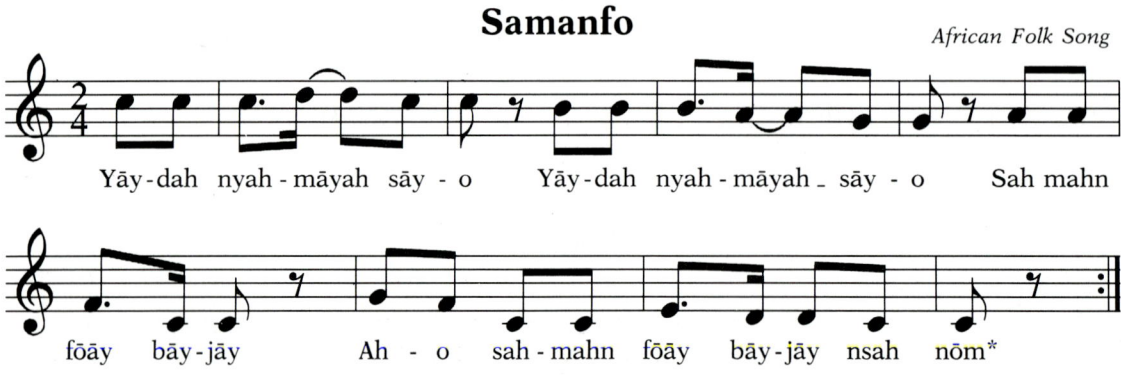

Yāy-dah nyah-māyah sāy-o Yāy-dah nyah-māyah sāy-o Sah mahn fōay bāy-jāy Ah-o sah-mahn fōay bāy-jāy nsah nōm*

*Phonetic

NARRATOR: Many years ago, life on earth was not as we know it today. The great and mighty Sun **(Sun Motif)** and his wife the Moon **(Moon Motif)** lived together on earth. They were great friends and were never seen apart. **(Sun and Moon Motifs)**

Sun Motif

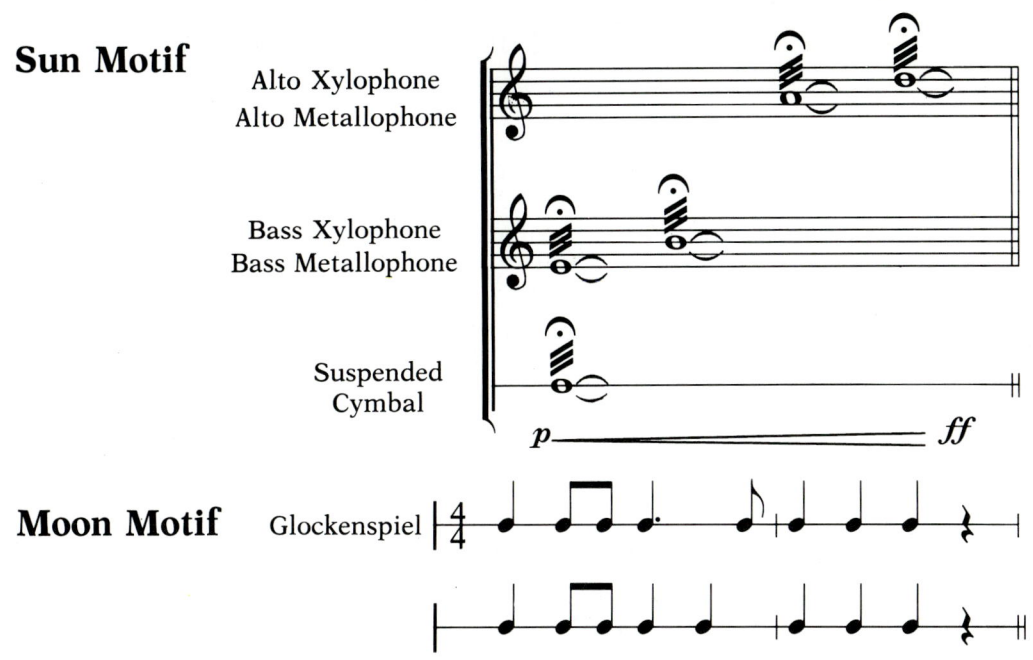

Moon Motif

NARRATOR: Every day the Sun and Moon Children played together.

Ibo

Nigerian Folk Song

Eim - a, Eim - a, I - bo - i-day-a-day Eim - a, Ei - i Ei - i - ei - i - ei - i - bo

NARRATOR: The Sun and the Moon were good friends with the Water. They visited the Water almost every day.

Benue

Nigerian Folk Song

105

NARRATOR: The Water never returned their visits. At last, the Sun and Moon asked the Water why it was that he never came to visit. The Water replied, "Before I can come to visit, you will have to build a house large enough to hold all of me and all who come with me." The very next day the Sun and the Moon began building a large house.

Building the House

NARRATOR: When the house was completed, the Sun and Moon invited the Water to come visit. Very soon, the Water had filled the first floor of the house. He asked the Sun if he might continue to come in. The Sun and Moon said, "Yes."

Water Theme

NARRATOR: The Water continued flowing with no end in sight. Once again, he asked if he might continue to come in. The Sun and the Moon answered, "Yes."
(Repeat "Water Theme")

By this time the Water had filled most of the house. The Sun and the Moon had to perch themselves on top of the roof. Again the Water questioned the Sun and once more received the same reply. So more of the Water rushed in.
(Repeat "Water Theme")

The Water very soon overflowed the top of the roof. The Sun and Moon were forced to go up into the sky, where they have remained ever since. And that is why the Sun and the Moon live in the sky.
(Repeat "Benue")

THE END

UNIT 5

SCALES

NIGHT

Stars over snow,
And in the west, a planet
Swinging below a star—
Look for a lovely thing and you will find it,
It is not far—
It will never be far.
— *Sara Teasdale*

INSPIRATION

The night sky has inspired artists, poets, and composers. The composer of this song admired the beauty of the constellation Orion. He was concerned that someday the stars might be hidden from us by air pollution.

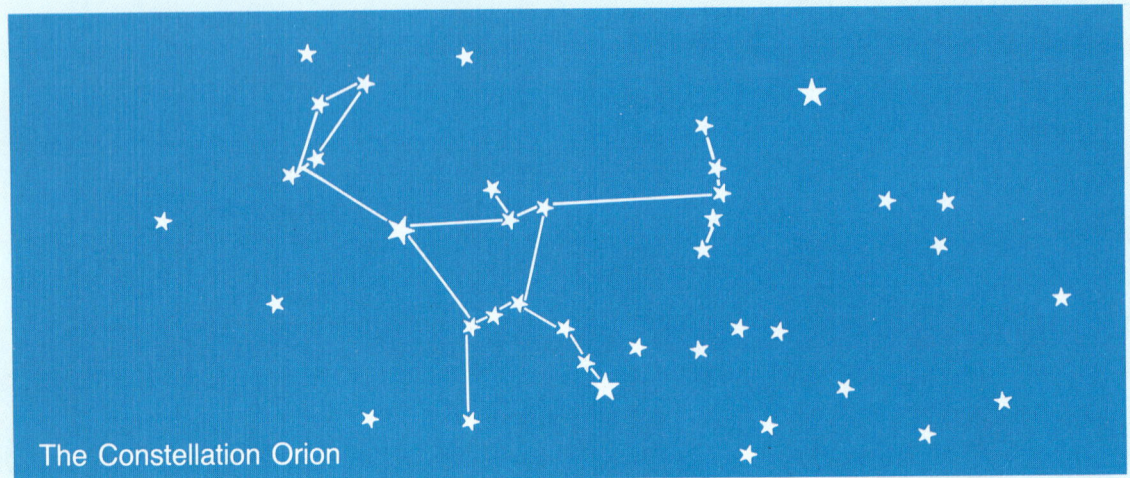

The Constellation Orion

 Listen to the song. What change does the composer make in the middle of the song? Why do you think he made this change?

Orion

Words and music by James Zimmermann

1. O - ri - on is a - ris - ing, You can see his stars a - blaz - ing in the mid - dle of a clear - eyed coun - try sky. And it's nev - er too sur - pris - ing that the sky is still a - maz -
(2.) day is get - ting cold - er, And I real - ly start to won - der why they're cloud - ing all the coun - try skies to gray. The world is get - ting old - er, You can hear it in the thun -

Gustav Holst (1874–1934), a British composer, wrote a **suite** called *The Planets* which has seven movements. Each of the seven movements is about a planet in our solar system. (Pluto had not yet been discovered. Earth is not included in the suite.)

- Listen to the first movement of *The Planets,* "Mars." Decide if there is a change of meter.

 "Mars" from *The Planets* by Gustav Holst

- Compare "Mars" with "Orion." How are they alike? How are they different?

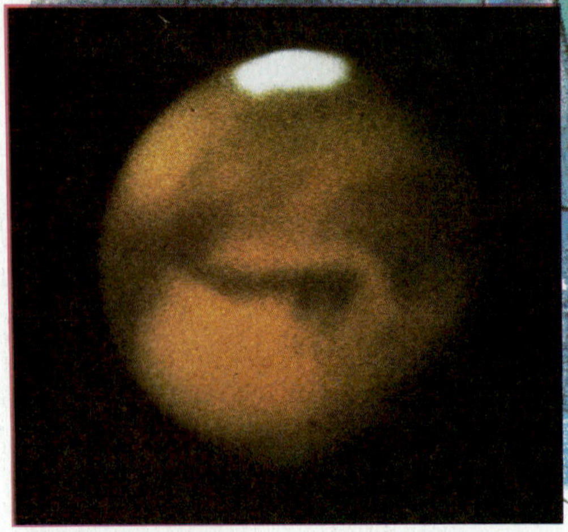

A photograph of Mars taken by Viking I, an unmanned spacecraft that landed on the planet and sent pictures and data back to Earth

Mars, the mythical Roman god

Photographs of Mars taken by Viking I: great volcano (*top left*), sand dunes on Mars (*top right*), first color photo of Mars (*middle left*), Martian sunset (*bottom*).

A SCALE-WISE MELODY

Did you know that falling stars are not really stars at all? They are meteors that glow when they enter the earth's atmosphere. Some people believe that seeing a falling star will bring them good luck.

In "Catch a Falling Star" there is a solo part for *cambiatas* (boys' changing voices). Since this is a lower voice, it is written in the **bass clef** (𝄢). Parts for higher voices are always written in the **treble clef** (𝄞).

- As you listen to the song, notice that the first two phrases of the melody move **scale-wise.**

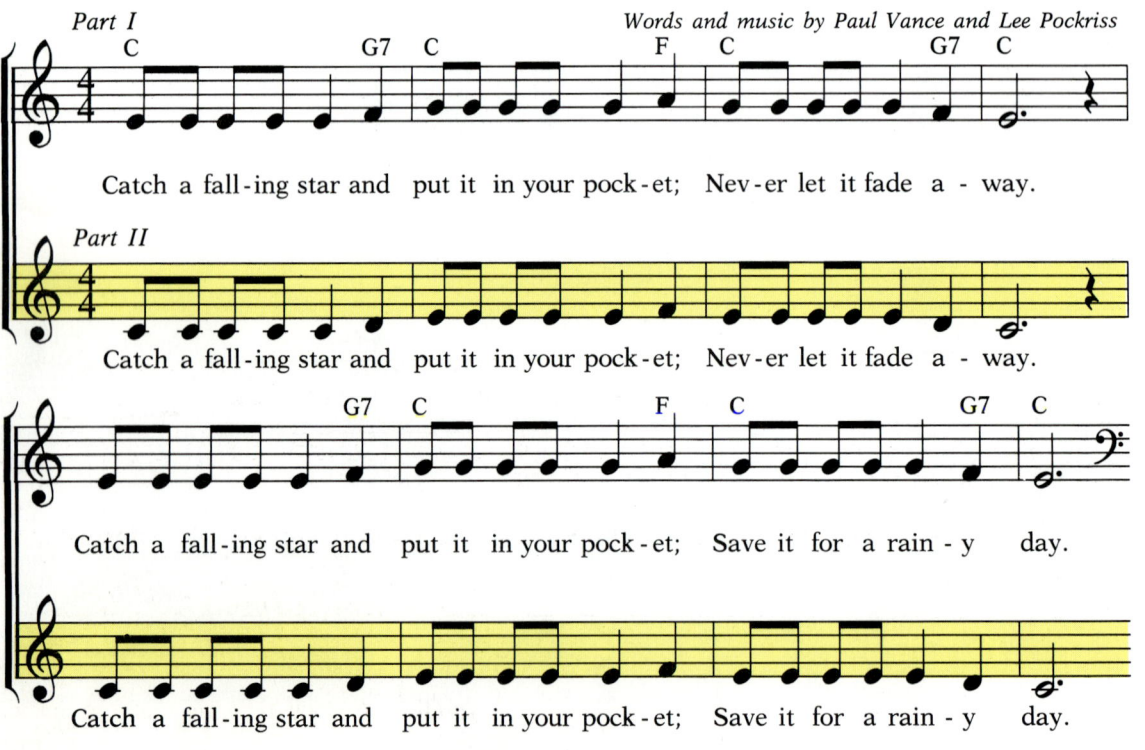

Catch a Falling Star

Words and music by Paul Vance and Lee Pockriss

Catch a fall-ing star and put it in your pock-et; Nev-er let it fade a-way.

Catch a fall-ing star and put it in your pock-et; Nev-er let it fade a-way.

Catch a fall-ing star and put it in your pock-et; Save it for a rain-y day.

Catch a fall-ing star and put it in your pock-et; Save it for a rain-y day.

Boy's changing voice (Cambiata)
F
C
For love may come and tap you on the shoul-der Some star-less night, And
F
Treble Voices
C
G7
just in case you feel you want to hold her, You'll have a pock-et full of star-light.
You'll have a pock-et full of star-light.

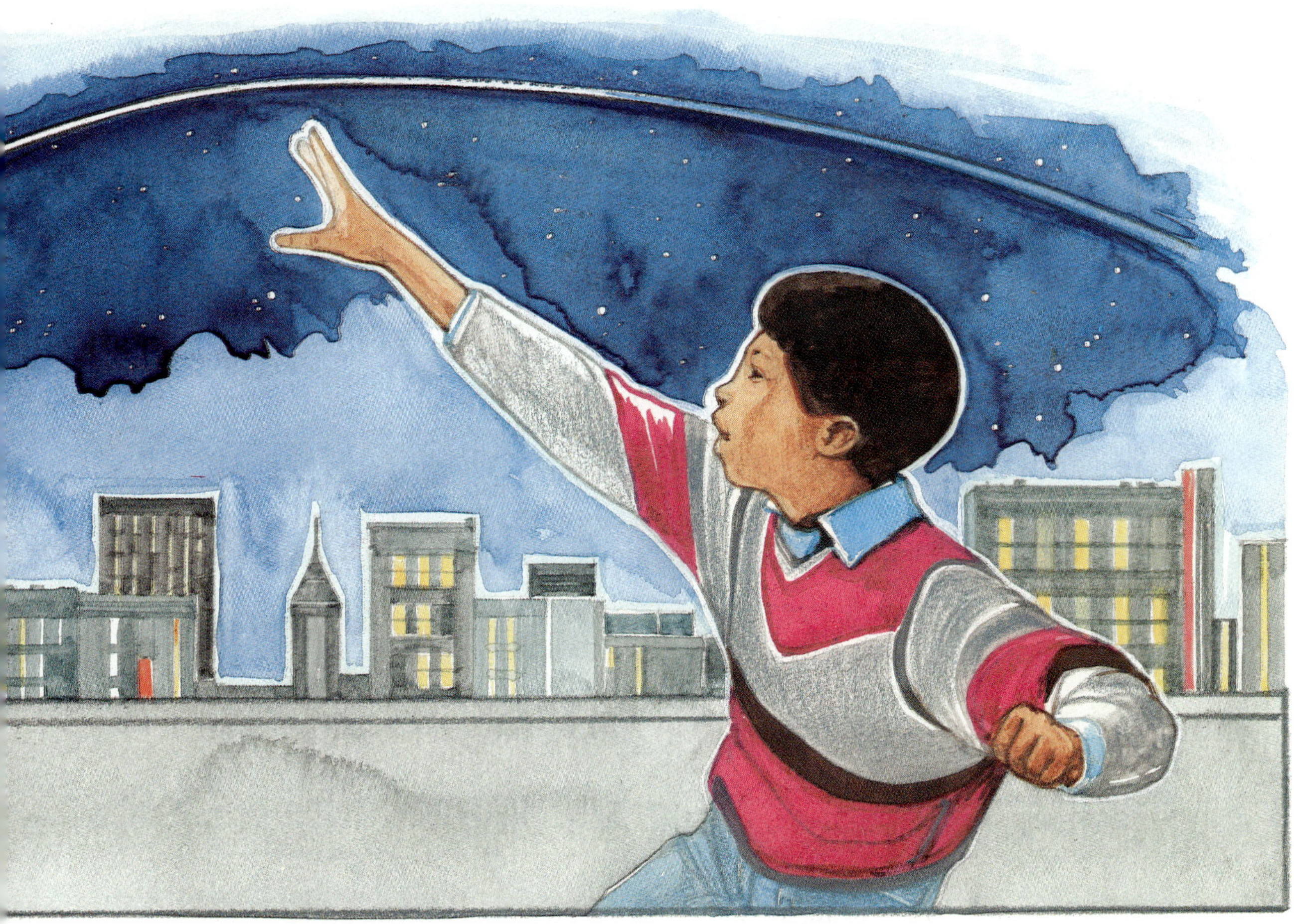

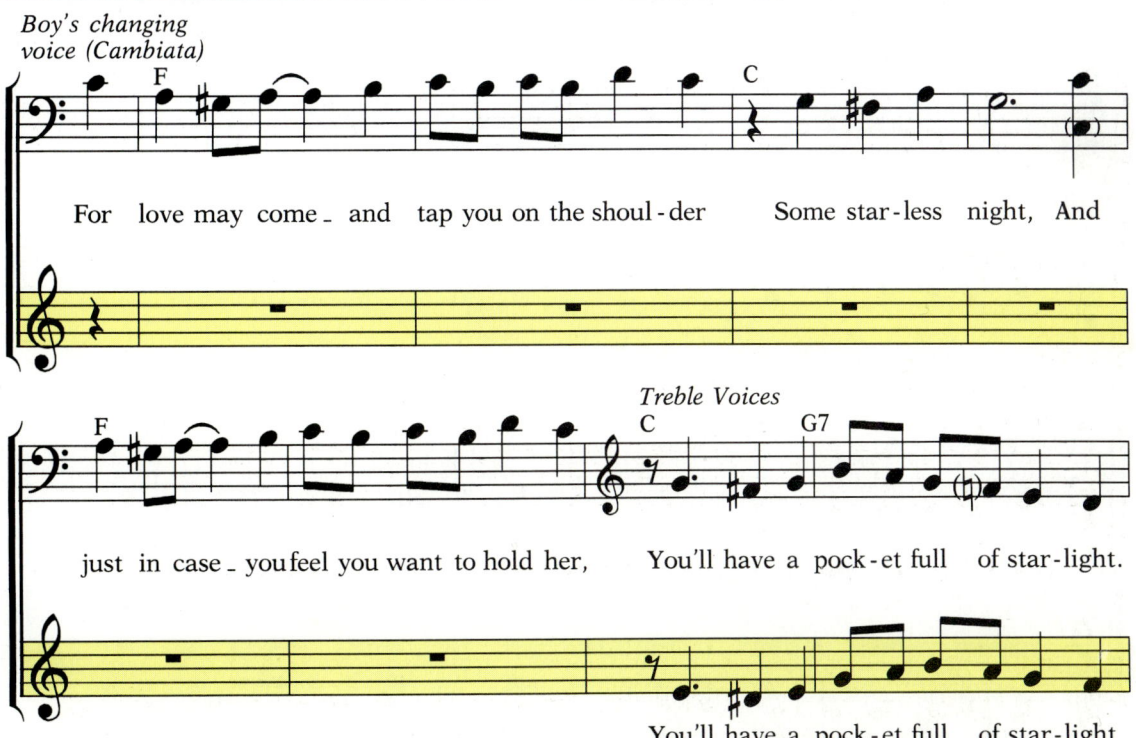

The Starry Night, 1889, Vincent van Gogh, Oil on canvas, 29 x 36¼". Acquired through the Lillie P. Bliss Bequest Collection, THE MUSEUM OF MODERN ART, NY

The Starry Night by Vincent van Gogh was painted in 1889 while the artist was living in Saint-Rémy, France. The painting is the result of van Gogh's efforts to create a picture that was constantly on his mind—that of a starry night.

- Play the first phrase of "Catch a Falling Star" below. Use a keyboard instrument or bells.

- Name the pitches.

The distance between two pitches which are right next to each other on the keyboard is called a **half step**.

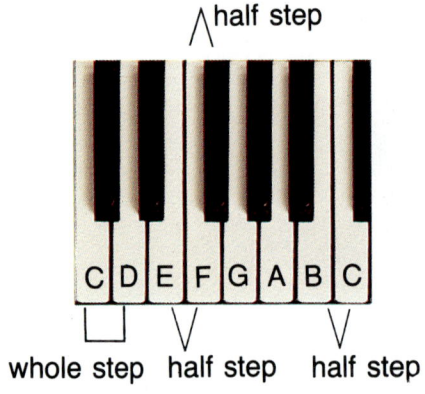

- Name the half step you played.

The distance between two pitches which have one key between them is called a **whole step**.

- Name two whole steps you played.

Most melodies are based on certain patterns of pitches or scales.

The **major scale** is the most frequently used scale. It is made up of half steps and whole steps between the pitches in the scale.

- Look at the half steps in the C major scale.

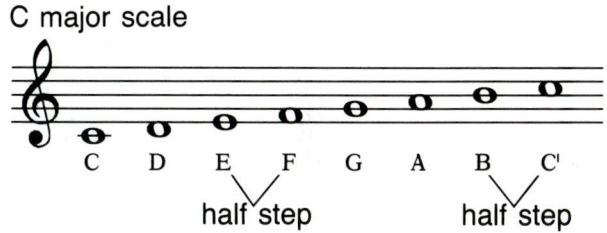

All the other pitches are a whole step apart.

- Play the C major scale on a keyboard instrument or on bells. Play it both **ascending** (upward) and **descending** (downward).

Songs that use the C major scale have C as their **tonal center**. The melody tends to return to C as the home base or resting place.

119

MELODIES BUILT ON A MAJOR SCALE

When melodies, or parts of melodies, are based on a scale, they are easier to play and sing.

- Look at the notation for "Lean on Me." Find two lines that are mostly scale-wise.
- Find the **D.S.**, or *dal segno*, symbol in the first ending. This means to repeat from the sign, 𝄋.

Lean on Me

Words and music by Bill Withers

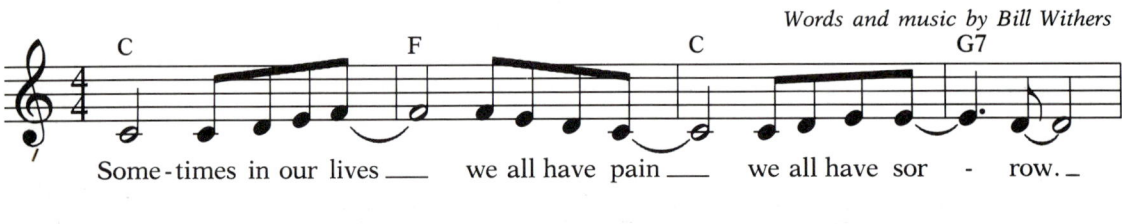

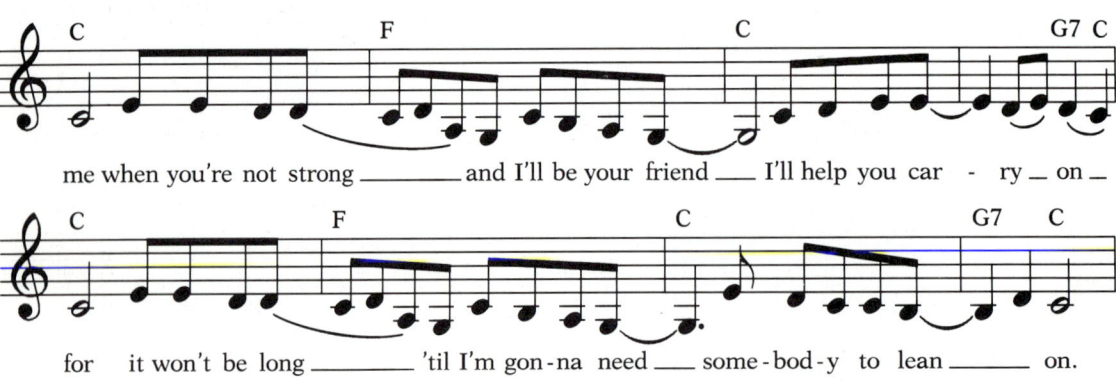

- How do the first four pitches in the C major scale relate to "Lean on Me"?

Scale-wise melodies can have chords added below them that also move scale-wise. Chords create harmony.

The melody of "Lean on Me" is the top line of notes. The harmony notes are added below.

- Play the first chord on a keyboard instrument. Using your right hand, place your thumb on E, your first finger on G, and your little finger on C. Keep your fingers "frozen" in this position.

- Now play the whole pattern using your "frozen hand."

Petrushka is a ballet about a puppet in a show at a fair. The music was composed by Igor Stravinsky (ē′gôr strə-vin′skē) in 1911. The "Russian Dance" is from this ballet. It is performed by three puppets: Petrushka, the Blackamoor, and the Ballerina.

Below is the main theme of "Russian Dance." Like the melody of "Lean on Me," this theme (top line of notes) also moves scale-wise.

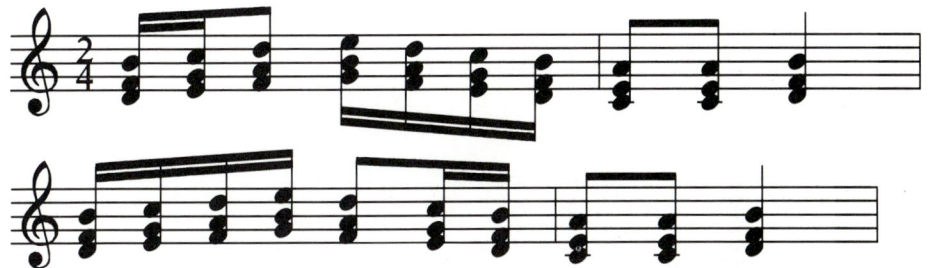

- Use your "frozen hand" to play this theme. What are the pitches of the first chord?
- Listen for the main theme in "Russian Dance." Raise your right hand when you hear it at a fast tempo. Raise your left hand when you hear the theme at a slower tempo.

   "Russian Dance" from *Petrushka* by Igor Stravinsky

Three scenes from the ballet *Petrushka.*

STEPS AND SKIPS

Most melodies move scale-wise at times and by skips at other times.

- In which way do the tinted portions of this song move?
- Find the parts of the melody that move scale-wise.
- Find the lines of the melody that are exactly, or almost exactly, the same.

Oliver Cromwell

English Folk Song

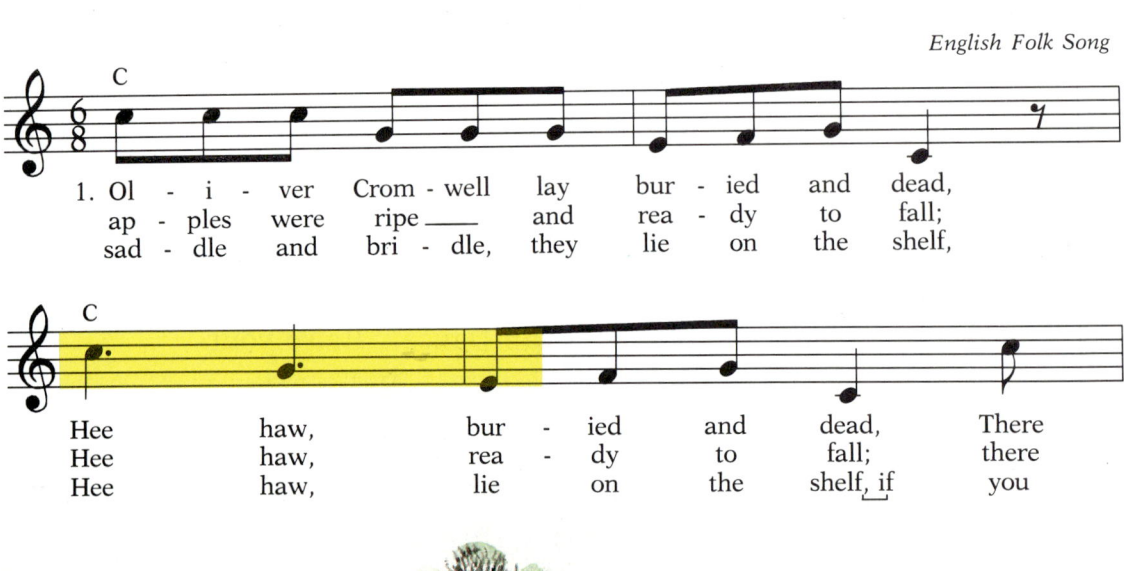

C
1. Ol - i - ver Crom - well lay bur - ied and dead,
ap - ples were ripe ___ and rea - dy to fall;
sad - dle and bri - dle, they lie on the shelf,
C
Hee haw, bur - ied and dead, There
Hee haw, rea - dy to fall; there
Hee haw, lie on the shelf, if you

OLIVER
CROMWELL

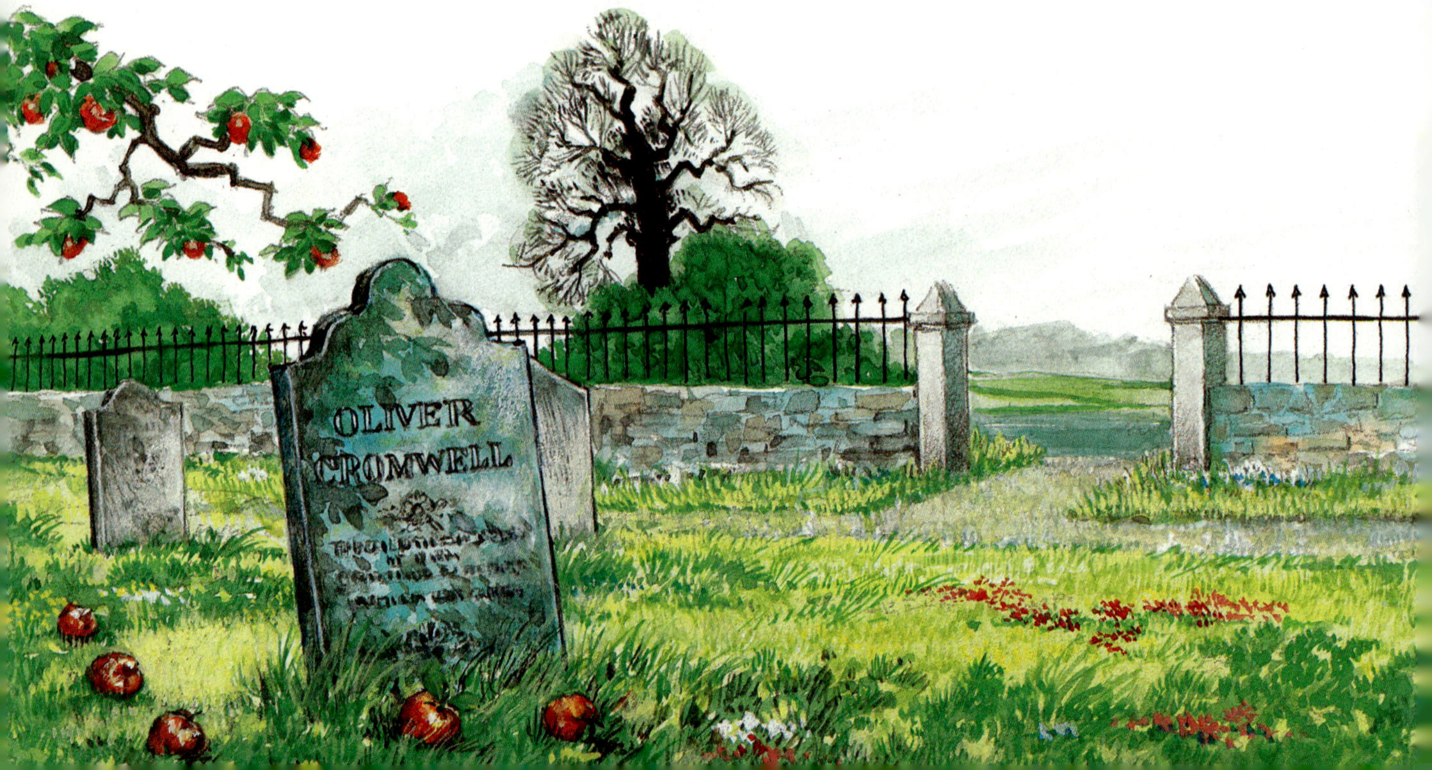

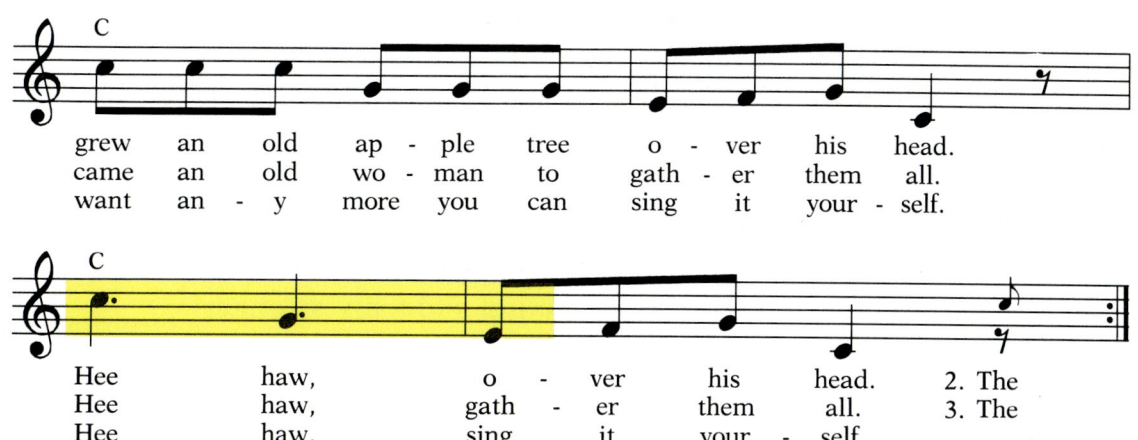

grew an old ap - ple tree o - ver his head.
came an old wo - man to gath - er them all.
want an - y more you can sing it your - self.

Hee haw, o - ver his head. 2. The
Hee haw, gath - er them all. 3. The
Hee haw, sing it your - self.

- Follow the notation of these two themes from "Mars" as you listen. Decide which theme moves by skips and which moves scale-wise.

Theme 1

Theme 2

125

A MELODY BUILT ON THE F MAJOR SCALE

Composers often express their thoughts and feelings in the music they write. To make certain ideas more important, a composer will accent them. The musical symbol > represents an **accent.** Accented notes sound suddenly stronger than the notes around them.

- As you listen, identify the accented notes in this song.

I Shall Sing

Words and music by Van Morrison
Arranged by N.F.

Part I

1. 3. I shall sing, sing my song, Be it right,
2. With my heart, with my soul, For the young,

Part II (3rd time only)

I shall sing, sing my song,

___ be it wrong. In the night, in the day,
___ for the old. When I'm high, when I'm low,

Be it right, be it wrong. In the night,

"I Shall Sing" is built on the F Major Scale.

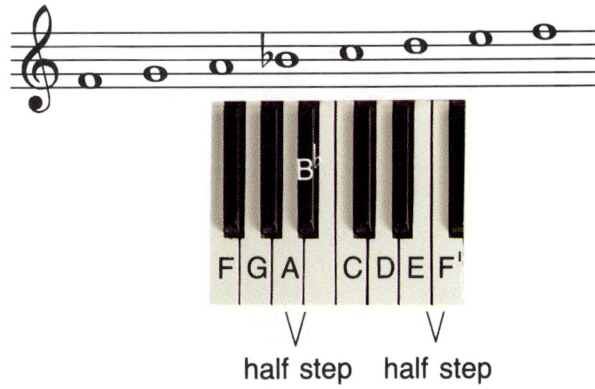

The B in this scale is a B flat. The **flat** symbol (♭) lowers the pitch one half step.

- Test your ears by playing the F major scale. Use the pitches above. Then play the scale substituting B for B♭. Which scale sounds right? Why?

The F major scale must have a B♭ because of the whole step-half step pattern. There is a half step between the third and fourth steps (A-B♭) and the seventh and eighth steps (E-F').

A MELODY BUILT ON THE D MINOR SCALE

The sound of the minor scale and the words of a great poet, Walter de la Mare, were the inspiration for this canon.

- Listen for the sound of the minor scale.

The Horseman

Music by M.D.
Words by Walter de la Mare

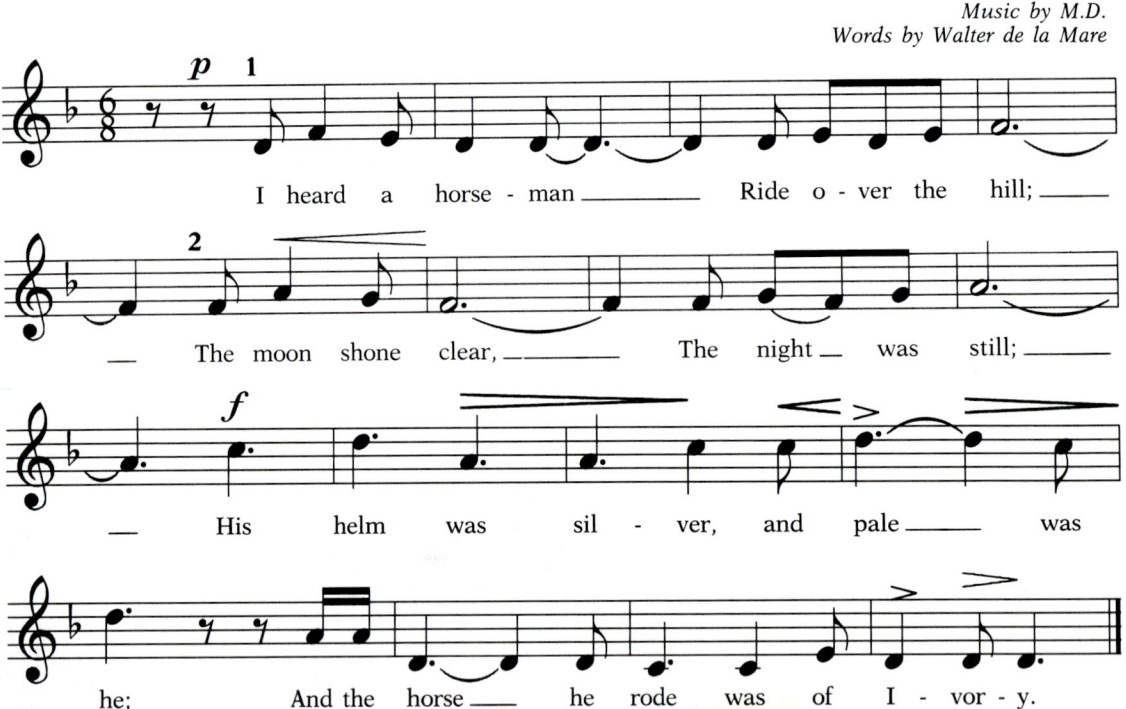

I heard a horseman __ Ride o-ver the hill; __
__ The moon shone clear, __ The night __ was still; __
__ His helm was sil-ver, and pale __ was
he; And the horse __ he rode was of I-vor-y.

The **minor scale,** like the major scale, is made up of half steps and whole steps. In the D minor scale, the half steps are between E and F and between A and B♭. The other pitches are a whole step apart.

The D minor scale uses the same pitch names as the F major scale (page 127). Because of this, it is also called the **relative minor** of F major.

D minor scale

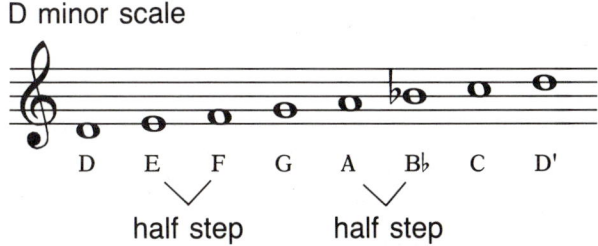

- Play the D minor scale on a keyboard instrument or on bells. Play an ascending scale and a descending scale.

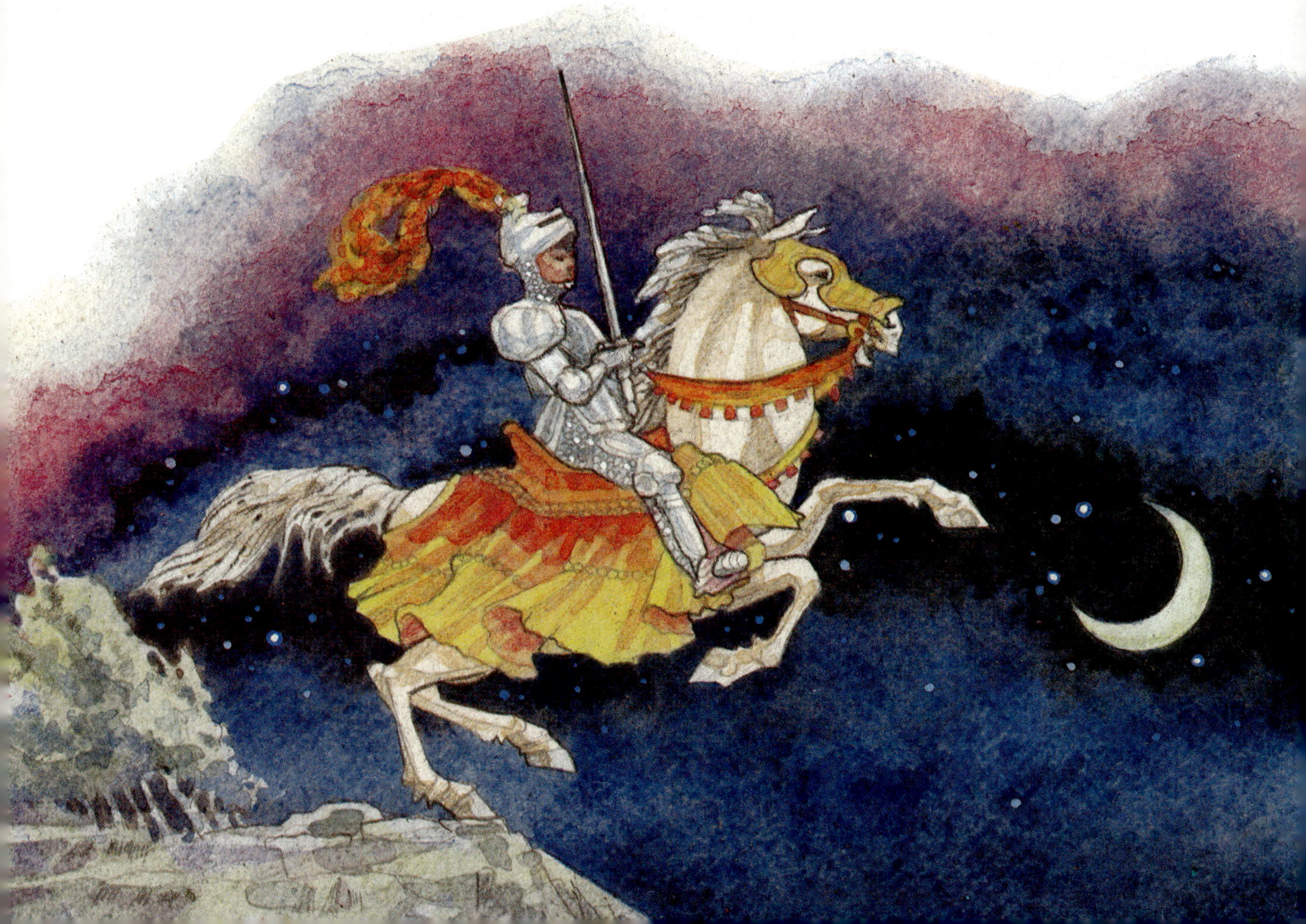

MELODIES BUILT ON A CHROMATIC SCALE

- On a keyboard instrument or on bells, play every pitch moving downward. Begin on C. You will be playing half steps, or **chromatics** (krō-mat′iks).

- Listen for the sound of chromatics in the song "Tumbling Tumbleweeds." Does the harmony part also move downward by half steps?   yes

- Follow the words as you listen.

Tumbling Tumbleweeds

See them tumbling down,
Pledging their love to the ground,
Lonely but free I'll be found,
Drifting along with the tumbling tumbleweeds.

Cares of the past are behind,
Nowhere to go, but I'll find
Just where the trail will wind,
Drifting along with the tumbling tumbleweeds.

I know when night has gone
That a new world's born at dawn.

I'll keep rolling along,
Deep in my heart is a song,
Here on the range I belong,
Drifting along with the tumbling tumbleweeds.

Words and music by Bob Nolan

A **chromatic scale** is made up of all half steps.

In the ascending scale, **sharps** (♯) show that the pitch is one half step higher. In the descending scale, flats show that the pitch is one half step lower.

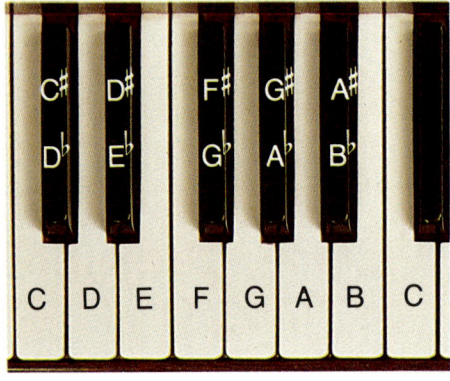

- Play a chromatic scale on a keyboard instrument or on bells. Begin on C and play every key or bell in order—black and white.
- Listen to "Flight of the Bumblebee" by the Russian composer Nicolai Rimsky-Korsakov (nik′ō-lī rim-skē-kôr′sə- kôf). It uses many chromatic tones to give the effect of the sound of a flying bee.

 "Flight of the Bumblebee" by Nicolai Rimsky-Korsakov

NICOLAI RIMSKY-KORSAKOV

Nicolai Rimsky-Korsakov was one of the best-known Russian composers. He was born in 1844 and died in 1908. He attended the Naval College in St. Petersburg (now Leningrad), but he also continued to study music. In 1871, even though he was officially serving in the Navy, Rimsky-Korsakov was appointed Professor of Composition at the St. Petersburg Conservatory.

Rimsky-Korsakov is known especially for his imaginative way of using orchestral instruments. He also did much to preserve the musical heritage of his country. His music was strongly influenced by Russian folk songs.

Rimsky-Korsakov's works include 15 operas and three symphonies. One of his most famous works is the symphonic suite *Scheherazade*.

A nineteenth-century engraving of the imperial bank in St. Petersburg

A MELODY BUILT ON A WHOLE-TONE SCALE

Another kind of scale is the **whole-tone scale.** It uses nothing but whole steps. The scale does not sound either major or minor.

- Build a whole-tone scale beginning on F. Here are the pitches you will need:

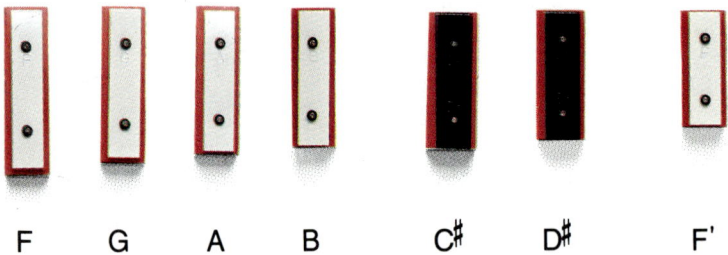

- Play the scale ascending, then descending.
- Listen for the special sound of the whole-tone scale in this version of a familiar round.

Oh, How Lovely Is the Evening
(Whole-Tone Version)

Traditional Round

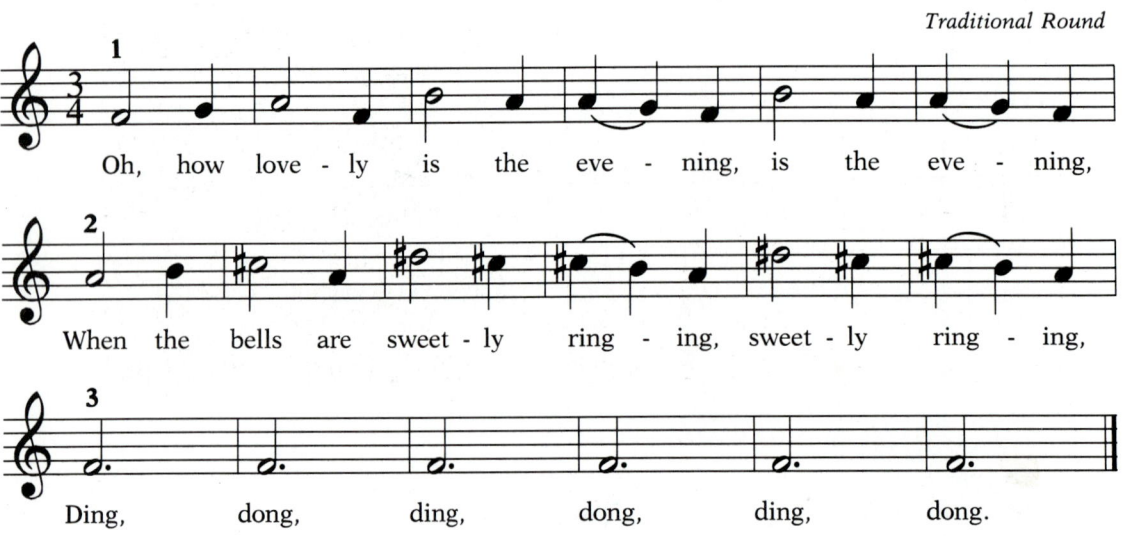

Claude Debussy (klôd deb-yoo-sē′) was a French composer who lived from 1862 to 1918. Debussy composed music in the impressionist style that developed in France in the late nineteenth and early twentieth centuries. Impressionist composers tried to use sounds that would create a certain mood or atmosphere.

• Listen to "Play of the Waves" from the suite *La Mer (The Sea)* by Debussy. It uses the parts of the whole-tone scale in some places. It also has many chromatics. Listen for these sounds and for the way the music suggests the sparkling movement of the ocean.

 "Play of the Waves" (excerpt) from *La Mer* by Claude Debussy

Etretat, the Beach and Port of Amont was painted by the French artist Claude Monet (1840–1926). Monet worked in the impressionist style of painting. The picture is made up of many dots or dabs of different color, which seem to blend into a solid scene.

SOMETHING DIFFERENT

Sometimes composers use two or more different scales, each with its own tonal center, at the same time. This is called **polytonal** music.

- Try polytonality on your own. Set up bells in two different scales.

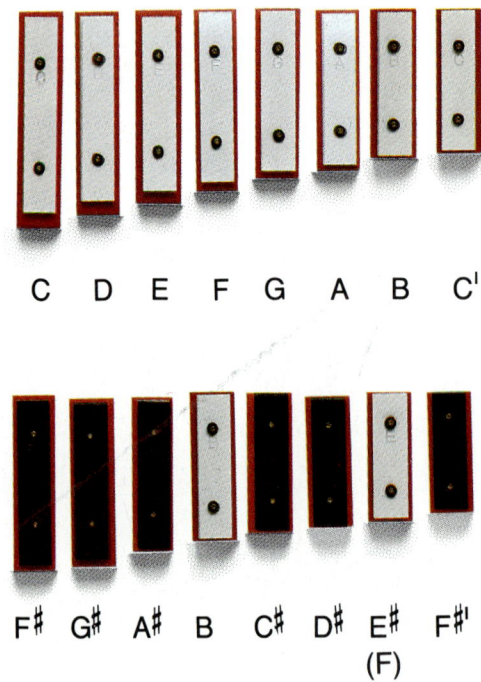

C D E F G A B C'

F# G# A# B C# D# E# F#'
                                       (F)

- Play a song you know using just the white bells.
- Then play the same song using the other scale.
- Listen to the combination of the song played on the two scales.
- Listen for the way Charles Ives (1874–1954) used polytonality to describe the scene of a Revolutionary War campground.

 "Putnam's Camp, Redding, Connecticut" from *Three Places in New England* by Charles Ives

Tonal music focuses the sound around one tonal center. Some composers make *all* the tones in a scale equally important. This music is called **atonal** because it has no tonal center.

Composers of atonal music may use all twelve pitches within an **octave.** They arrange the pitches in a special **tone row** to make their main theme. This is called **twelve-tone music.**

- Create your own tone row. Scramble all twelve bells in the chromatic scale (every pitch from C to C).
- Arrange the twelve bells in any order. Play them one by one from left to right using any rhythmic pattern. If you hear the sound focusing toward a tonal center, change the order of the bells.

Notice that wide skips between pitches make the scale sound restless. In twelve-tone music there is always that restless feeling of never returning home to a tonal center.

- Listen to three short pieces that Anton Webern (vā′bərn), who lived from 1883 to 1945, composed using this system.

 Three Pieces from *Eight Fragments* by Anton Webern

A MASTER COMPOSER USES MUSICAL ACCENTS

Igor Stravinsky was one of the outstanding composers of the twentieth century. His music often shows an exciting use of accents.

Symphony of Psalms, a composition written for chorus and orchestra, was first performed in 1930. The words of the first movement are from Psalm 39 and are sung in Latin.

- Follow the listening map as you listen to the music. Listen for the accented sounds. What symbol on the map represents these sounds?

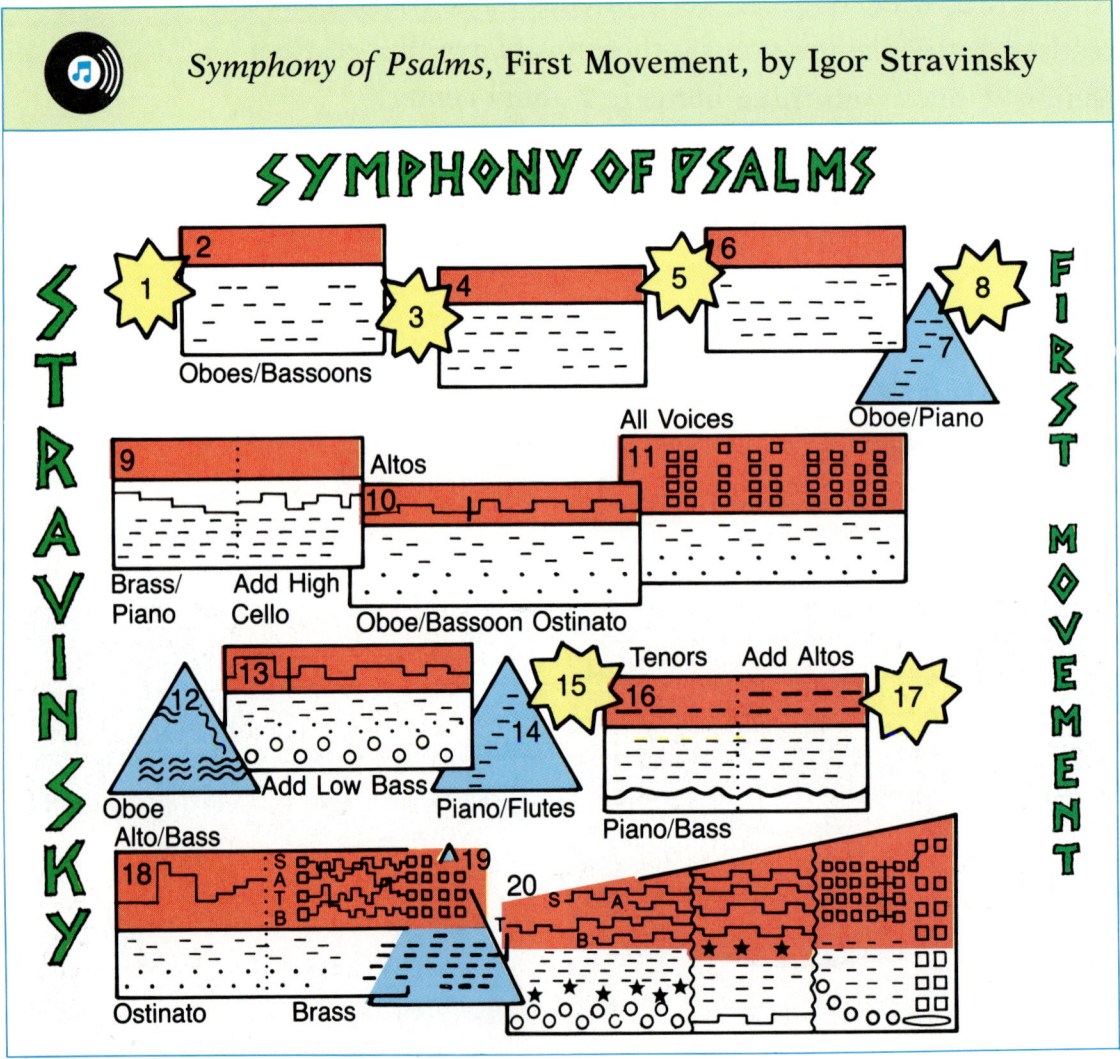

Symphony of Psalms, First Movement, by Igor Stravinsky

IGOR STRAVINSKY

Igor Stravinsky was born near St. Petersburg, Russia, in 1882 and died in 1971. He took piano lessons as a child. When he grew up his father decided that he should study law. In 1902, however, Stravinsky left St. Petersburg University and became a private student of the composer Rimsky-Korsakov.

Stravinsky's first success was music for the ballet *The Firebird* (1910). The next year, Stravinsky became world-famous with his daring music for the ballet *Petrushka*. He followed these successes with *The Rite of Spring*. When it opened in 1913, it caused a riot. The sounds of the music were unlike anything anyone had ever heard.

From 1918 to about 1950, Stravinsky composed in the **Neo-Classic style,** using musical styles from the past in modern ways. From 1952 on, he wrote music based on the twelve-tone system. Stravinsky's main works include eleven ballets, three operas, five compositions for chorus and orchestra, and many pieces for orchestra.

A scene from *The Firebird*

TAKE ANOTHER LOOK

- Sing your favorites of these songs. Think about how the melodies are put together. Do they move by steps or by skips? Are they built on a major scale or a minor scale?

Catch a Falling Star

The Horseman   I Shall Sing   Orion

- Listen again for the movement of the melody and the use of accent to emphasize a sound.

Mars   Symphony of Psalms

JUST CHECKING

- How much do you remember? Choose the best answer for each question.

1. Which measure shows scale-wise motion?

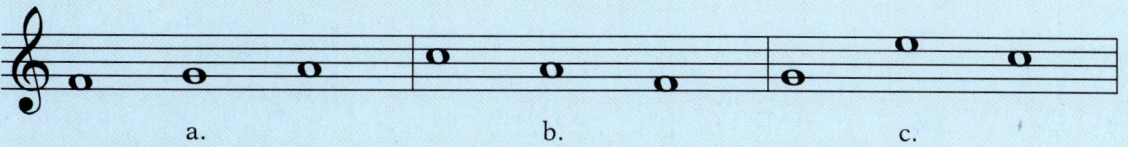

    a.   b.   c.

2. In which scale are the second and third notes a half step apart?
   a. major   b. minor   c. major and minor

3. Which musical symbol means to accent, or bring out more strongly, a single note?

   a. 𝄢   b. ♭   c. >

Use the major scale below for questions 4 and 5.

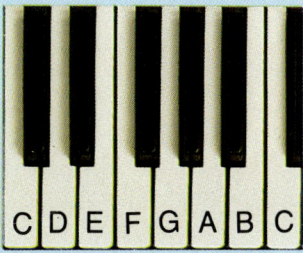

4. Which of these pitches are a half step apart?
   a. F and G   b. E and F   c. A and B

5. Which of these pitches are a whole step apart?
   a. C and D   b. E and F   c. B and C

UNIT 6
AMERICA'S OWN SOUND

143

SPIRITUALS

Spirituals are one of the best-known types of African American music. These songs originated in the South before the Civil War.

Spirituals usually have a strong rhythm that often includes **syncopation** (sounds or silences where you do not normally expect them).

• Listen for the syncopation in this song.

- Look and listen for syncopation. On what words does syncopation occur?

This Train

African American Spiritual

1. This train is bound for glo-ry, this train,____
2. This train don't pull no sleep-ers, this train,____
3. This train is bound for glo-ry, this train,____

This train is bound for glo-ry, this train,____
This train don't pull no sleep-ers, this train,____
This train is bound for glo-ry, this train,____

This train is bound for glo-ry, If you ride it,
This train don't pull no sleep-ers, Don't pull noth-ing
This train is bound for glo-ry, If you ride it

you must be ear-ly, This train.____
but the righ-teous peo-ple, This train.____
you must be ho-ly, This train.____

SINGING THE BLUES

Blues is a style of music that began in America in the early twentieth century. Its roots can be found in African American spirituals and work songs.

Most blues songs tell of feelings of loneliness and sadness. The tempo is usually slow.

- Listen to the story in "Joe Turner Blues." Notice which lines have the same words. Which line of words is different?

Joe Turner Blues

American Blues

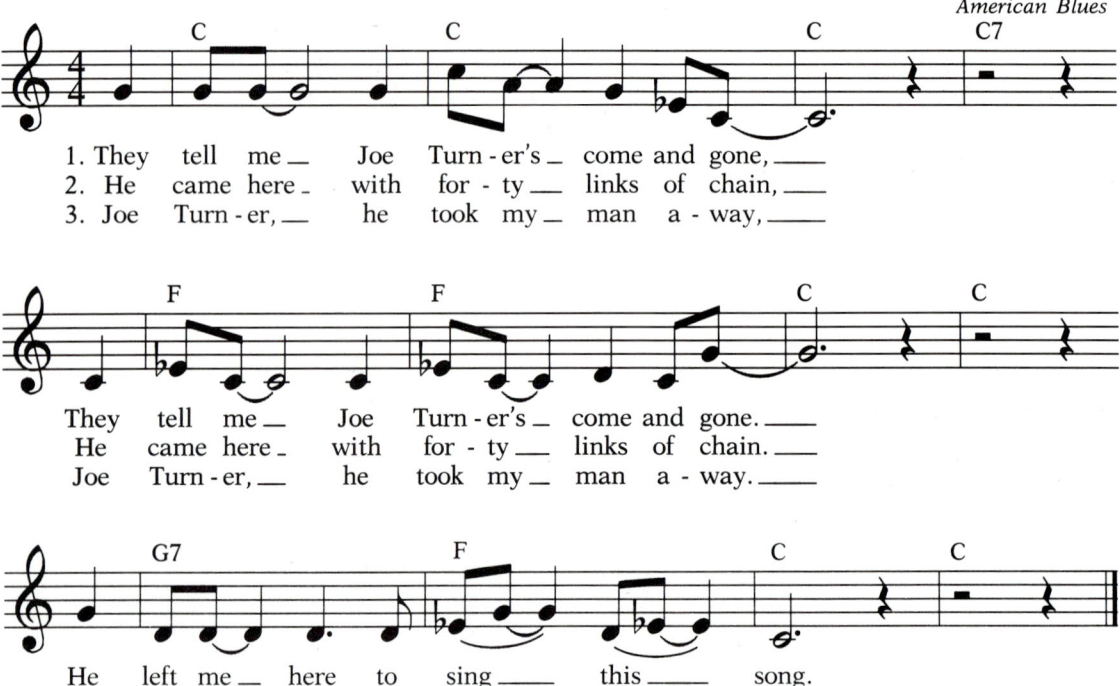

1. They tell me Joe Turner's come and gone,
   They tell me Joe Turner's come and gone.
2. He came here with forty links of chain,
   He came here with forty links of chain.
3. Joe Turner, he took my man away,
   Joe Turner, he took my man away.

He left me here to sing this song.

In blues some pitches are lowered one half step. These are called **blue notes**.

"Joe Turner Blues" is built on the C major scale. Notice in the C scale below that one pitch has been lowered. This lowered pitch is the third step.

- Listen again for the effect of the blue notes in "Joe Turner Blues." Find the blue notes in the song. Remember that a ♭ lowers a pitch one half step.

Chicago 1955 by Ben Shahn

You can accompany "Joe Turner Blues" by using a chord pattern called the **twelve-bar blues progression.** (**Bar** is another word for measure.) Each chord lasts four beats. In C major, the chord pattern is:

   C C C C7

   F F C C

   G7 F C C

- Practice these chords on an autoharp or guitar. Then play them as you sing "Joe Turner Blues."

Blues takes on a different style in this tale about traveling across America.

- Listen for the blue notes in this folk blues song. Raise your hand when you hear a blue note.

The City Blues

American Folk Blues

1. Cloud-y in the west, Looks like rain; I spent all my mon-ey on the sub-way train in New York Cit-y, In New York Cit-y, In New York Cit-y, you real-ly got to know your way.

2. Went to Detroit, it was fine,
   I watched the cars movin' off th' assembly line,
   In Detroit City, in Detroit City,
   In Detroit City, you really got to know your way.

3. I looped the loop, I rocked and reeled,
   I thought the Cubs played ball in Marshall Field,
   In the Windy City, in the Windy City,
   In the Windy City, you really got to know your way.

4. Went a little south, St. Louis (Loo-ee),
   A piece of Missouri on the Mississippi.
   In old St. Louis, in old St. Louis,
   In old St. Louis, you really got to know your way.

5. I moved on down, New Orleans (Or-leens).
   I had my first taste of its pecan pralines,
   In New Orleans, in New Orleans,
   In New Orleans, you really got to know your way.

Chicago

6. I headed West, to "L.A."
   It really is a city where it's fun to stay,
   In old "L.A.," in old "L.A.,"
   In old "L.A.," you really got to know your way.

7. Headed up the coast, "Golden Gate."
   I went out to the wharf to eat a "Fisherman's Plate,"
   In San Francisco, in San Francisco,
   In San Francisco, you really got to know your way.

8. Went on North, Seattle,
   I gave its Space Needle a mighty pull.
   In old Seattle, in old Seattle,
   In old Seattle, you really got to know your way.

• Create your own verse about a favorite city.

San Francisco

New York City

SINGING IN HARMONY

A **ballad** is a song that tells a story. Rock singer and composer Billy Joel chose the story of a well-known outlaw of the Wild West for his composition "The Ballad of Billy the Kid."

- Listen for the contrasting sounds of the rock group and the orchestra.

   "The Ballad of Billy the Kid" by Billy Joel

Another American composer, Woody Guthrie, wrote more than 1,000 ballads. In this ballad, he tells of the days of the "Dust Bowl" in the Southwest.

- Listen for the harmony in this song.

So Long

Words and music by Woody Guthrie

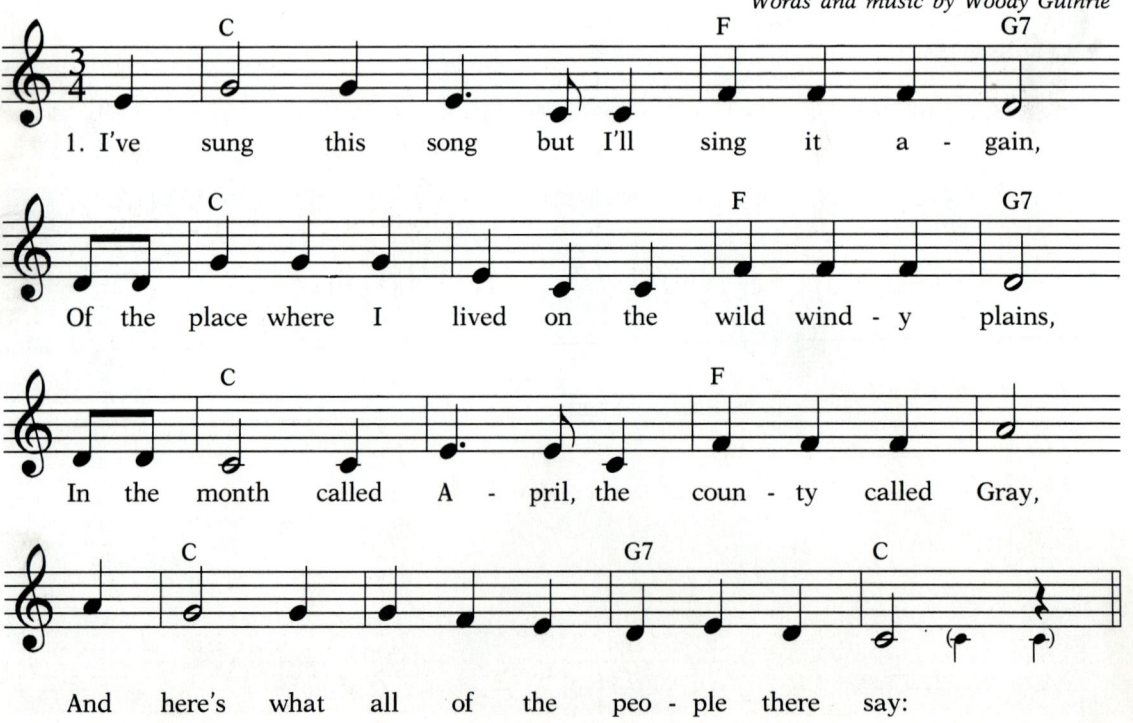

Refrain

"So long, it's been good to know you,
So long, it's been good to know you,
So long, it's been good to know you,
This dust-y old dust is a-get-ting my home,
I've got to be mov-ing a-long."

2. A dust storm hit and it hit like thunder,
   It dusted us over and covered us under,
   It blocked out the traffic and blocked out the sun,
   And straight for home all the people did run, singing:
   Refrain

3. We talked of the end of the world, and then
   We'd sing a song, and then sing it again.
   We'd set for an hour and not say a word,
   And then these words would be heard:
   Refrain

SO LONG It's Been Good to Know Yuh (Dusty Old Dust)
Words and Music by Woody Guthrie.
TRO—Copyright © 1940 (renewed 1968), 1950 (renewed 1978) and 1963 Folkways Music Publishers, Inc., New York, N.Y. Used by permission.

• Can you name this familiar song? Study the melody and rhythm.

Katharine Lee Bates (1859–1929), on a visit to Pike's Peak in Colorado, was so inspired by the beauty around her that she wrote a poem, "America, the Beautiful." Her poem was published in 1893 and was set to music by several composers. The most widely known version is this one.

- Practice singing the harmony parts for "America, the Beautiful."

America, the Beautiful

Music by Samuel Ward
Words by Katharine Lee Bates
Arranged by Mary Val Marsh

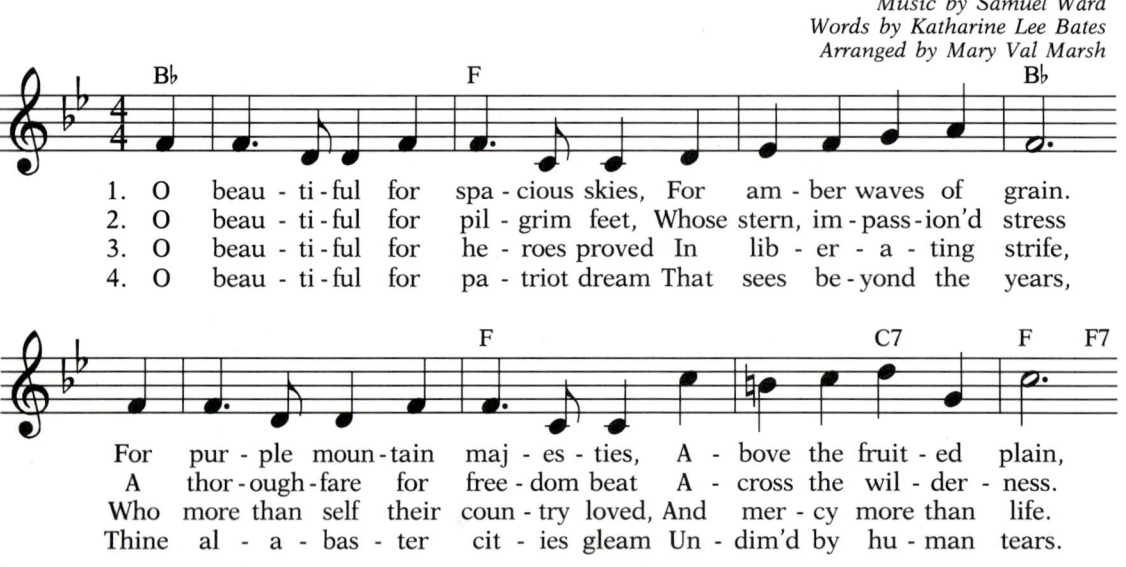

1. O beau-ti-ful for spa-cious skies, For am-ber waves of grain.
2. O beau-ti-ful for pil-grim feet, Whose stern, im-pass-ion'd stress
3. O beau-ti-ful for he-roes proved In lib-er-a-ting strife,
4. O beau-ti-ful for pa-triot dream That sees be-yond the years,

For pur-ple moun-tain maj-es-ties, A-bove the fruit-ed plain,
A thor-ough-fare for free-dom beat A-cross the wil-der-ness.
Who more than self their coun-try loved, And mer-cy more than life.
Thine al-a-bas-ter cit-ies gleam Un-dim'd by hu-man tears.

Arrangement Copyright © 1979 by Mary Val Marsh

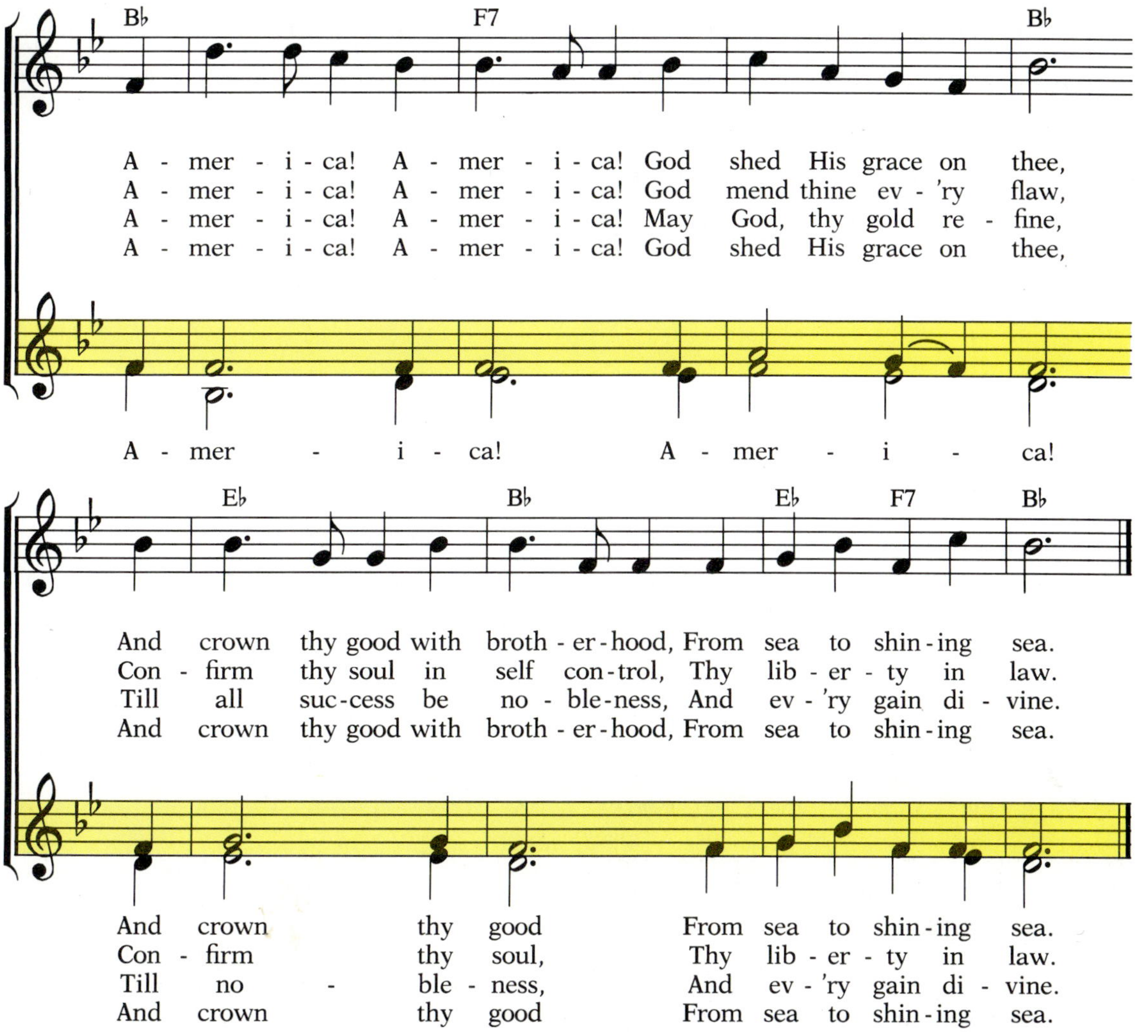
B♭
F7
B♭
A - mer - i - ca! A - mer - i - ca! God shed His grace on thee,
A - mer - i - ca! A - mer - i - ca! God mend thine ev - 'ry flaw,
A - mer - i - ca! A - mer - i - ca! May God, thy gold re - fine,
A - mer - i - ca! A - mer - i - ca! God shed His grace on thee,
A - mer - i - ca! A - mer - i - ca!
E♭
B♭
E♭
F7
B♭
And crown thy good with broth - er - hood, From sea to shin - ing sea.
Con - firm thy soul in self con - trol, Thy lib - er - ty in law.
Till all suc - cess be no - ble - ness, And ev - 'ry gain di - vine.
And crown thy good with broth - er - hood, From sea to shin - ing sea.
And crown thy good From sea to shin - ing sea.
Con - firm thy soul, Thy lib - er - ty in law.
Till no - ble - ness, And ev - 'ry gain di - vine.
And crown thy good From sea to shin - ing sea.

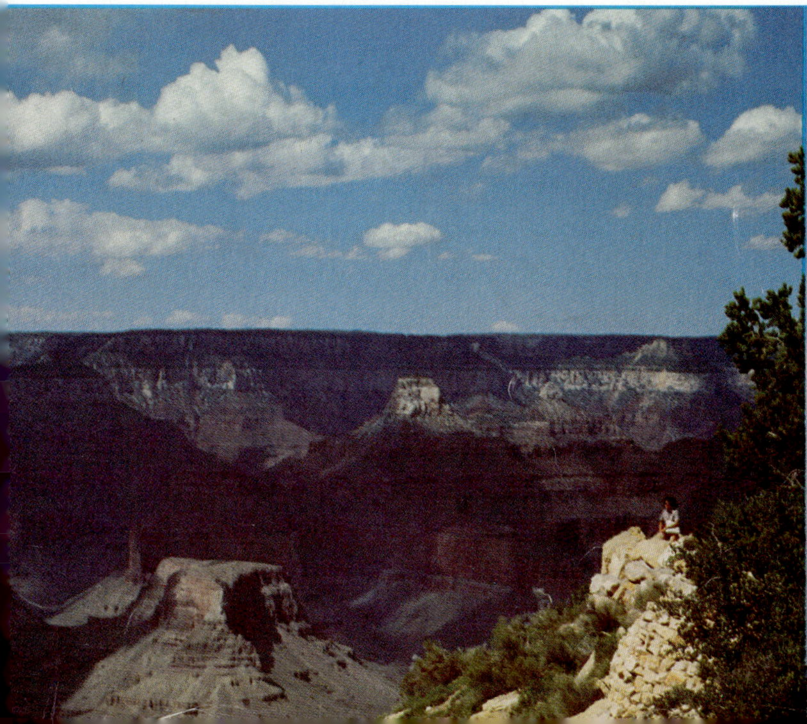

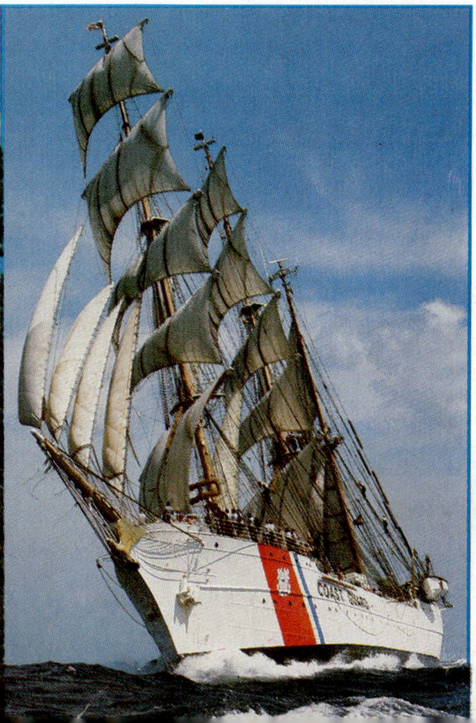
COAST GUARD

SINGING IN UNISON AND IN PARTS

The melody of "America" is the same as that of "God Save the Queen," the British national anthem.

- Listen for the combination of unison voices accompanied by a band. What is the musical texture?

America (Version 1)

Music by Henry Carey
Words by Samuel F. Smith

1. My country, 'tis of thee, Sweet land of liberty, Of thee I sing. Land where my fathers died! Land of the pilgrims' pride! From ev'ry mountain side, Let freedom ring!
2. My native country thee, Land of the noble free, Thy name I love. I love thy rocks and rills, Thy woods and templed hills; My heart with rapture thrills, Like that above.
3. Let music swell the breeze, And ring from all the trees Sweet Freedom's song; Let mortal tongues awake, Let all that breathe partake, Let rocks their silence break, The sound prolong.
4. Our fathers' God, to Thee, Author of liberty, To Thee we sing. Long may our land be bright With Freedom's holy light; Protect us by Thy might, Great God, our King!

- Listen to this version of "America."

 "America" (version 2) performed by the Mormon Tabernacle Choir

- How is the vocal arrangement different from that in the first version of "America"?

- How are the accompaniments different?

FROM RAGTIME TO JAZZ

The highly syncopated rhythms of Scott Joplin's piano compositions strongly influenced the development of jazz. His style became known as ragtime.

In **ragtime style,** the melody is strongly syncopated while the accompaniment keeps a steady beat.

- Tap a steady beat as you listen for syncopation in the melody of *Maple Leaf Rag*.

 Maple Leaf Rag by Scott Joplin

Scott Joplin

Scott Joplin was born in Texas in 1868, the son of an ex-slave, and died in 1917. He taught himself to play the piano. By 1885, Joplin had moved to St. Louis, where he played piano in small clubs and developed his ragtime style. In 1893, Joplin settled in Sedalia, Missouri. His famous *Maple Leaf Rag* was published in 1899. *Maple Leaf Rag* influenced many composers who were trying out the new ragtime style.

Altogether, Joplin published more than 30 piano "rags." He also published a set of six exercises called *The School of Ragtime* (1908) to show pianists how real rag should be played. Joplin's ragtime music became popular again in the 1970s when it was featured in the film *The Sting*.

Ragtime swept the country in the 1890s. It was originally a piano style, but soon instrumental groups began to create ragtime arrangements. "Hello! My Baby" was a popular ragtime song. It was written shortly after the telephone was invented.

- Look and listen for this syncopated pattern in the song.

Hello! My Baby

Music by Joseph E. Howard
Words by Ida Emerson

Hel-lo! my ba-by, hel-lo! my hon-ey, hel-lo! my rag-time gal;
Send me a kiss by wire, ba-by my heart's on fire!
If you re-fuse me, hon-ey, you'll lose me, then you'll be left a-lone. Oh, ba-by,
tel-e-phone and tell me I'm your own.

Jazz is America's contribution to the music of the world. With its roots in African American spirituals, blues, and ragtime, it borrowed rhythms from Africa and Latin America and melodies from the hymns of Europe. It was popular music and was played in dance halls and on vaudeville stages.

George Gershwin at work, left. Above, part of Gershwin's original score of his Second Rhapsody.

The American composer George Gershwin (1898–1937) grew up in New York City. He loved jazz and brought it to the concert hall.

- Listen for blue notes and syncopated rhythms played in *legato* style.

 Prelude for Piano, No. 2 by George Gershwin

Miles Davis (b. 1926) is an American jazz trumpet player. He developed a jazz style in the 1940s that became known as "cool jazz." Davis moved from traditional jazz into a style of music that combined jazz and rock.

Miles Davis on trumpet

Syncopation, blue notes, and improvisation are the basic elements of jazz. Miles Davis uses the twelve-bar blues progression as the basis for this improvisational jazz style. His artistry on the trumpet is the identifying feature of his jazz.

- As you listen to "Freddie Freeloader," tap the steady beat softly. Can you feel the contrast of the syncopated rhythm?

 "Freddie Freeloader" by Miles Davis

A COMPOSER'S CHOICE

Thelonious Monk (thə-lō′nē-əs məngk), who lived from 1920 to 1982, was a composer and pianist. Monk's jazz was abstract and unpredictable. He used the twelve-bar blues progression but then extended and developed it, improvising to suit his style. His unique style often included using chromatics (moving pitches up and down by half steps). The term "cool" was used to describe Monk's style of music.

- Listen for the way Monk's melodies "ease" up and down the piano.

 "Blue Monk" by Thelonious Monk

A composer has to make many choices when writing a song. If you were composing a song . . .

- Would you start with the words? Or would you start with the melody?

- What choices would you make in each of these categories?

Subject	a serious subject	a funny subject
Accompaniment	guitar	piano
Rhythm	a steady beat	syncopation
Tempo	fast	slow
Dynamics	loud	soft
Texture	thick	thin
Form	AB form	ABA form
Melody	major	minor
Style	a ballad	the blues
Tone Color	solo voice	chorus

- Are there other choices to be made?

- Every time you sing a song or listen to music, think about how its musical elements might apply to writing a song.

Part of Gershwin's original score of his Second Rhapsody

TAKE ANOTHER LOOK

- Sing your favorites of these songs that gave us America's own sound.

Ev'ry Time I Feel the Spirit   This Train
Joe Turner Blues   The City Blues   Hello! My Baby

- Listen for syncopation.

Freddie Freeloader   Prelude for Piano, No. 2
Maple Leaf Rag

- Identify syncopation and sixteenth notes in these examples.

JUST CHECKING

- How much do you remember? Choose the best answer for each question.

1. Which rhythm combination shows syncopation?

2. Blue notes are ___.
   a. tones that are raised one half step
   b. tones that are lowered one whole step
   c. tones that are lowered one half step

3. Which of these songs is in blues style?
   a. "Hello! My Baby" (page 157)
   b. "Joe Turner Blues" (page 146)
   c. "Ev'ry Time I Feel the Spirit" (page 144)

4. Which is a characteristic of traditional blues style?
   a. grew out of work songs and spirituals
   b. based on 12-bar form
   c. usually has a slow tempo
   d. all of the above

5. In blues, which step of the scale is usually a blue note?
   a. third   b. first   c. second

6. Ragtime music is ___.
   a. always played in legato style
   b. strongly syncopated
   c. usually played in a slow tempo

SONG SLEUTH

Music by
Neil Fishman

Book and Lyrics by
Harvey Edelman

© 1987 by Sammy Smile Music

CAST

Sherlock Holmes	Annie	Regina	Karen
Dr. Watson	Michael	Katie	Lisa
Debbie	Cindy	Corey	Sam
Justin	Rebecca	Sean	Jason

Musical Numbers

As the musical opens, a group of students is sitting listening to a popular song. After it ends, they talk about how to. . .

Write a Song *(pages 166–167)*

Everyone agrees that it would be great fun to write a song. However, no one has a clue as to how to solve the mystery of songwriting. Just then, the world's greatest detectives, Sherlock Holmes and Dr. Watson, arrive. Holmes's first clue is the way Corey is absently tapping his ruler against his leg. They all. . .

Listen to the Rhythm *(page 168)*

Efforts to start a ball game get everyone going. . .

On a Melody *(page 169)*

By now, everyone is hungry for more. Jason's lunch just happens to provide them with a. . .

Harmony Sandwich *(page 170)*

Holmes is still tracking clues. Tone color and dynamics aren't enough until the students. . .

Find the Words *(page 171)*

All that is left is to put it all together. Everyone discovers that. . .

We Can Do It If We Try *(pages 172–173)*

Write a Song

Music by Neil Fishman
Words by Harvey Edelman

write a song!

Would-n't it be great to write a

song   Would-n't it be great to write a song!

Find the Words

Music by Neil Fishman
Words by Harvey Edelman

1. Find the words and you will see how words can fit thoughts to a "T." No matter what is on your mind, the right words are right there to find.
   Find the words that will explain the ideas that are in your brain. You may want to spread some news or just chase away the blues.

Refrain
Find the words *(response)* Rhyme the words *(response)* Shine the words *(response)* Refine the words *(response)* Design the words *(response)* Combine the words *(response)* All kinds of words Come on and find the words!

June moon tune

2. Find the words,
   The verbs and nouns,
   What they say and how they sound.
   A well-placed word will give a twist,
   To meanings that we might have missed.

   Find the words,
   The adjectives,
   That color in your narratives,
   Certain words will illustrate,
   The mood that you want to create.
   Refrain

UNIT 7

CHECK THE METER

LISTENING FOR BEAT

This song, from the musical show *Barnum*, tells how to succeed at any job. Just take one day (or "one brick") at a time.

• Tap the beat as you listen to this show tune.

One Brick at a Time

Music by Cy Coleman
Words by Michael Stewart

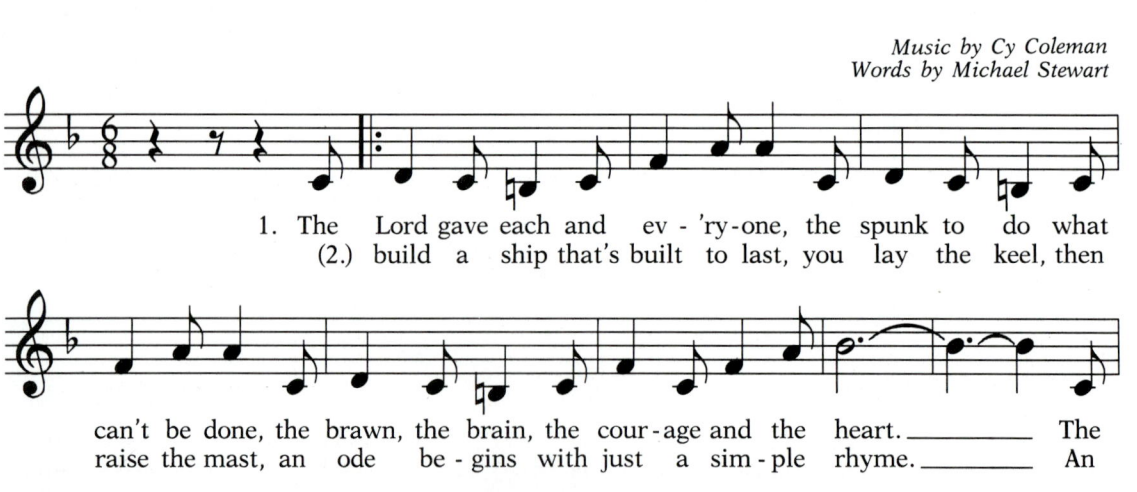

1. The Lord gave each and ev-'ry-one, the spunk to do what
(2.) build a ship that's built to last, you lay the keel, then

can't be done, the brawn, the brain, the cour-age and the heart._____ The
raise the mast, an ode be-gins with just a sim-ple rhyme._____ An

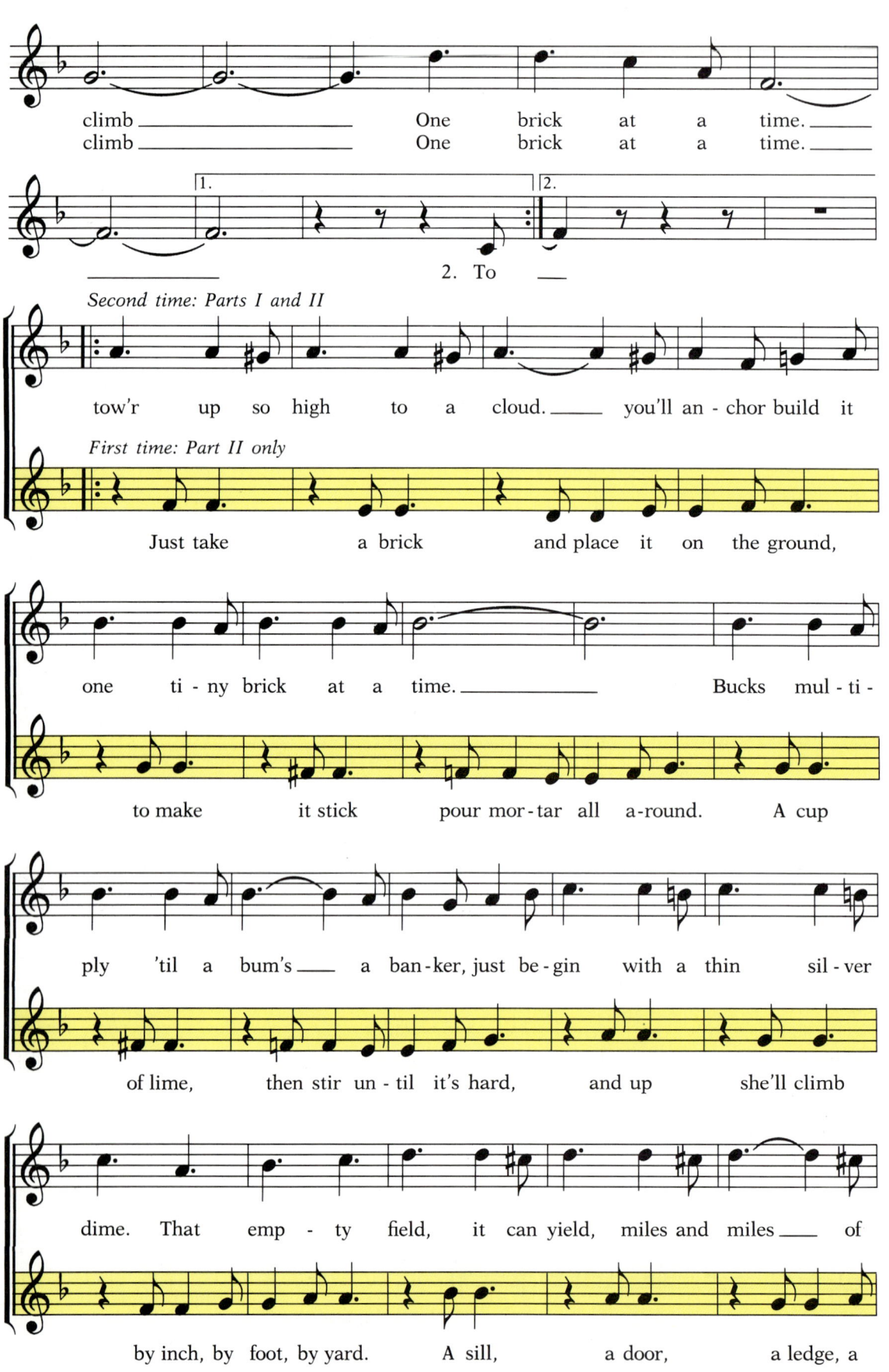

NOTATION THEN AND NOW

The only existing music manuscript for "Summer Is A-Comin' In" is in the British Museum. This reproduction shows the thirteenth-century notation and the Middle English and Latin words.

- Compare the old notation to the modern notation on page 181. Follow the shape of the melody as you sing.

Sumer is icumen in, BRITISH MUSEUM, London

Summer Is A-Comin' In

English Folk Song

Summer is a-comin' in, Loud-ly sing cuck-oo; Grow-eth seed and blow-eth mead and spring-eth wood a-new, Sing cuck-oo. Ewe now bleat-eth af-ter lamb, low'th af-ter calf the cow, Bull-ock start-eth, buck now vert-eth, Mer-ry sing cuck-oo, Cuck-oo, cuck-oo, Well now sing thou cuck-oo, nor cease thou nev-er nu.

• Try this ostinato with "Summer Is A-Comin' In."

Sing cuck-oo. Now sing cuck-oo.

The rock group Pink Floyd became very popular in the late sixties. The group used elements of classical music in their songs. Their most successful album was *Dark Side of the Moon*, which was released in 1973 and stayed on pop music charts for over a decade.

Through electronics, sounds can be produced in ways for which there is no standard notation.

- Listen for the unusual sounds in "The Gunners Dream." What instruments do you think were used to create them?

 "The Gunners Dream" from *The Final Cut* by Pink Floyd

The Polish composer Krzysztof Penderecki (krshi′shtof pen-də-ret′skē), born in 1933, tried to express the tragedy of war in his music. He wrote a **threnody** (thren′əd-ē), or song of mourning, for 52 stringed instruments. There is no feeling of beat in this composition. The sounds are not meant to be pleasing. Penderecki's unusual orchestral sounds required a new kind of notation.

- Look at this section of the score as you listen. The triangles represent the highest pitches of each group of stringed instruments.

 Threnody for the Victims of Hiroshima (excerpt) by Krzysztof Penderecki

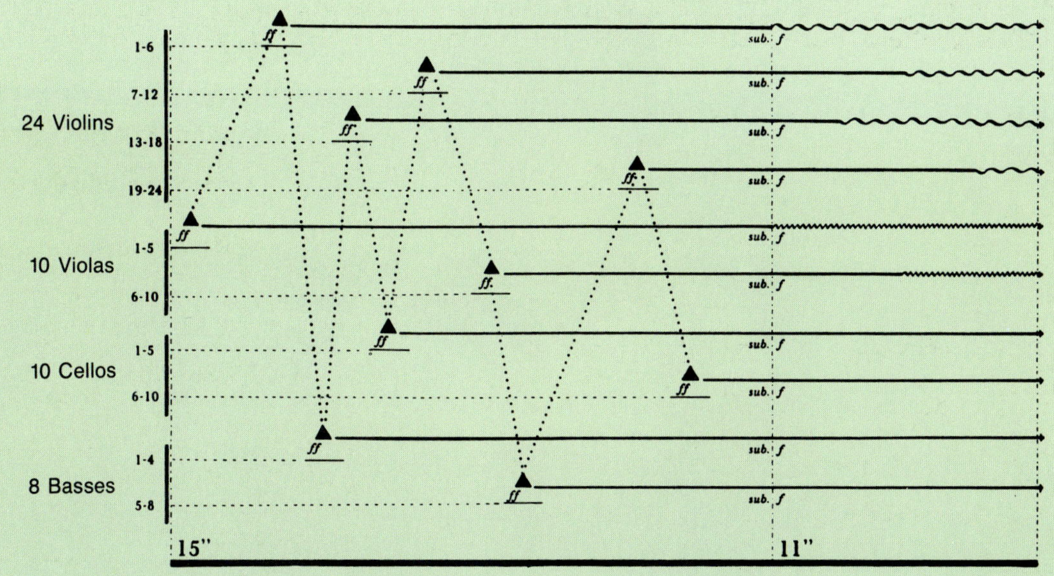

GETTING STARTED

To reach a goal, you need to start somewhere. Here are some starting suggestions for writing a song.

- Arrange five bells on a table. Use the following combination (or decide on a combination of your own).

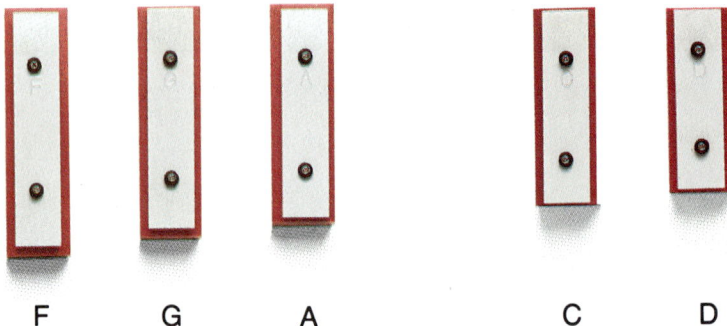

- Play several notes until you find a combination of sounds that you like. Write the letter names of the pitches in order.

- Draw a staff. Add a treble clef and meter signature of $\frac{4}{4}$, or choose your own meter. Your staff will look like this:

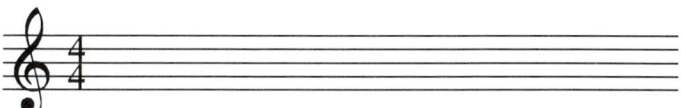

- Write your melody on the staff you drew. Be sure that you have four beats in each measure. Your notation might look something like this:

- Use your notation to play your melody on the bells. Does it sound the way you thought it would? If not, you may need to change it. You may want to add to your melody to make it longer.

MAJOR OR MINOR?

- As you listen, decide if this song is in major or in minor.

Promised Land

Words and music by Natalie Sleeth

First time: Part I only

Broth-er, sis-ter,* lend an ear, — I'm head-in' for the prom-ised land!

Second time: Parts I and II

Broth - er, sis - ter,* lend an ear, for soon our

Trou-bles soon will dis-ap-pear, — I'm head-in' for the prom-ised land!

trou - bles all will dis - ap-pear. One day there's

When I reach it there will be love and hap-pi-ness a-wait-in' for me, —

bound to be great love for you and me, just

come a-long and you will see! — I'm head-in' for the prom-ised land!

wait and see! I'm head-in' for the prom-ised land!

*Alternate: Sister, brother, All you children, All you sisters (brothers).

*Alternate: sisters, brothers

- Describe the form of this song.

THE MUSICAL THEATER

- Listen for the strong beat in this show tune. Notice the meter signature. ¢ (cut time) means the same as 2/2.

Give My Regards to Broadway

Words and music by George M. Cohan

1. Did you ev-er see two Yan-kees part up-on a for-eign shore, When the good ship's just a-bout to start for old New York once more? With tear-dimmed eye, they say good

2. Say hel-lo to dear old Co-ney Isle, if there you chance to be, When you're at the Wal-dorf, have a smile and charge it up to me. Men-tion my name ev-'ry place you

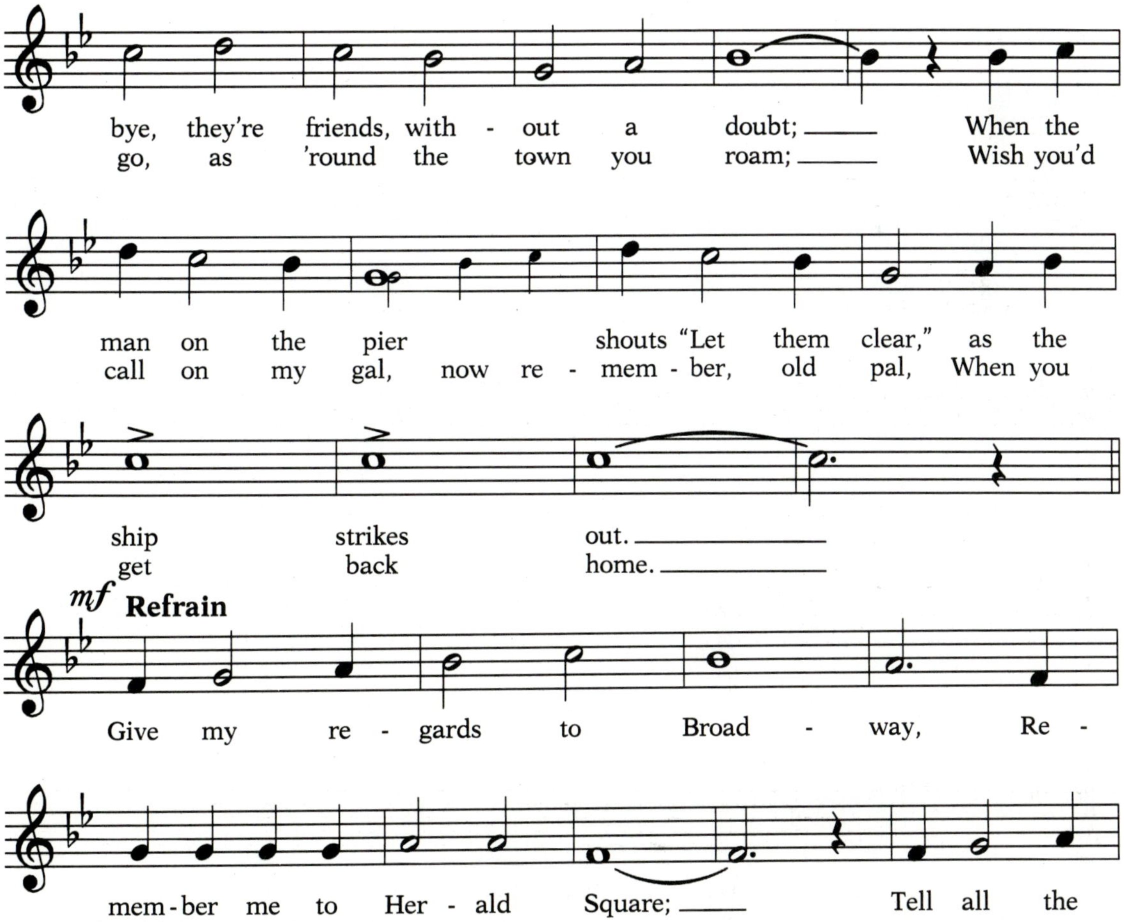

bye, they're friends, with - out a doubt; _____ When the
go, as 'round the town you roam; _____ Wish you'd

man on the pier shouts "Let them clear," as the
call on my gal, now re - mem - ber, old pal, When you

ship strikes out. _____
get back home. _____

mf **Refrain**

Give my re - gards to Broad - way, Re -

mem - ber me to Her - ald Square; _____ Tell all the

191

gang at For-ty - Sec-ond Street that I will soon be there. ___ Whis-per of how I'm yearn-ing to min-gle with the old time throng; ___ Give my re-gards to old Broad-way and say that I'll be there, ere long. ___

George M. Cohan (1878–1942), the composer of "Give My Regards to Broadway," was also a director, dancer, and singer. He often starred in his own musicals. The syncopated rhythm and the strong feeling of the meter are typical of Cohan's songs. His best-known songs include "You're a Grand Old Flag" and "The Yankee Doodle Boy."

The New York theater district became known as "The Great White Way" because of the brilliance of the lights around the theaters each evening.

The character pictured at left is from the Broadway musical *Cats*. Shown below are the stars of *A Chorus Line*, a musical about singers and dancers in Broadway shows.

Donny Osmond is shown at left in a scene from *Little Johnny Jones*, a musical written by George M. Cohan. The play was first performed in 1904 and features the song "Give My Regards to Broadway," which is sung by a character who is homesick for the United States.

193

STEADY BEAT

The musical show *Oliver!* was written by British author-composer Lionel Bart. It is based on the Charles Dickens novel *Oliver Twist*. The show was a hit on both the London and New York stages. This song from *Oliver!*, "Consider Yourself," has already passed the test of time.

- Do you feel the meter in two or six?

A scene from the musical *Oliver!*

Consider Yourself

Words and music by Lionel Bart

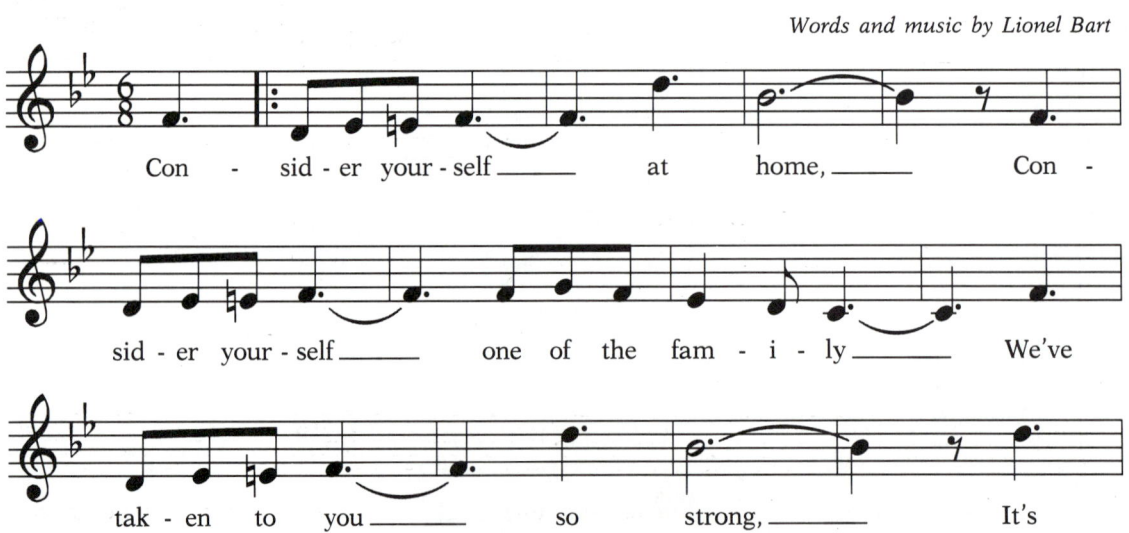

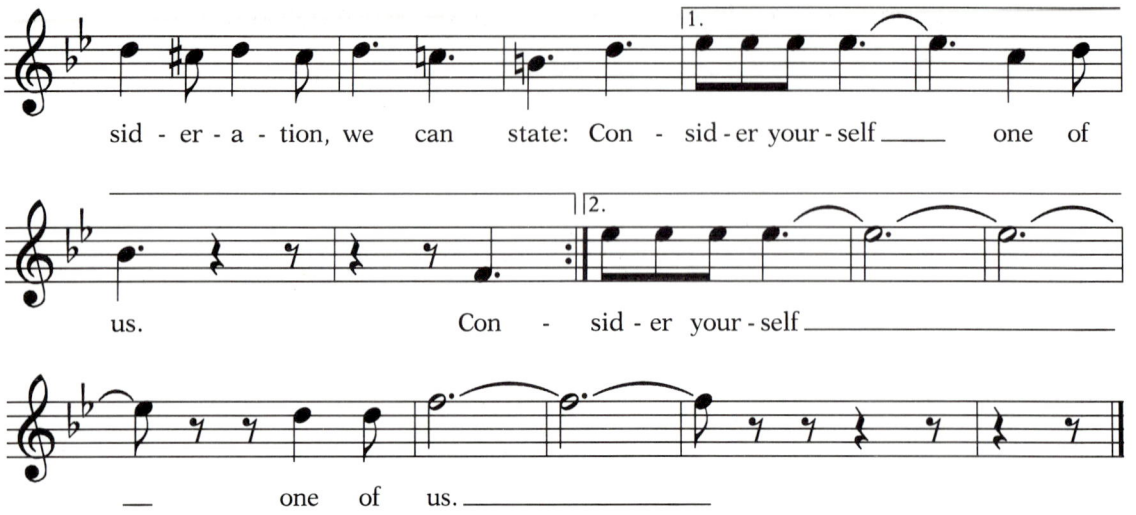

CONSIDER YOURSELF
From the Columbia Pictures–Romulus Film OLIVER!
Words and Music by Lionel Bart.
Copyright © 1960 Lakeview Music Co. Ltd., London, England. TRO—Hollis Music, Inc., New York, controls all publication rights for the U.S.A. and Canada. Used by permission.

The meter of this song is $\frac{6}{8}$. This tells that:

> **6** there are six beats in each measure
> **8** the eighth note (♪) equals one beat

• Did you feel the meter moving in sets of two?

When the tempo of music in $\frac{6}{8}$ meter is slow, all six beats are felt. The strong beats are the first and fourth beats. When the tempo is faster, the first and fourth beats are felt as the steady beat.

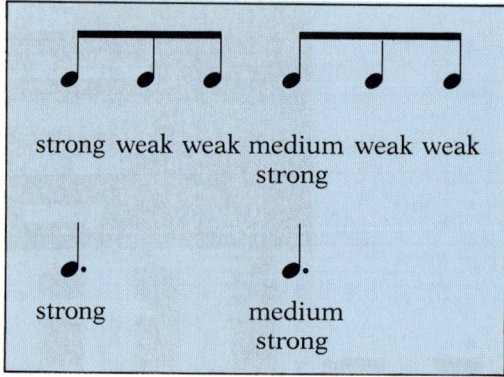

This is why you can feel $\frac{6}{8}$ meter moving in sets of two. The meter signature $\frac{6}{8}$ is another way of showing $\frac{2}{\text{♩.}}$ meter.

196

You can combine any of these rhythm "bricks" to make your own lines of rhythm.

If you put these four "bricks" together, you will have the rhythm for the first part of "Row, Row, Row Your Boat."

Row, Row, Row Your Boat

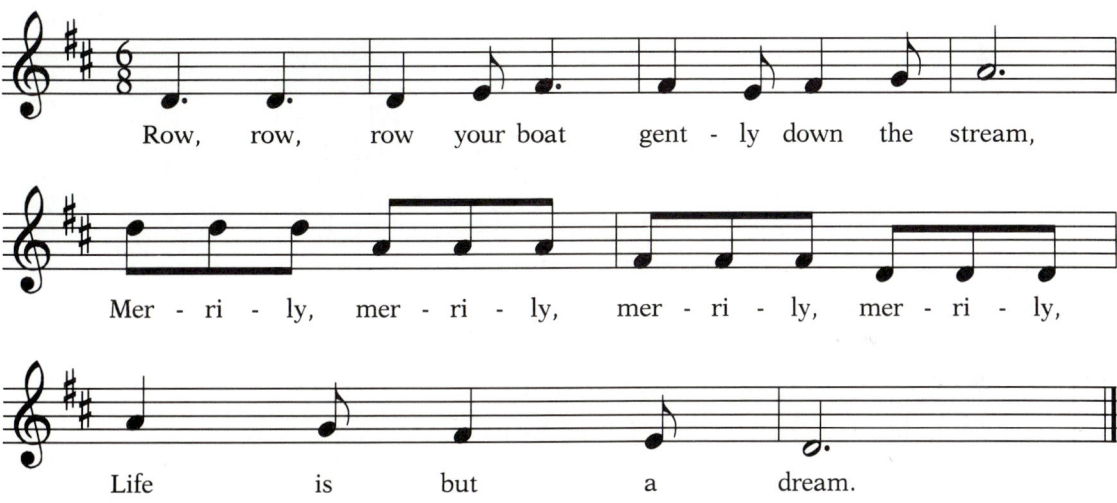

It may help to think of these words for each "brick."

- Practice clapping these combinations.

TARANTELLA

A **tarantella** is an Italian folk dance. It is a very fast dance that was thought to cure the bite of the tarantula.

This "Tarantella" was one of many pieces the Italian composer Gioacchino Rossini (jō-ə-kē′nō rô-sē′nē) wrote to entertain his friends. Rossini was born in 1792 and died in 1868. Fifty years after his death, Ottorino Respighi (ôt-tō-rē′nō rə-spē′gē), who lived from 1879 to 1936, arranged some of these pieces into a ballet called *The Fantastic Toyshop*.

These are the basic rhythms used in "Tarantella."

- Listen for the strongly accented beats in this music. Do you feel it move in two beats or six beats?

 "Tarantella" from *The Fantastic Toyshop (La Boutique Fantasque)* by Rossini-Respighi

- Did the tempo change?

"Tarantella" begins and ends in A minor.

The A minor scale uses these pitches.

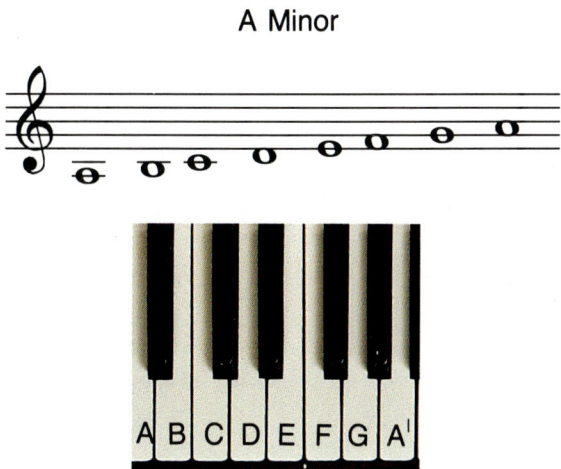

- Play the white keys from A to high A. Listen to the sound of the A minor scale.

In the A major scale, you must **sharp** three pitches. That means raise them one half step.

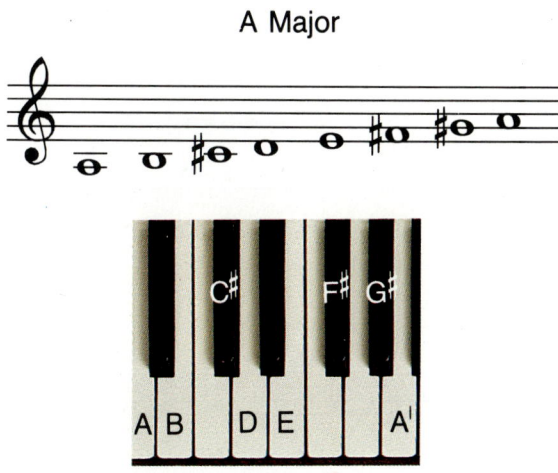

- Play the A major scale. Compare its sound with the sound of the A minor scale.
- Listen again to "Tarantella." Raise your right hand when the sound is in minor. Raise your left hand when the sound is in major.

RHYTHM PRACTICE

Robert Louis Stevenson wrote a poem called "Over the Sea to Skye." The poem told of Bonnie Prince Charlie, who tried to recapture the British throne for his family. After losing a battle in 1746, he took refuge on the Isle of Skye in Scotland.

Annie MacLeod composed this melody especially for the poem.

- Feel the rocking motion created by the melody and rhythm patterns. Do you feel the meter in two or six?

Over the Sea to Skye

Music by Annie MacLeod
Words by Robert Louis Stevenson

Refrain

Sing me a song of a lad that is gone, Say, could that lad be I?
Mer-ry of soul he sailed on a day o-ver the sea to Skye.

Verse

1. Give me a-gain all that was there, give me the sun that shone!
2. Bil-low and breeze, is-lands and seas, moun-tains of rain and sun.

D.C. (Last time al Fine)

Give me the eyes, give me the soul, give me the lad that's gone.
All that was good, all that was fair, all that was me is gone.

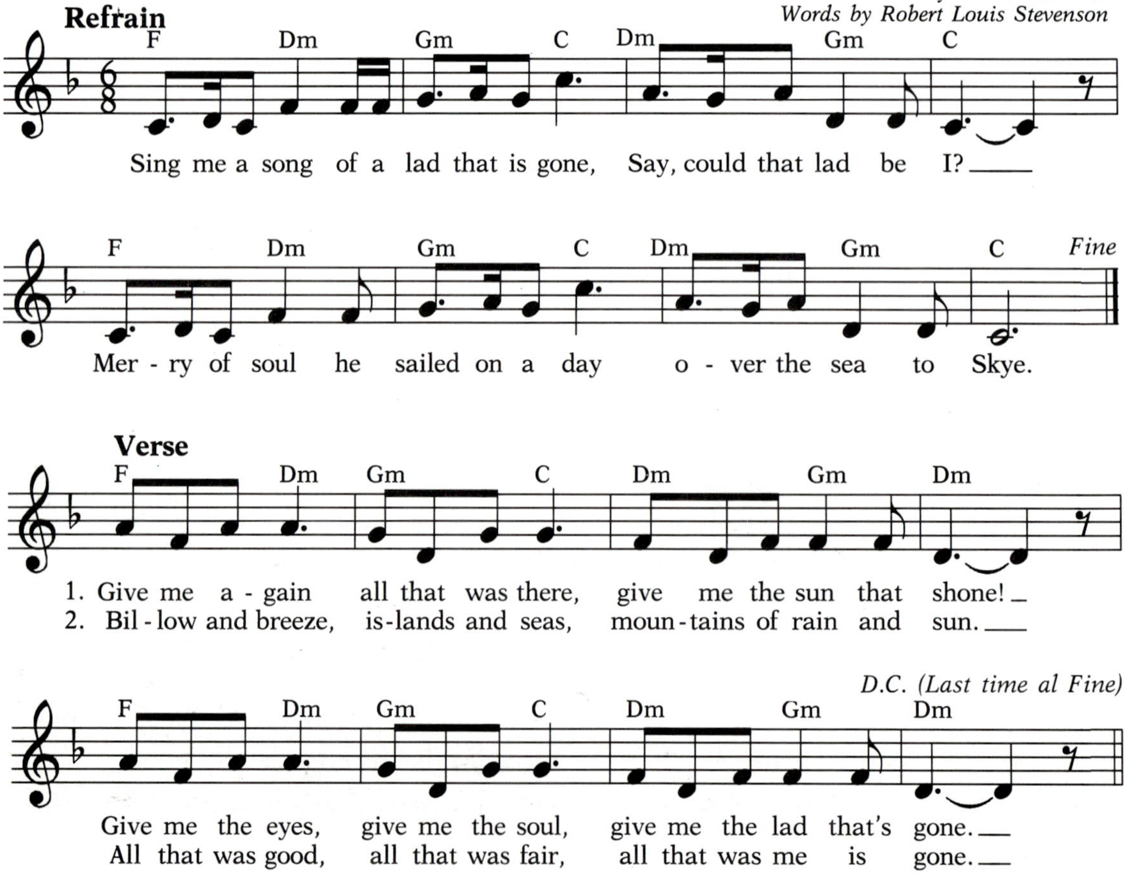

- Look at the notation for "Over the Sea to Skye." Find these rhythm combinations.

- Clap each combination to hear the difference in the rhythms.

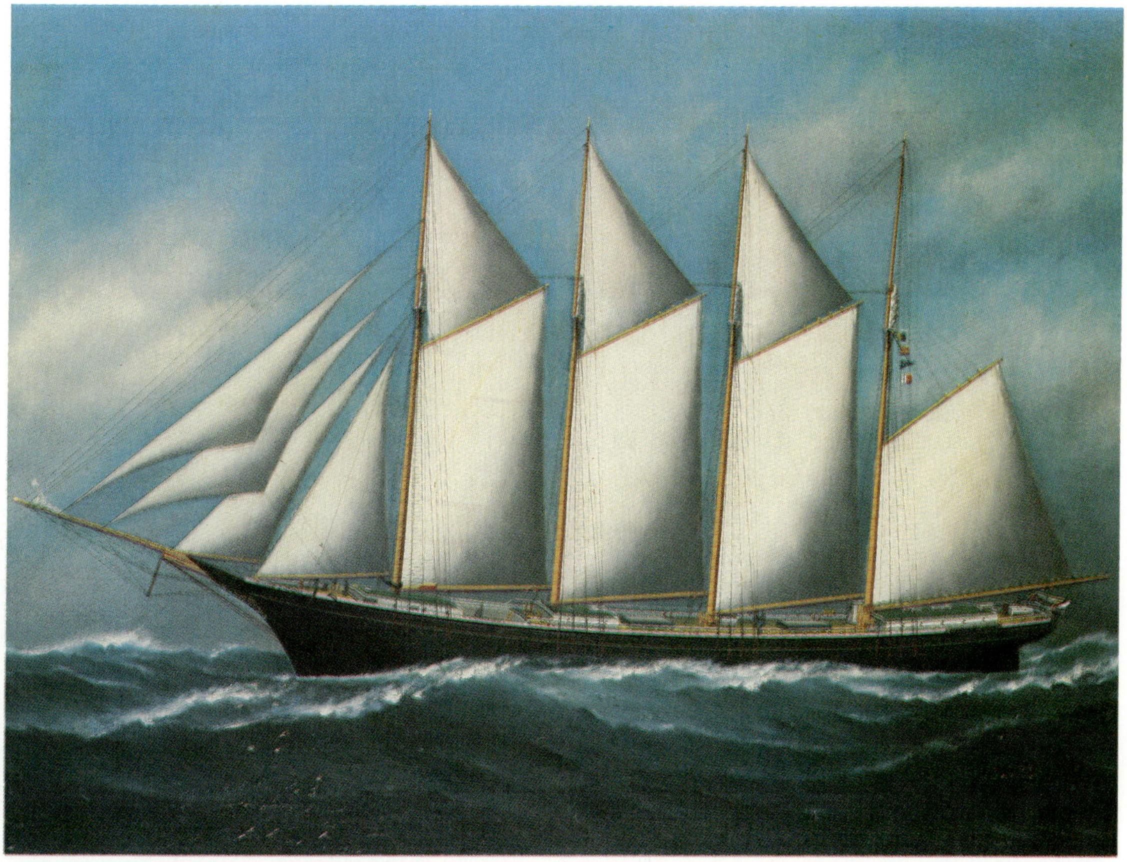

William H. Yerkes by Samuel F. M. Badger

STAY WITH THE BEAT

- Follow the meter signatures as you listen to this song. How many times does the meter change?

Scarborough Fair

English Folk Song

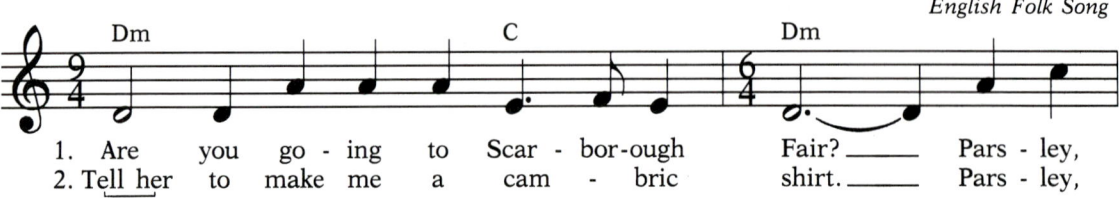

1. Are you go - ing to Scar - bor - ough Fair? ____ Pars - ley,
2. Tell her to make me a cam - bric shirt. ____ Pars - ley,

sage, rose - mar - y and thyme; ____ Re - mem - ber me to one that lives
sage, rose - mar - y and thyme; ____ With - out a seam or fine nee - dle

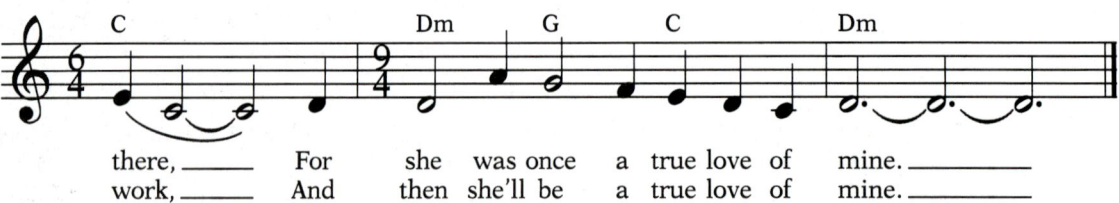

there, ____ For she was once a true love of mine. ____
work, ____ And then she'll be a true love of mine. ____

3. Tell her to wash it in yonder dry well,
   Parsley, sage, rosemary and thyme;
   Where water ne'er sprung, nor drop of rain fell,
   And then she'll be a true love of mine.

4. Tell her to dry it on yonder thorn,
   Parsley, sage, rosemary and thyme;
   Which never bore blossom since Adam was born,
   And then she'll be a true love of mine.

5. Tell him to find me an acre of land,
   Parsley, sage, rosemary and thyme;
   Between the sea foam and the sea sand,
   Or never be a true love of mine.

6. Tell him to plough it with a lam'd horn,
   Parsley, sage, rosemary and thyme;
   And sow it all over with one peppercorn,
   Or never be a true love of mine.

7. Tell him to reap it with a sickle of leather,
   Parsley, sage, rosemary and thyme;
   And tie it all up with a peacock's feather,
   Or never be a true love of mine.

8. When he has done and finished his work,
   Parsley, sage, rosemary and thyme;
   Then come to me for his cambric shirt,
   And he shall be a true love of mine.

- Now listen for the changing meter in this music. Use your right hand to tap the strong beat when you hear sets of three. Use your left hand to tap the strong beat when you hear sets of four.

 "Staywithit" by Barbara Staton

CREATING A SHORT MELODY

- Think of a rhythm from a poem or song you like. Clap the rhythm.
- Add a melody to the rhythm. Use one pitch for each rhythmic sound. Use the following pitches.

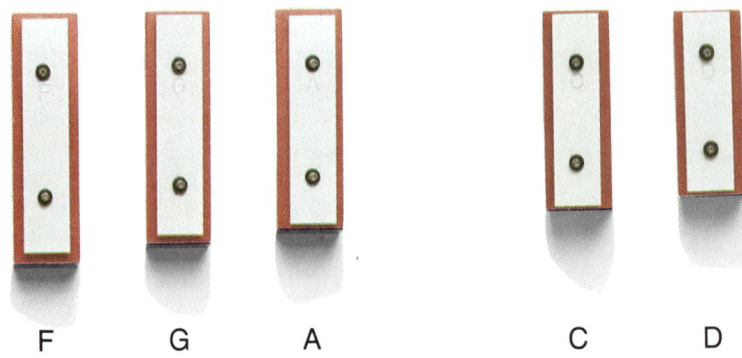

Remember that your melody can move by steps or skips, or may repeat a pitch.

- Hum your melody. Change it as you see fit.
- Write it down. Use traditional notation or make up your own symbols.

These are the elements from which you can build a song. Use this checklist as a guide.

CHECKLIST

- **rhythm**—each measure contains the correct number of beats
- **melody**—at least one note for each word or syllable
- **tone color**—voices or instruments (or both)
- **notation**—notes on a staff, or your own symbols, that help you remember the sound
- **dynamic markings**—symbols that show how loud or soft
- **tempo markings**—words that tell how fast or slow
- **harmony**—an accompaniment or second part
- **form**—contains some repetition and some contrast

TAKE ANOTHER LOOK

- Sing your favorites of these songs. Which ones are in $\frac{6}{8}$ meter? Which one is in minor?

Give My Regards to Broadway
Consider Yourself
One Brick at a Time
Row, Row, Row, Your Boat
Promised Land

- Read these rhythm bricks in any order—across, down, up, or diagonally.

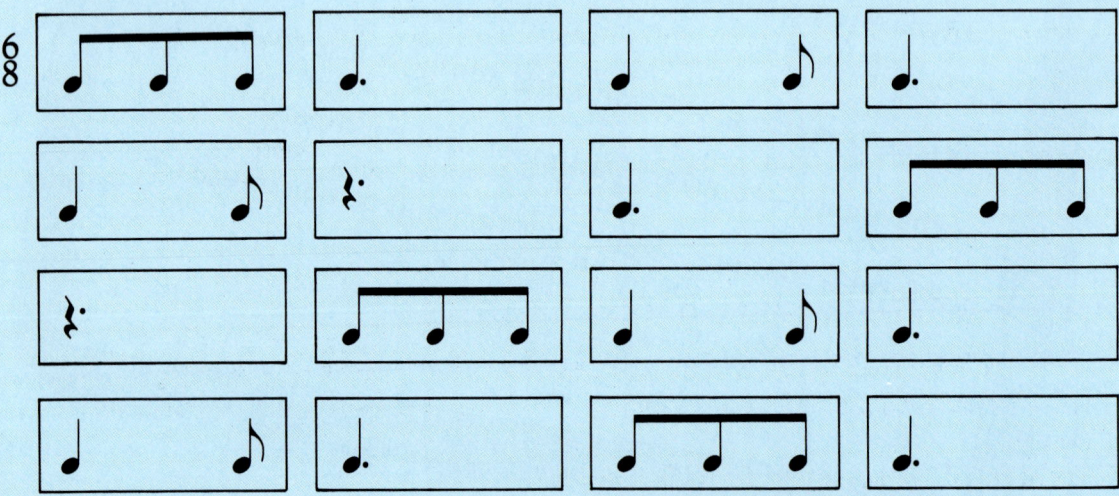

- Tap the rhythm combinations above as you listen to "Tarantella."

JUST CHECKING

- How much do you remember? Choose the best answer for each question.

1. Which staff shows a minor scale?

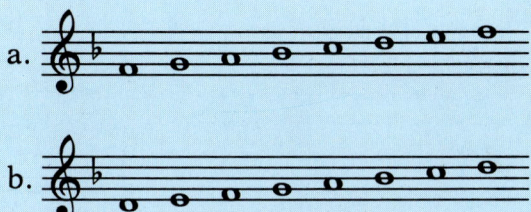

2. Which are the pitches for a minor scale beginning on A?

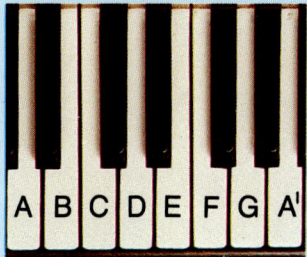

   a. A B C D E F G A'   b. A B C D E F G# A'   c. A B C# D E F G A'

3. Which shows the correct number of beats for a measure in 6/8 meter?

   a. ♩. ♩.   b. ♩ ♪ ♪   c. ♫ ♩

4. Which of these songs is built on a minor scale?
   a. "One Brick at a Time" (page 176)
   b. "Consider Yourself" (page 194)
   c. "Promised Land" (page 186)

5. Which of these songs is in 6/8 meter?
   a. "Promised Land" (page 186)
   b. "Consider Yourself" (page 194)
   c. "Give My Regards to Broadway" (page 190)

UNIT 8
SOUNDS AND STYLES

MUSIC

Music is a tale told in sounds
Of such infinite reach
All time, all life, all tongues
Are in its speech.
Music is the sound of events
So moving, in its classic or its blue,
The heart nods recognition: "I was there.
And I have felt that, too. . . ."
—Mary L. O'Neill

LISTENING FOR ELECTRONIC INSTRUMENTS

- Listen for the instruments that accompany this pop-style song.

I Can See Clearly Now

Words and music by Johnny Nash

1.,3. I can see clear - ly now, the rain has gone.
2. I think I can make it now, the pain has gone.

I can see all ob - sta - cles in my way,
All of the bad feel - ings have dis - ap - peared.

Gone are the dark clouds that had me blind
Here is the rain - bow I've been pray - ing for

To Coda

It's gon-na be a bright, bright sun-shin-y day,

It's gon-na be a bright, bright sun-shin-y day.

Some modern composers create new tonal effects in their compositions through electronic techniques. They also use standard instruments in unusual ways.

Atmospheres was written for orchestra by the Hungarian composer György Ligeti (jôrj lē-get′ē), who was born in 1923. This music was used to suggest space travel in the motion picture *2001: A Space Odyssey*. It features sounds made by playing wire brushes directly on the strings of a piano.

2001: A Space Odyssey

- Listen to *Atmospheres*.

 Atmospheres by György Ligeti

Shadowfax

The modern jazz group Shadowfax was formed in 1972 in Chicago. They tour in the United States and Canada and have recorded several albums. Shadowfax uses synthesizers in combination with other instruments. The composition "Shadowdance" uses electronic instruments such as the **lyricon** (an instrument that might be called an electronic clarinet) and a synthesizer. It uses standard instruments such as the drums, marimba, guitar, and vibraphone. You will also hear Asian instruments such as gongs, **angklung** (metal and bamboo shakers), and tuned wood blocks.

- As you listen to "Shadowdance," decide which instruments might be making some of the sounds that you hear.

 "Shadowdance" by Shadowfax

BLUEGRASS AND COUNTRY MUSIC

- Listen to the song. Sing the part that best suits your vocal range.

Rocky Top

Words and Music by Boudleaux Bryant and Felice Bryant
Arranged by P.W.

Wish that I was on ol' Rock-y Top, down in the Ten-nes-see hills;

Ain't no smog-gy smoke on Rock-y Top; Ain't no tel-e-phone bills;

Once I knew a girl on Rock-y Top; Half bear, oth-er half cat;

Wild as a mink, but sweet as so-da pop, I still dream a-bout that;

Refrain

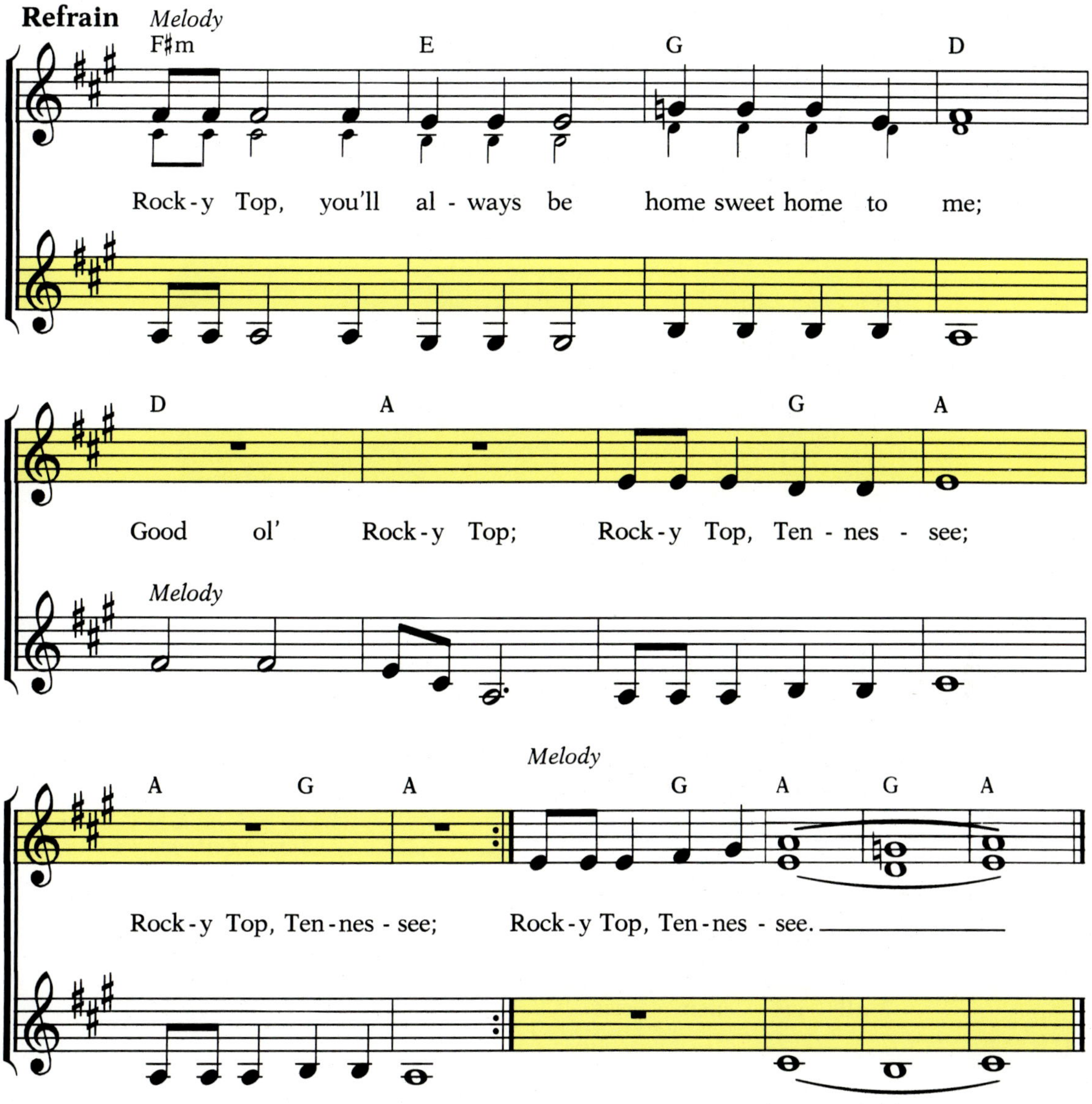

Melody
F♯m E G D
Rock-y Top, you'll al-ways be home sweet home to me;
D A G A
Good ol' Rock-y Top; Rock-y Top, Ten-nes-see;
Melody
A G A
Melody
G A G A
Rock-y Top, Ten-nes-see; Rock-y Top, Ten-nes-see.

Country music is a type of American music that began in the rural South. It had its roots in English and Scottish folk music. **Bluegrass** is a type of country music that became popular in the 1940s. A typical bluegrass band consists of fiddle, mandolin, guitar, five-string banjo, and bass.

- Listen and identify the instruments you hear.

"Rocky Top" and "Hickory Hollow" performed by Banks and Shane

The guitar is at home in pop, rock, folk, and country music, and even in the concert hall.

An acoustic guitar

- Listen for the sound of the guitar in "Take Me Home, Country Roads." This song is a crossover between country and pop music.

Take Me Home, Country Roads

Words and music by Bill Danoff, Taffy Nivert, and John Denver

1. Al - most Heav - en, West Vir - gin - ia, Blue Ridge Moun - tains, Shen - an - do - ah Riv - er. Life is old there, old - er than the trees, Young - er than the moun - tains, grow - ing like a breeze.
2. All my mem - 'ries gath - er 'round her, Min - er's la - dy, strang - er to blue wa - ters. Dark and dust - y painted on the sky. Mist - y rays of moon - shine, tear - drop in my eye.

SOUNDS OF OTHER LANDS

The **bouzouki** (boo-zōō′kē) is a stringed instrument used in traditional Greek folk music. Bouzouki music uses an unusual mixture of rhythms.

- Listen for the sound of the bouzouki.

Gerakina

Greek Folk Song
Words by M.S.

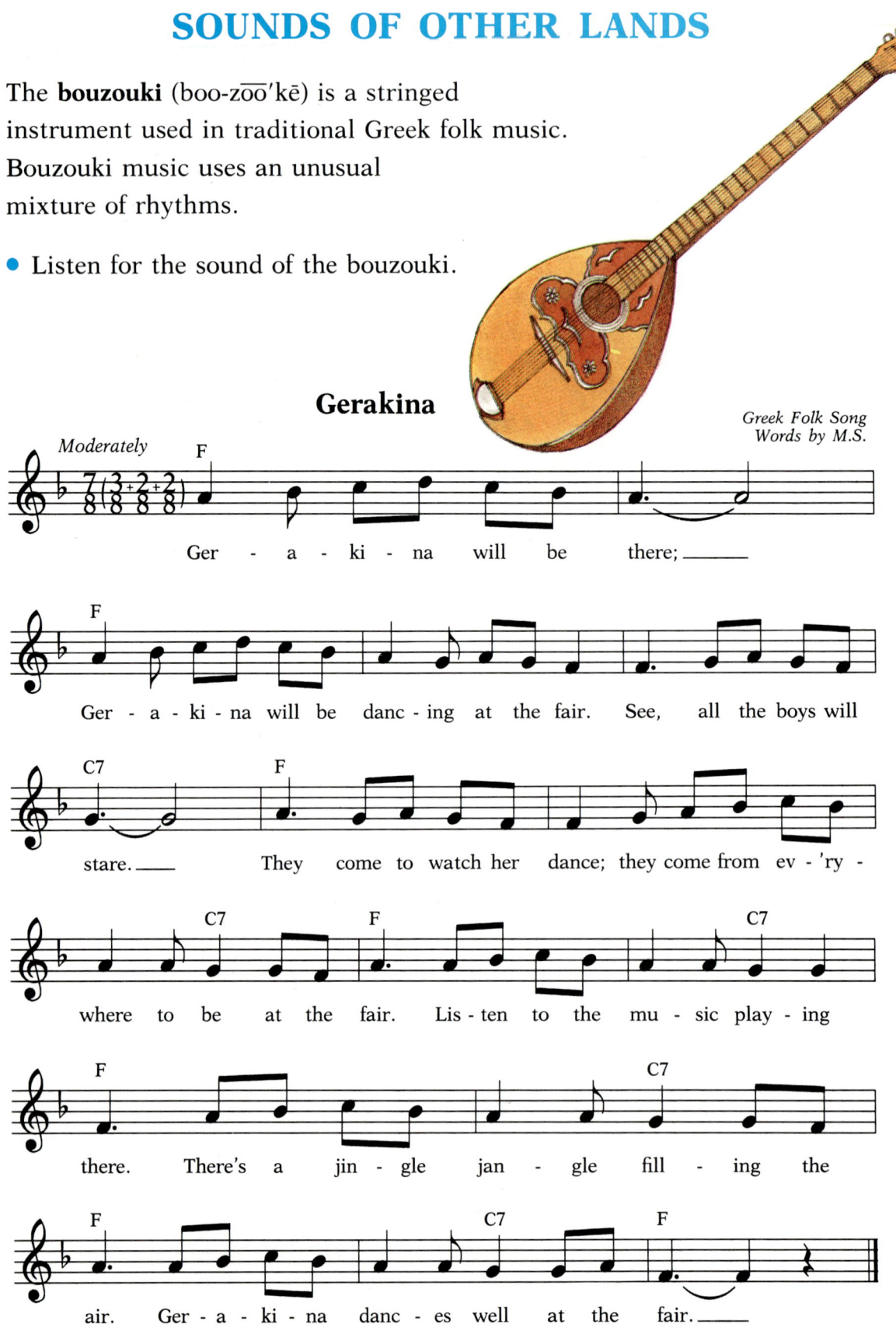

Ger - a - ki - na will be there;

Ger - a - ki - na will be danc - ing at the fair. See, all the boys will stare. They come to watch her dance; they come from ev - 'ry - where to be at the fair. Lis - ten to the mu - sic play - ing there. There's a jin - gle jan - gle fill - ing the air. Ger - a - ki - na danc - es well at the fair.

Still Life with Guitar by Pablo Picasso

Spanish folk music was greatly influenced by gypsies who wandered across Europe from India and settled in Spain around 1450. Their fiery music is known as **flamenco.** It is accompanied by guitar and often **castanets** (two small, hollow-shaped pieces of wood clicked together in one hand).

Flamenco was the inspiration for *Concierto de Aranjuez.* This concerto for guitar and orchestra was written in 1939 by the Spanish composer Joaquín Rodrigo (wä-kēn′ ro-drē′gō), who was born in 1901. Aranjuez is a town in Spain that was a favorite gathering spot of the nobility around 1800. The excitement and spirit of Spanish life at that time can be felt in the music.

- As you listen to the music, signal when you hear guitar alone, orchestra alone, or guitar and orchestra together.

 Concierto de Aranjuez, First Movement, by Joaquín Rodrigo

UNUSUAL RHYTHM EFFECTS

Accenting beats in unexpected places can make music more exciting. In Spanish folk music, a rhythm effect called **hemiola** (hem-ē-ō′lə) is often used. This is a pattern in $\frac{6}{8}$ meter in which two sets of three ($\overset{>}{1}$ 2 3 $\overset{>}{1}$ 2 3) alternate with three sets of two ($\overset{>}{1}$ 2 $\overset{>}{1}$ 2 $\overset{>}{1}$ 2).

- Practice clapping this hemiola pattern. Say all the numbers, but clap only on 1.

$$\|: \overset{>}{1}\ 2\ 3\ \overset{>}{1}\ 2\ 3\ \mid \overset{>}{1}\ 2\ \overset{>}{1}\ 2\ \overset{>}{1}\ 2\ :\|$$

In hemiola, the constant shifting of accents makes it sound as if the meter is changing.

- Listen to *Concierto de Aranjuez* again. Clap the strong beat during the introduction. Listen for the hemiola in the music.

Another unusual meter is used in Greek folk music.

- Notice the $\frac{7}{8}$ meter in "Gerakina" on page 218. The seven beats in each measure may be accented in sets of three and sets of two.

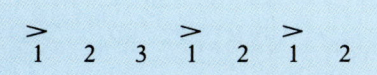

- Practice clapping this pattern. Say all the numbers, but clap only on 1.

- Now practice clapping this pattern as you listen to "Gerakina" again. Then step in place on the strong beats instead of clapping. Finally, do a step called a "grapevine" step. Step to the side with your right foot, cross behind with your left, step again with your right, then cross in front with your left. This step is used in many Greek dances.

CALYPSO AND SALSA

Calypso is a style of music which originated in Trinidad, an island in the Caribbean Sea. Calypso songs are usually lively, rhythmic, and humorous. They began as protest songs against the harsh life of those who worked on the sugar plantations. Calypso music stresses certain words or syllables that are normally unaccented.

- Listen for the words that are accented in calypso style.
- Find the measures in the refrain that have a syncopated pattern.

Island in the Sun

Music by Harry Belafonte
Words by Lord Burgess

1. This is my is-land in the sun where my peo-ple have toiled since time be-gun. Though I may sail on man-y a sea. Her shores will al-ways be home to me.

Refrain
Oh, is-land in the sun. Willed to me by my

Optional Cambiata

father's hand. All my days I will sing in praise of your forests, waters, your shining sand. *Fine*

2. I hope the day will never come that I can't awake to the sound of drum. Never let me miss carnival With calypso songs philosophical. *D.S. al Fine*

Steel drums are often used to accompany calypso songs. These drums were originally made by hammering the tops of oil drums into different shapes until the desired pitches could be played. Instruments commonly used in Latin American music are shown below.

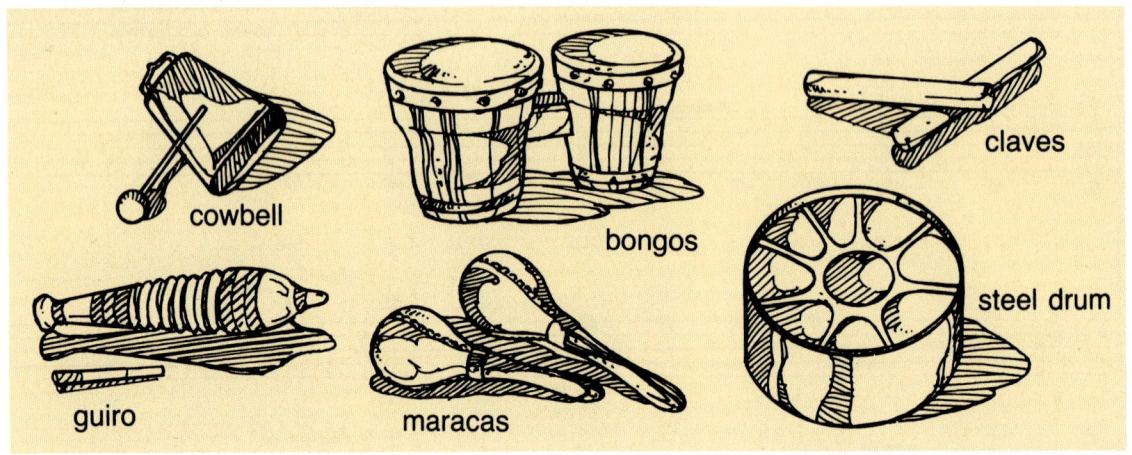

- Clap the rhythm and speak the chant for each instrument.

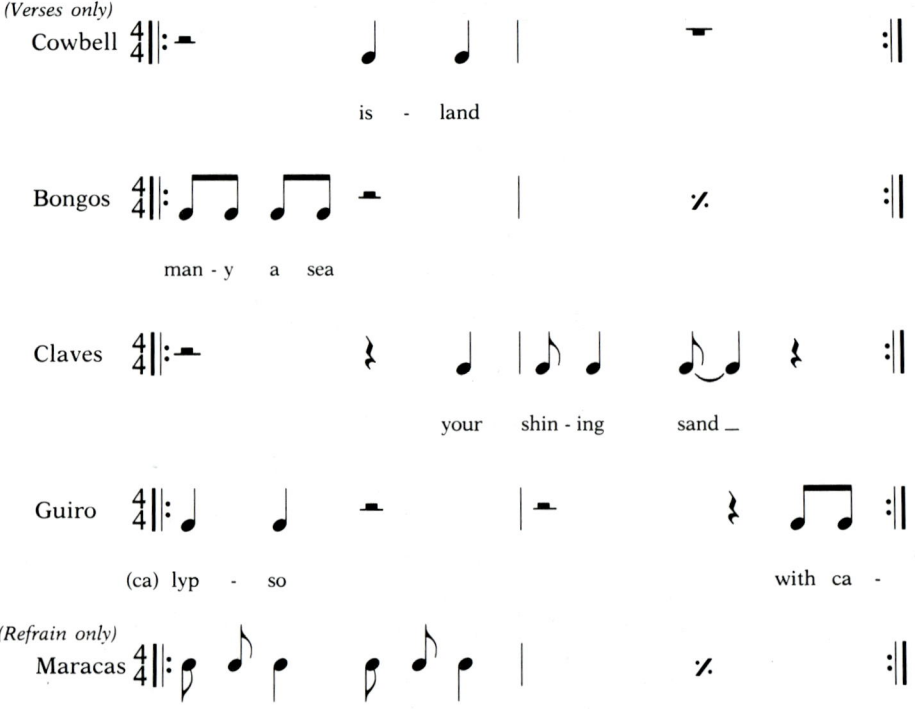

- Play the instruments as you speak the chant again. Then use the instruments as you sing "Island in the Sun" on pages 222 and 223.

Lee Ritenour

Latin American rhythms are especially effective with electronic instruments.

Lee Ritenour is a jazz musician who uses elements of folk music and electronic instruments. In "The Sauce," Lee plays electric guitar and electronic classical guitar. A synthesizer may also be heard, along with standard percussion instruments. The sauce referred to in the title is hot sauce, or *salsa*, often added to foods. **Salsa** is also the name used for an exciting style of Latin American dance music.

- Listen for the electronic sounds and for the Latin American rhythms in "The Sauce."

    "The Sauce" performed by Lee Ritenour

THE FOUR FAMILIES OF THE ORCHESTRA

Instruments of the orchestra may be grouped into four families: brass, woodwind, string, and percussion.

Young Person's Guide to the Orchestra by the English composer Benjamin Britten (1913–1976) was composed to introduce these four families. It is a set of variations on the theme below by the seventeenth-century English composer Henry Purcell (1659–1695).

• Listen to this composition. Follow the listening map so that you will know what instruments are playing.

 Young Person's Guide to the Orchestra ("Variations and Fugue on a Theme of Purcell") by Benjamin Britten

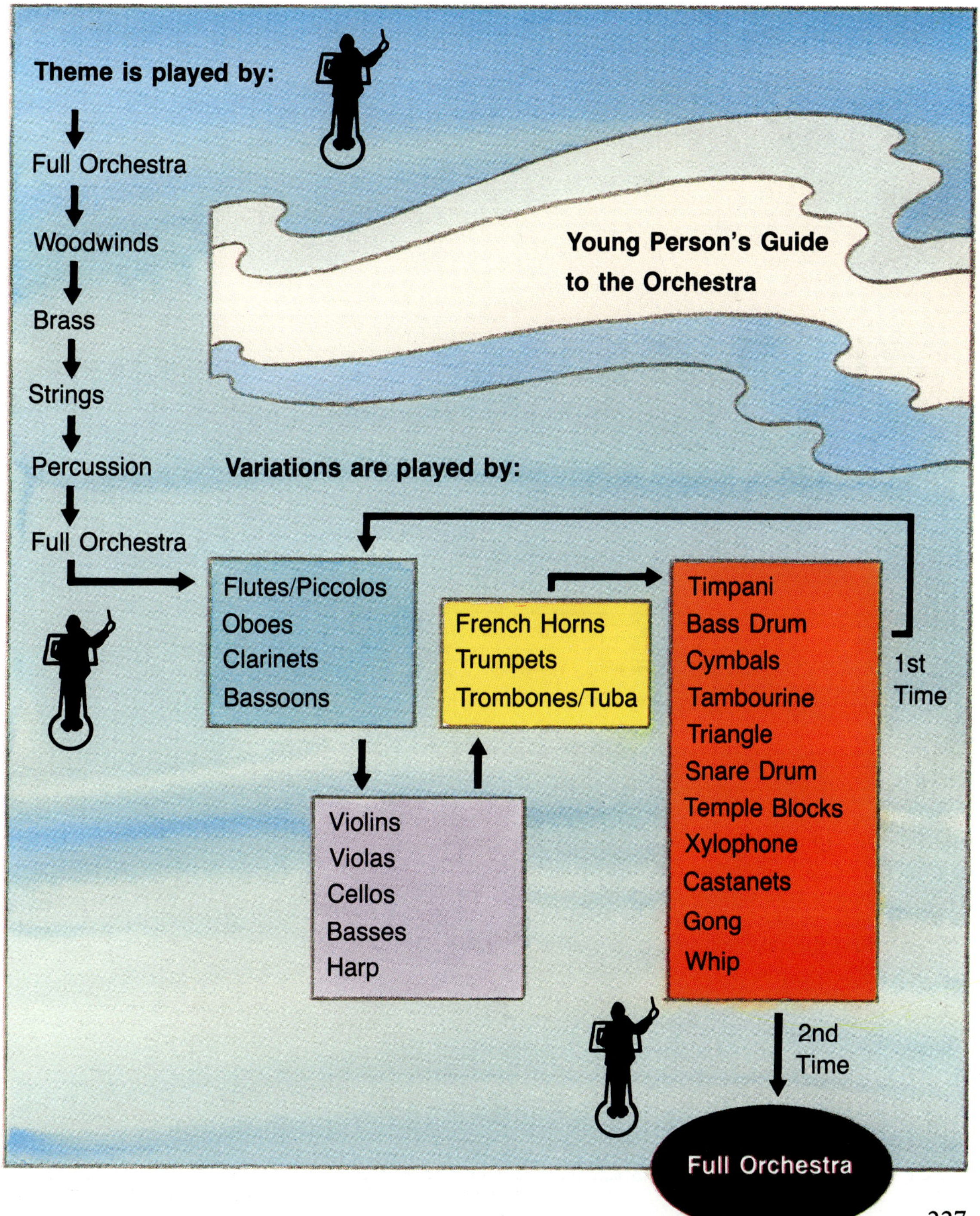

Theme is played by:
- Full Orchestra
- Woodwinds
- Brass
- Strings
- Percussion
- Full Orchestra

Young Person's Guide to the Orchestra

Variations are played by:

Flutes/Piccolos, Oboes, Clarinets, Bassoons

French Horns, Trumpets, Trombones/Tuba

Timpani, Bass Drum, Cymbals, Tambourine, Triangle, Snare Drum, Temple Blocks, Xylophone, Castanets, Gong, Whip — 1st Time

Violins, Violas, Cellos, Basses, Harp

2nd Time → Full Orchestra

CHORDAL MOVEMENT

The melody of "Matilda" can be accompanied with three chords.

- Use an autoharp to discover the pitches that make up the chords in this folk song. Find the measures that use only chord tones.

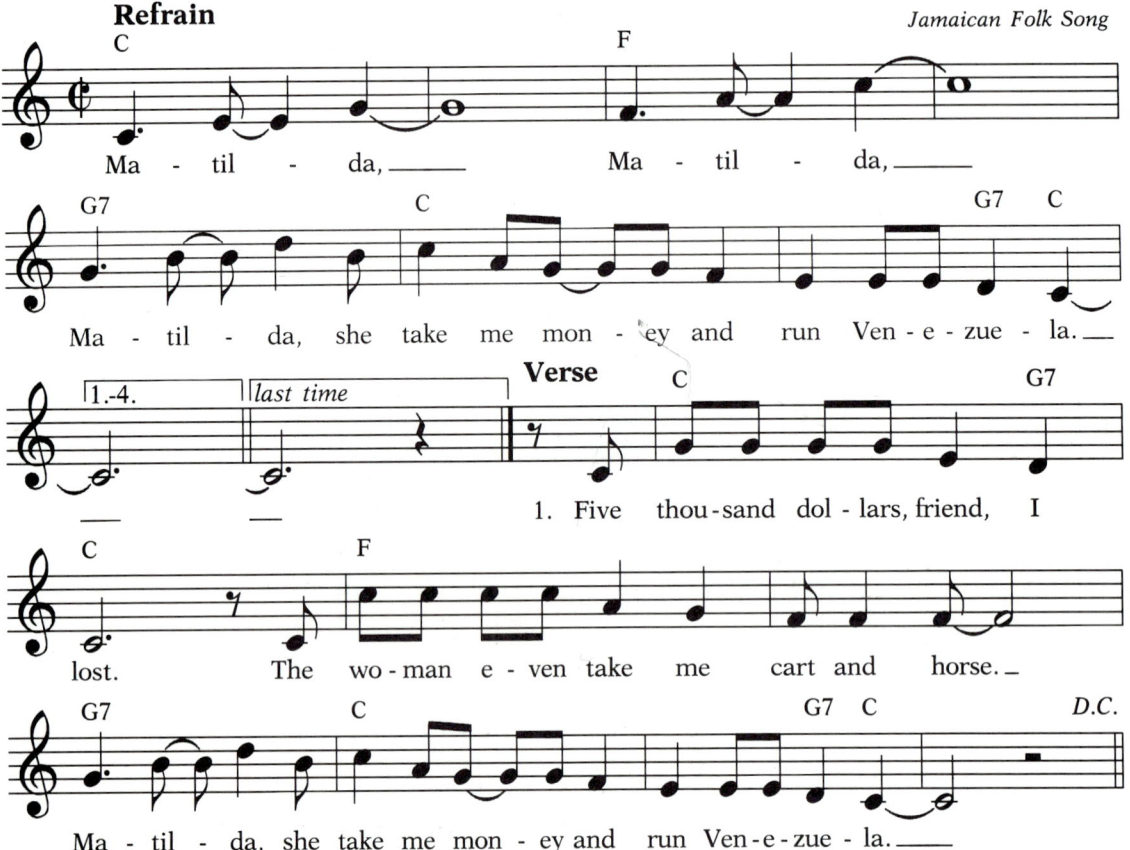

2. My money was to buy me house and land,
   The woman she got a serious plan.
   Matilda, she take me money and run Venezuela.
   Refrain

3. Now the money was safe in me bed,
   Stuck in the pillow beneath me head,
   But Matilda, she find me money and run Venezuela.
   Refrain

4. Never will I love again,
   All me money gone in vain
   'Cause Matilda, she take me money and run Venezuela.
   Refrain

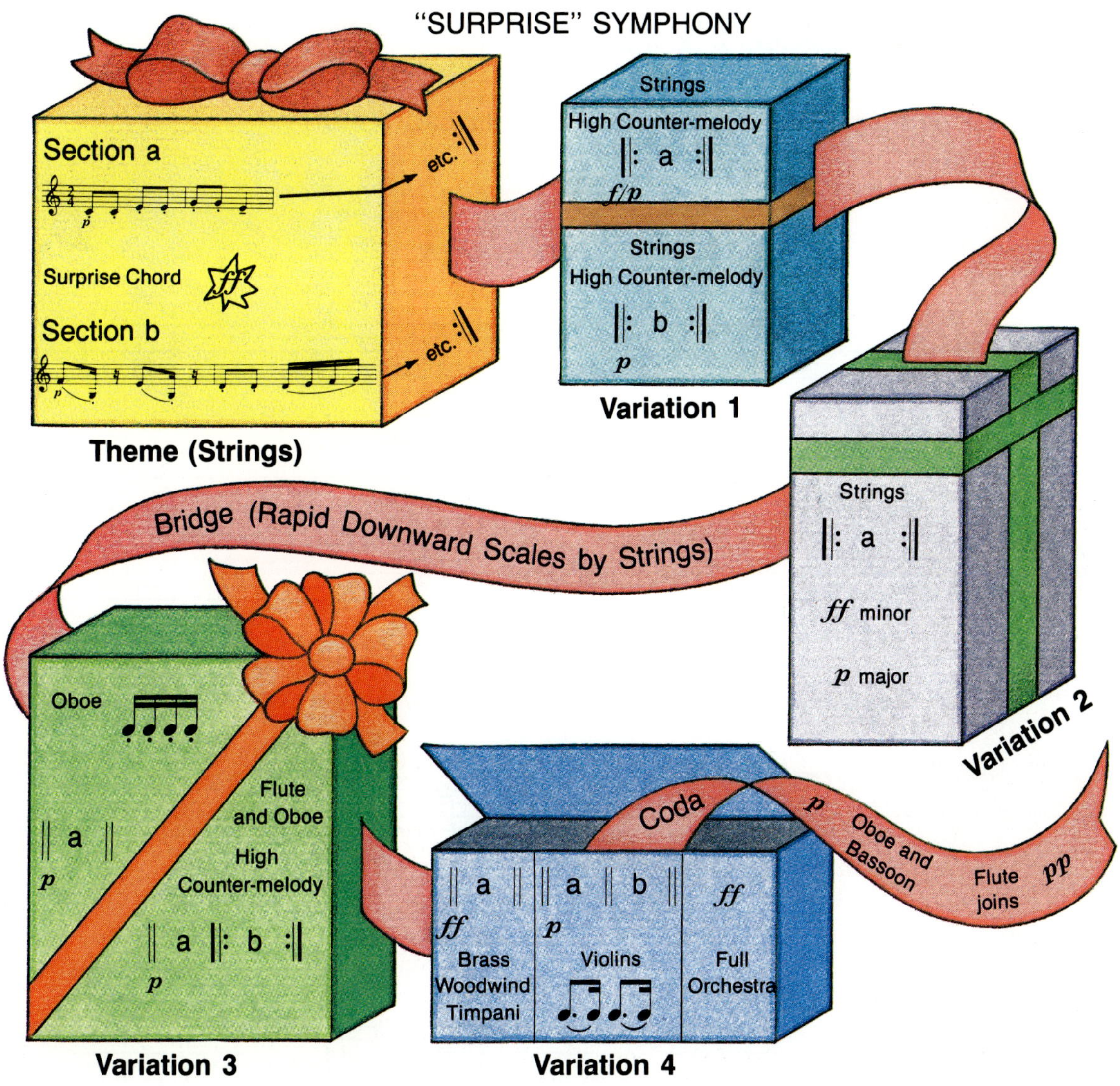

"SURPRISE" SYMPHONY

The great Austrian composer Franz Joseph Haydn (1732–1809) composed 104 symphonies. One of the best-known is Symphony No. 94. When you hear it, you will discover why it has always been called the "Surprise" Symphony.

- Which theme in this composition moves in chordal fashion? Following the listening map will help you to hear the way that the theme is varied.

 Symphony No. 94 ("Surprise" Symphony), Second Movement, by Franz Joseph Haydn

A VARIETY OF TONE COLORS

- What instruments are often used for American country music?

Mama Don't 'Low

American Folk Song
Arranged by P.W.

1.
2. } Ma-ma don't 'low no { gui-tar play-in' round here, _____
3.   ban-jo pick-in' round here, _____
                              har-mo-niz-in' round here, _____

no play-ing round here
no pick-ing round here
no har-mo-ny here

Ma-ma don't 'low no { gui-tar play-in' round here, _____
                       ban-jo pick-in' round here, _____
                       har-mo-niz-in' round here, _____

no play-ing round here
no pick-ing round here
no har-mo-ny here

I don't care what Ma-ma don't 'low, Gon-na { play my gui-tar an-y-how,
                                               pick my ban-jo an-y-how,
                                               har-mo-nize songs an-y-how,

I don't care, I don't care, { play gui-tar an-y-how,
                                pick ban-jo an-y-how,
                                har-mo-nize an-y-how,

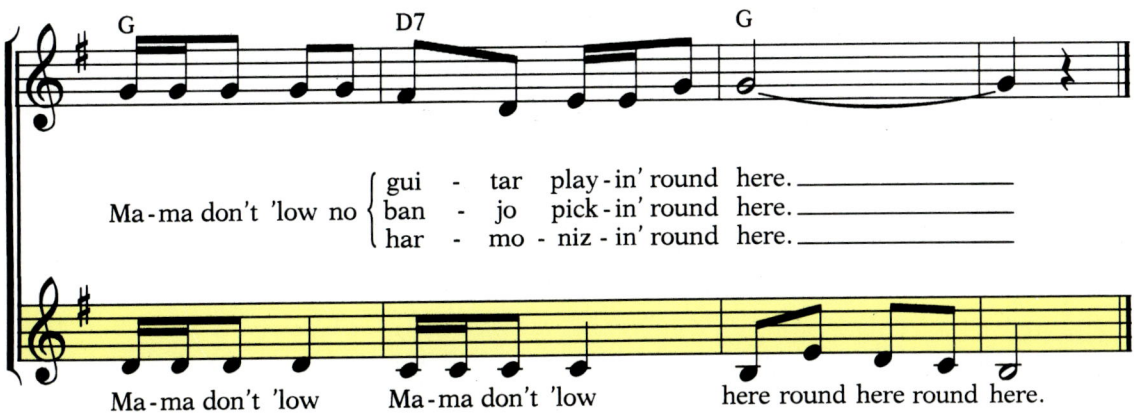

- Listen for the variety of instruments the Banks and Shane Band demonstrates with this song.

 "Mama Don't 'Low" performed by Banks and Shane

The Banks and Shane Band performs a variety of American music styles using traditional country instruments along with other instruments such as bass and drums.

"Copacabana" was inspired by a trip to South America at carnival time. The composer liked the local popular music. He used its sound to describe the mood of a Brazilian beach. "Copacabana" is part of a suite named *Saudades do Brasil* *(Recollections of Brazil)*.

- Listen for the different instruments in each section of the music.

"Copacabana" (excerpt) from *Saudades do Brasil* by Darius Milhaud (dä-ryo͞os' mē-ō')

A gargoyle on top of Notre Dame cathedral in Paris

The American composer Otto Luening (ä'tō lōōn'ing), born in 1900, wrote music for the synthesizer. This composition suggests gargoyles on a great cathedral coming to life.

- Listen for the sounds made by the synthesizer in "Gargoyles." No other instrument could create quite the same effects.

 "Gargoyles" (excerpt) by Otto Luening

CHOOSING APPROPRIATE TONE COLORS

- What instruments would you choose to accompany this calypso song?

MAKING A MUSIC VIDEO

A **music video** combines music and visual images and is played on a television. Some videos show people performing a song. Others show pictures or scenes telling a story along with the song.

- Think about one of your favorite music videos. What do you like about it? How does the video or picture add to your enjoyment of the music? What music videos do others in your class like?
- Plan a music video in your class. Decide what small groups will be needed to do this. You might want to have a script group, a music group, a costume group, a prop group, a scenery group, and an equipment group.

The script group writes the **script,** the description needed for the actors, singers, and musicians to portray the song on the screen. Then the group makes a **storyboard** that shows in drawings (like cartoons) how each shot in the video will look. This will help the person who uses the camera to get the best shots for the video.

The music group is responsible for planning who will sing and play in the music video. This group decides on the kinds of musical instruments and the number of singers needed.

The costume group is responsible for finding or making costumes appropriate for the music video.

The prop group collects the objects needed to help the actors and singers act out the song.

The scenery group helps to decide whether the music video will be performed outside or inside. They also put together any scenery needed to provide the backgrounds for the acting and singing.

The equipment group gets and learns how to use the camera, lights, and other equipment needed to produce the music video.

- Divide into small groups and plan a schedule for each group. Then follow your schedule to make the music video. When it's finished, invite friends to watch the show.

TAKE ANOTHER LOOK

- Sing your favorites of these songs.

    I Can See Clearly Now   Rocky Top
    Take Me Home, Country Roads
    Island in the Sun   Mama Don't 'Low
    John B. Sails

- Name two musical elements or styles that you recognize in these compositions.

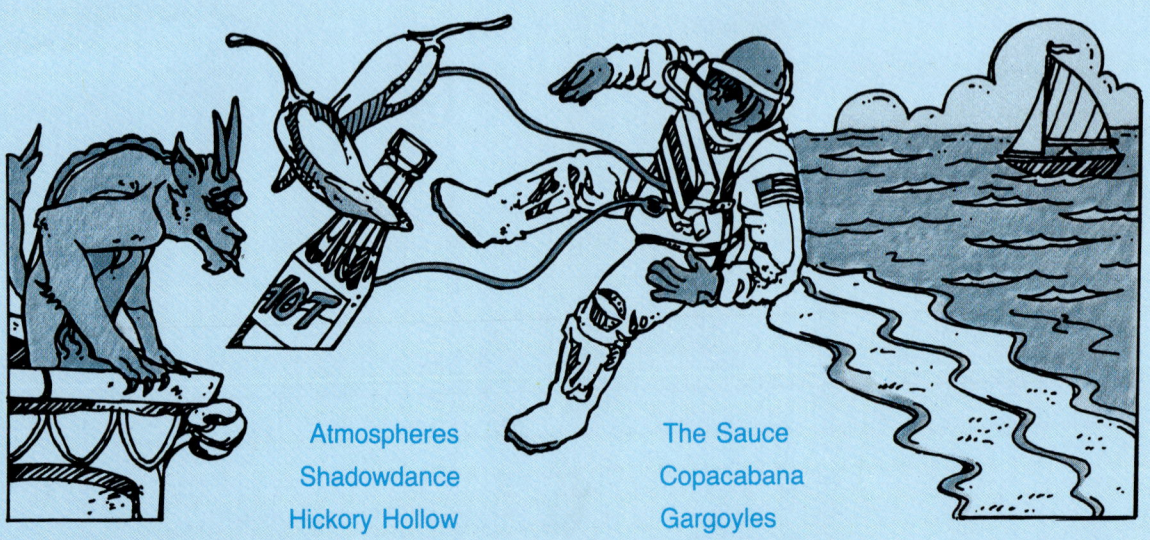

Atmosphere   The Sauce
Shadowdance   Copacabana
Hickory Hollow   Gargoyles

- Listen again to *Young Person's Guide to the Orchestra.* Name as many instruments as you can in each of the four families of the orchestra.

JUST CHECKING

- How much do you remember? Choose the best answer for each question.

1. Which style of music often features a banjo?
    a. calypso music
    b. American country music
    c. rock music

2. Which group of instruments would be used in Latin American music?
    a. maracas, bongos, cowbell, steel drum
    b. bass, cello, violin
    c. guitar, banjo, fiddle

3. A synthesizer is ___.
    a. a type of cymbal
    b. an electronic instrument
    c. always used in calypso music

4. A symphony orchestra is made up of ___ families of instruments.
    a. 6   b. 3   c. 4

5. Which group of instruments belongs to the woodwind family?
    a. bass, cello, violin, viola, harp
    b. piccolo, flute, clarinet, oboe, bassoon
    c. bass drum, cymbals, snare drum, gong

SONGBOOK

Who's That Yonder?

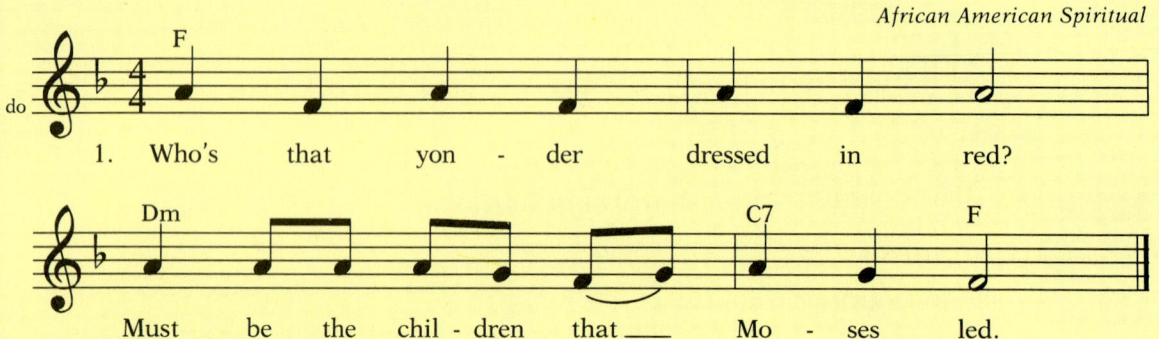

African American Spiritual

1. Who's that yonder dressed in red?
   Must be the children that Moses led.

2. Who's that yonder dressed in white?
   Must be the children of the Israelite.

3. Who's that yonder dressed in blue?
   Must be the children that are comin' through.

4. Who's that yonder dressed in black?
   Must be the hypocrites a-turnin' back.

Dinah

1850 Minstrel Song

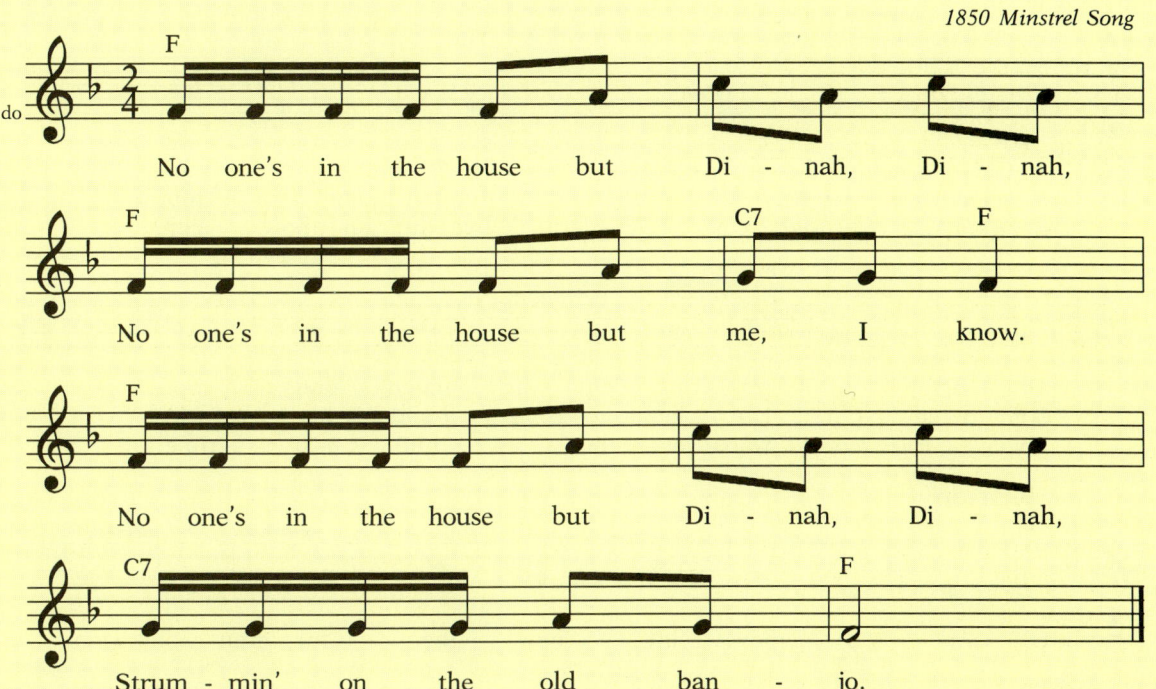

241

The Old Ark

I Spurred My Horse

American Nonsense Song

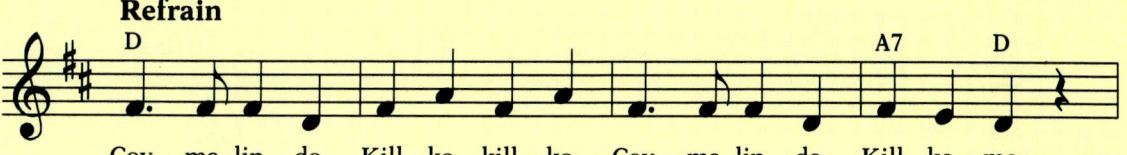
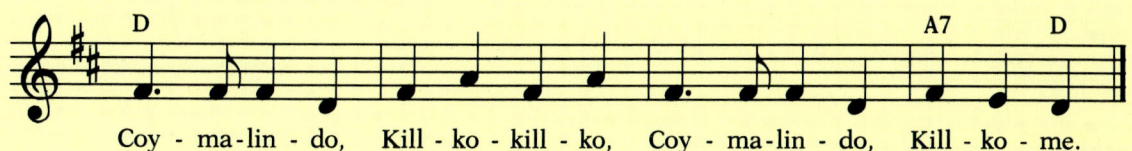

2. I grabbed those reins and held them tight,
   I grabbed those reins and held them tight,
   I grabbed those reins and held them tight,
   And rode that horse with all my might.

   Refrain

3. I fed my horse in a poplar trough,
   I fed my horse in a poplar trough,
   I fed my horse in a poplar trough,
   And there he got the whooping cough.

   Refrain

4. I fed my horse with a silver spoon,
   I fed my horse with a silver spoon,
   I fed my horse with a silver spoon,
   And then he kicked it o-ver the moon.

   Refrain

5. When my horse is dead and gone,
   When my horse is dead and gone,
   When my horse is dead and gone,
   I'll use his jaw-bone to plow my corn.

   Refrain

Land of the Silver Birch

Canadian Folk Song

1. Land of the sil-ver birch, home of the bea-ver,
   Where still the might-y moose wan-ders at will,
   Blue lake and rock-y shore, I will re-turn once more.
   Boom de de boom boom, Boom de de boom boom, Boom de de boom boom, Boom.

2. Down in the for-est, deep in the low-lands,
   My heart cries out for thee, hills of the north.

3. High on a rock-y ledge, I'll build a wig-wam,
   Close by the wa-ter's edge, si-lent and still.

Perry Merry Dictum Dominee

Appalachian Folk Song

1. I had four brothers over the sea,
   Perry merry dictum Dominee;
   And they each sent a present unto me,
   Partum quartum perry dicentum, Perry merry dictum Dominee.

2. The first sent me cherries without any stones,
   Perry merry dictum Dominee;
   The second sent a chicken without any bones,
   Partum quartum perry dicentum, Perry merry dictum Dominee.

3. The third sent a blanket that had no thread,
   Perry merry dictum Dominee;
   The fourth sent a book that could not be read,
   Partum quartum perry dicentum, Perry merry dictum Dominee.

4. When the cherries are in bloom they have no stones,
   Perry merry dictum Dominee;
   When the chicken's in the egg it has no bones,
   Partum quartum perry dicentum, Perry merry dictum Dominee.

5. When the blanket's in the fleece it has no thread,
   Perry merry dictum Dominee;
   When the book's in the press it cannot be read,
   Partum quartum perry dicentum, Perry merry dictum Dominee.

Cotton Eye Joe

Alabama Folk Song

2. Come for to see you, come for to sing,
   Come for to show you my diamond ring.

3. Where did you get it? How did it glow?
   Who could've made it, Cotton Eye Joe?

4. Comes from the mine field, comes from the ground,
   Comes from the darkness with night all around.

5. Why does it sparkle? What makes it glow?
   Why is it gleaming, Cotton Eye Joe?

6. Light makes it glitter, sun from the skies,
   Wants to be shining like your bright eyes.

2. She's nearing now the station
   O sister, don't be vain
   But come and get your ticket
   And be ready for the train.
   Refrain

3. The fare is cheap and all can go
   The rich and poor are there;
   No second class on board this train,
   No difference in the fare.
   Refrain

Camptown Races

Words and music by Stephen C. Foster

1. Camp-town la-dies sing this song, Doo-dah, doo-dah.
   Camp-town race track five miles long, Oh, doo-dah-day.
   Went down there with my hat caved in, Doo-dah, doo-dah.
   Came back home with a pock-et-ful of tin, Oh, doo-dah-day.

   Refrain
   Goin' to run all night, Goin' to run all day,
   Bet my mon-ey on the bob-tailed nag, Some-bod-y bet on the bay.

2. Long tail fil-ly and the big black horse, Doo-dah, doo-dah!
   Flew the track and both cut a-cross, Oh, doo-dah-day.
   Blind horse stick-ing in a big mud hole, Doo-dah, doo-dah!
   Could-n't touch bot-tom with a ten-foot pole, Oh, doo-dah-day.
   Refrain

Oh, How Lovely Is the Evening

Traditional Round

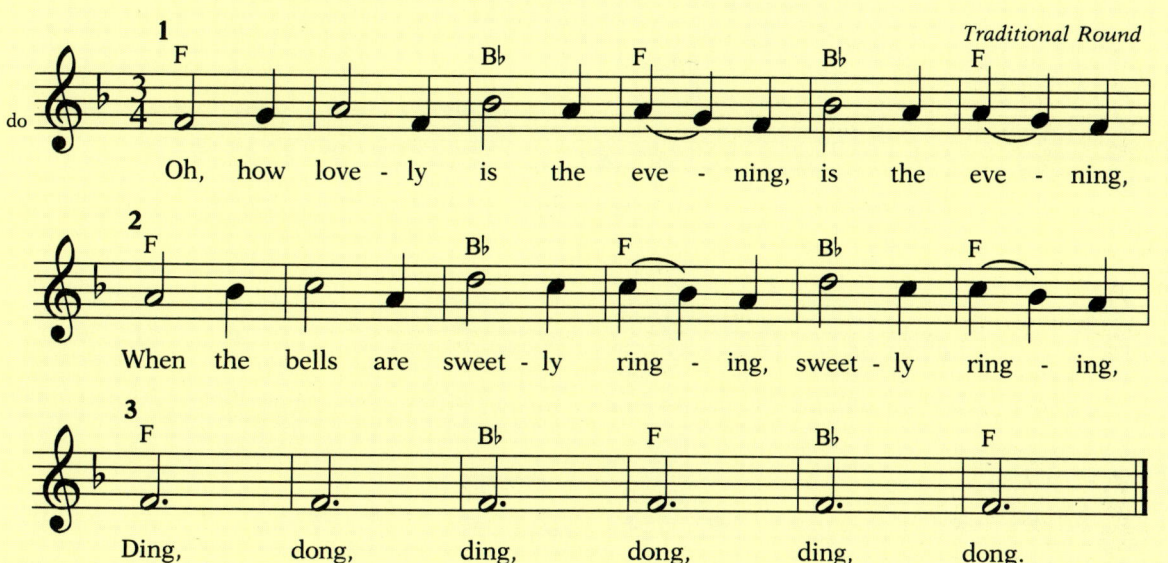

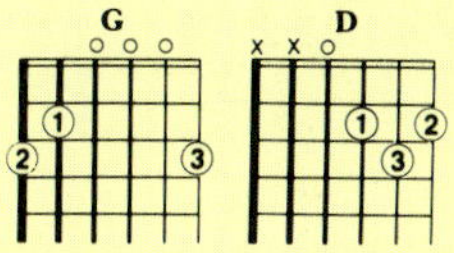

Kookaburra

Australian Round
Words by M. Sinclair

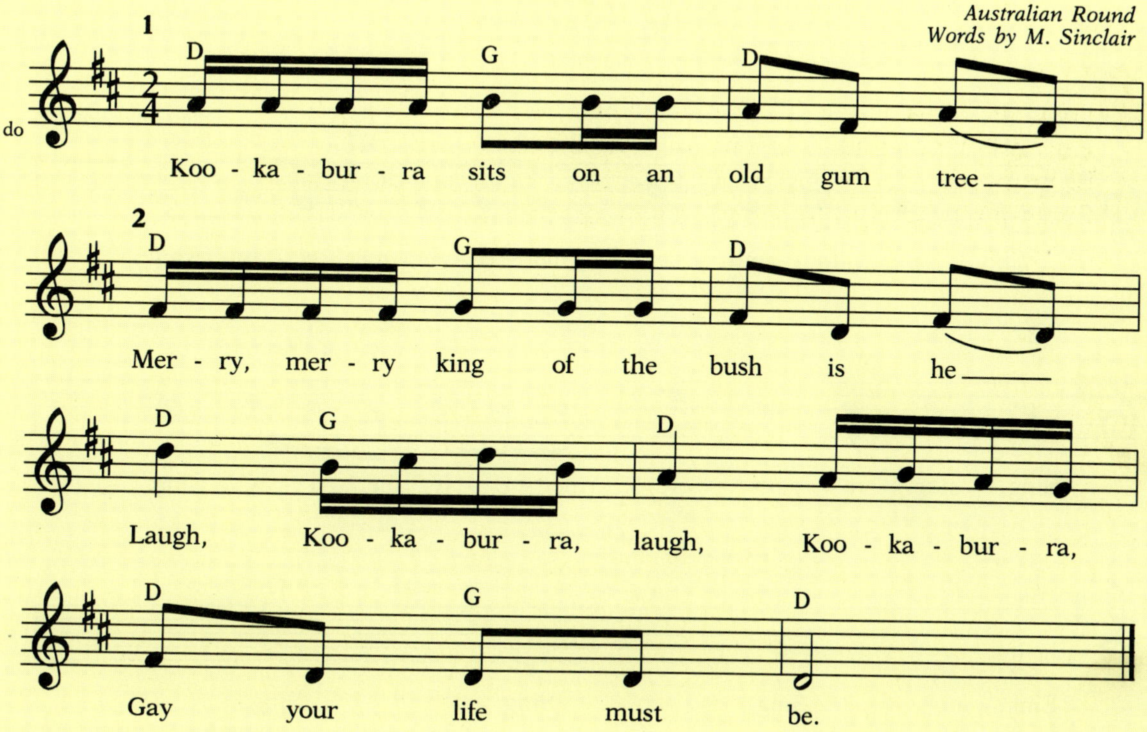

A Ram Sam Sam

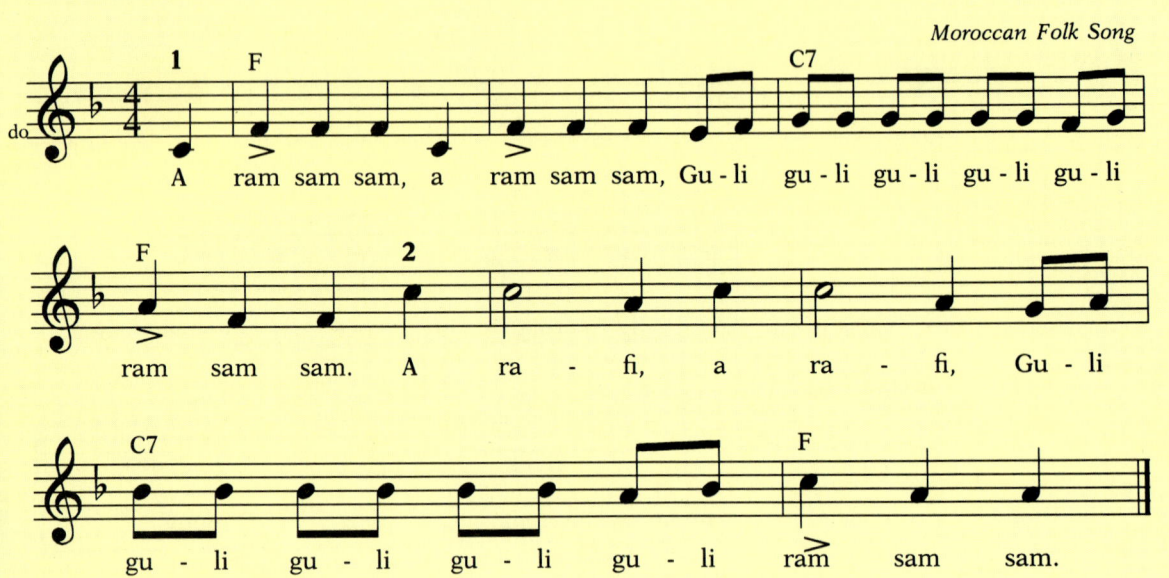

Sing Together

Autumn Canon

Words and music by L. Bardos
Translated by Sean Deibler

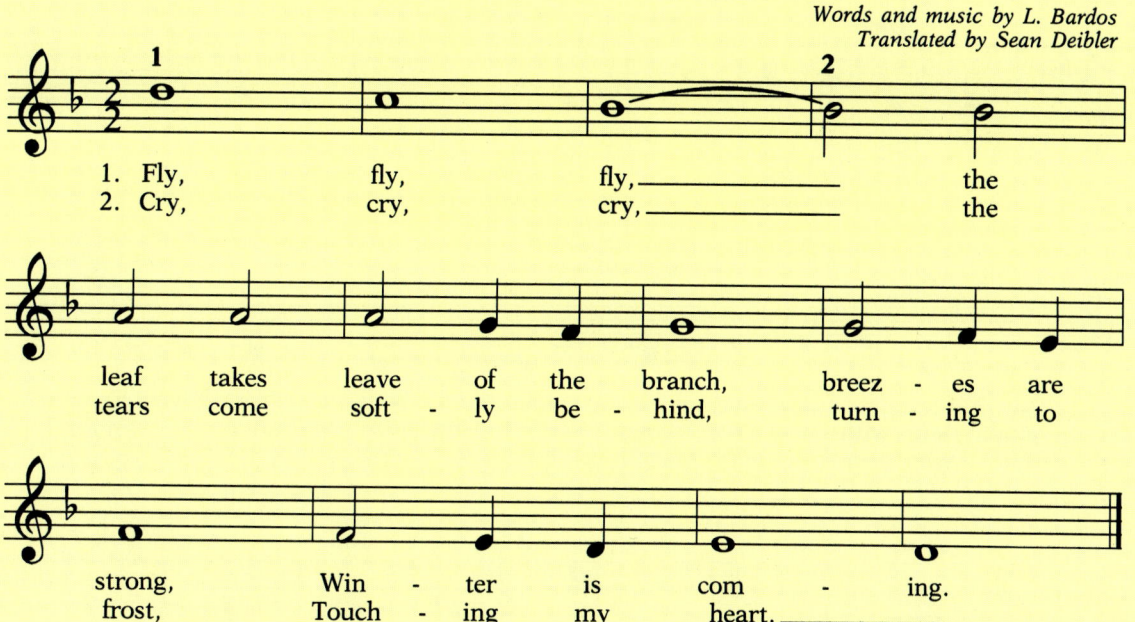

1. Fly, fly, fly, the leaf takes leave of the branch, breezes are strong, Winter is coming.
2. Cry, cry, cry, the tears come softly behind, turning to frost, Touching my heart.

God Rest You Merry, Gentlemen

Hark! The Herald Angels Sing

Music by Felix Mendelssohn
Words by Charles Wesley

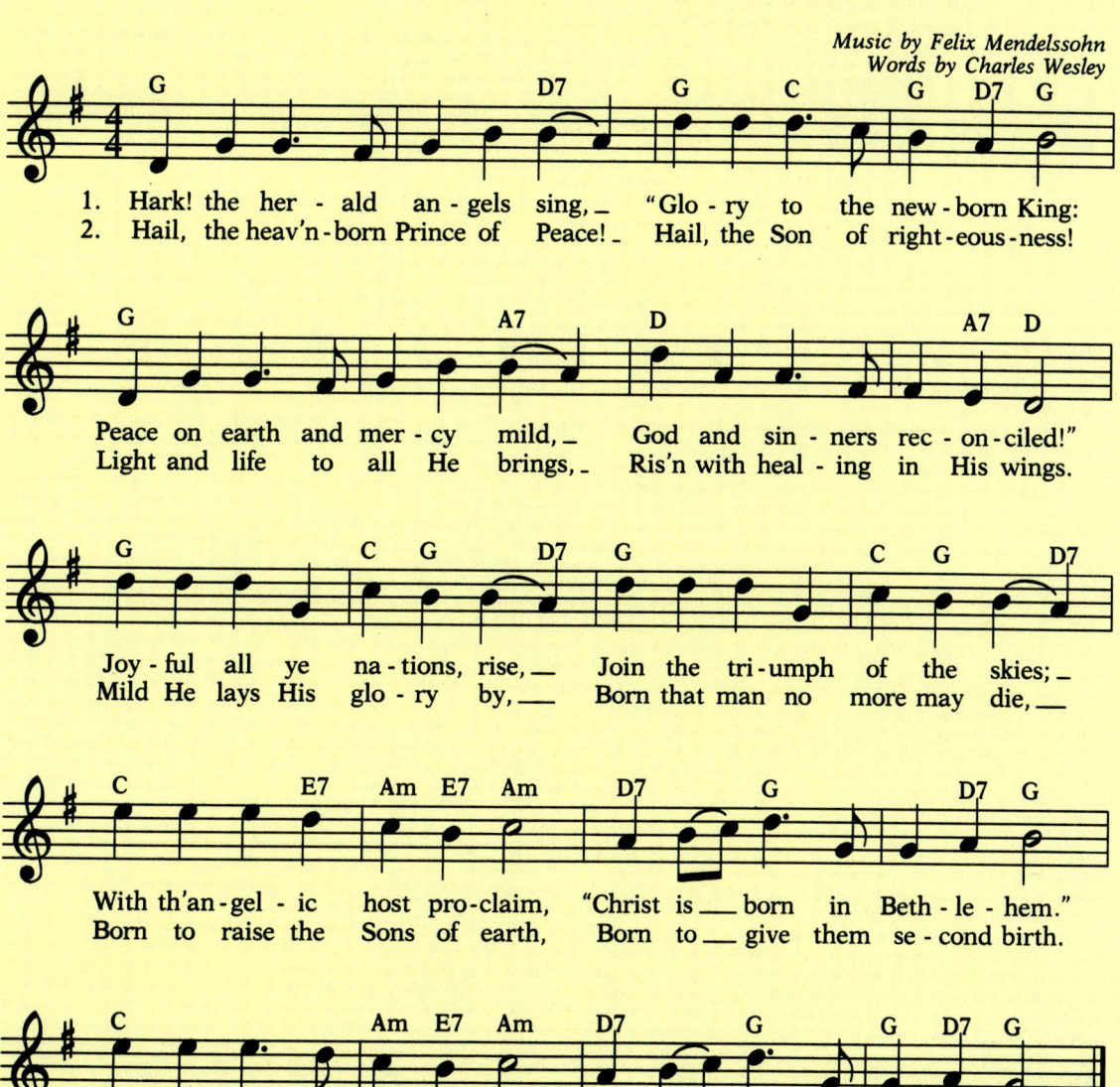

1. Hark! the her-ald an-gels sing,— "Glo-ry to the new-born King:
2. Hail, the heav'n-born Prince of Peace!— Hail, the Son of right-eous-ness!

Peace on earth and mer-cy mild,— God and sin-ners rec-on-ciled!"
Light and life to all He brings,— Ris'n with heal-ing in His wings.

Joy-ful all ye na-tions, rise,— Join the tri-umph of the skies;—
Mild He lays His glo-ry by,— Born that man no more may die,—

With th'an-gel-ic host pro-claim, "Christ is— born in Beth-le-hem."
Born to raise the Sons of earth, Born to— give them se-cond birth.

Hark! the her-ald an-gels sing, Glo-ry— to the new-born King.

253

Carol of the Drum

Dona Nobis Pacem

Hava Nagila

Harvest Time

Finnish Folk Song
Words by Tossi Aaron

Bring the wheat and bar-ley in,
Fill the si-lo, fill the bin,
From the field and mea-dow,
Ay, liu-liu-u liu-liu-liu, Ga-ther in the har-vest! har-vest!

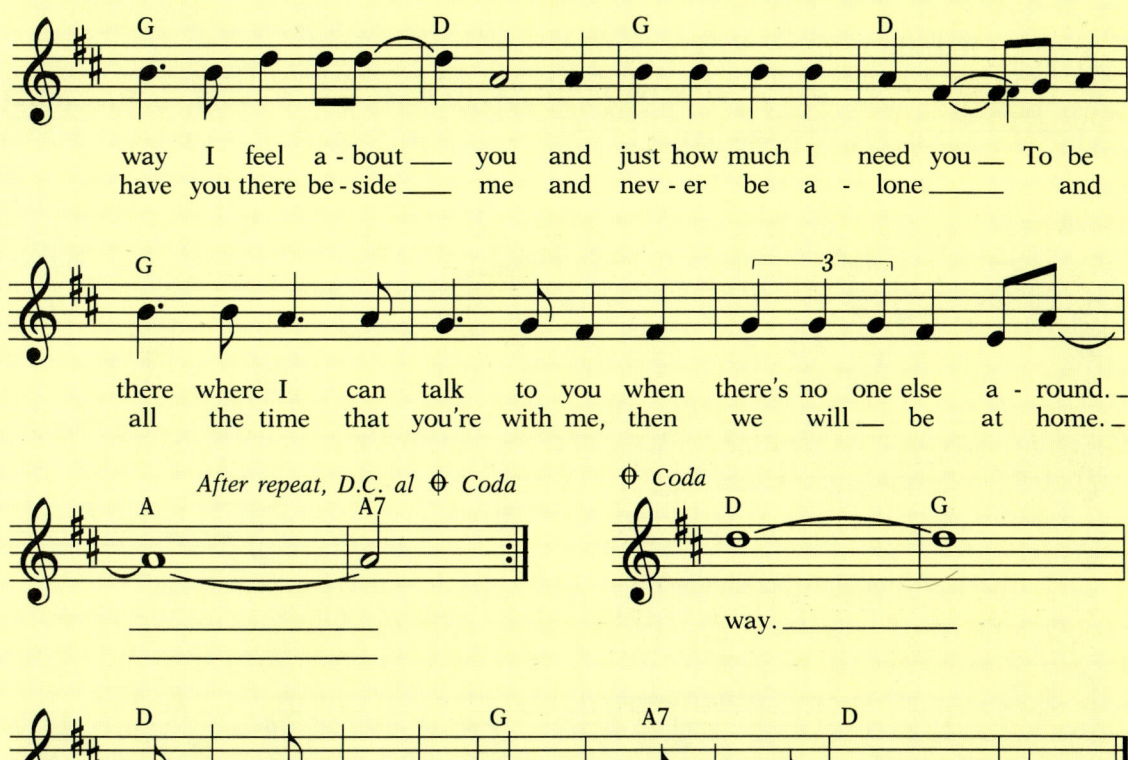

Guantanamera

Words and music by José Fernandez Dias
Lyrics adapted by Julian Orbon
Music adapted by Hector Angulo and Pete Seeger

2. Mi verso es de un verde claro,
   Y de un carmin encendido,
   Mi verso es de un verde claro,
   Y de un carmin encendido,
   Mi verso es un cierro herido,
   Que busca en el monte amparo.
   Refrain

3. Con los pobres de la tierra,
   Quiero yo mi suerte echar,
   Con los pobres de la tierra,
   Quiero yo mi suerte echar,
   El arroyo de la sierra,
   Me complace más que el mar.
   Refrain

"Guantanamera Guajira Guantanamera." Original lyrics and music by José Fernandez Dias (Joseito Fernandez). Music adaptation by Hector Angulo, Pete Seeger & Julian Orbon, Lyric adaptation by Julian Orbon. Based on a poem by Jose Marti. Copyright © 1963, 1966 by Fall River Music, Inc., New York. All rights reserved. Used by permission.

Ifca's Castle

Czechoslovakian Folk Song

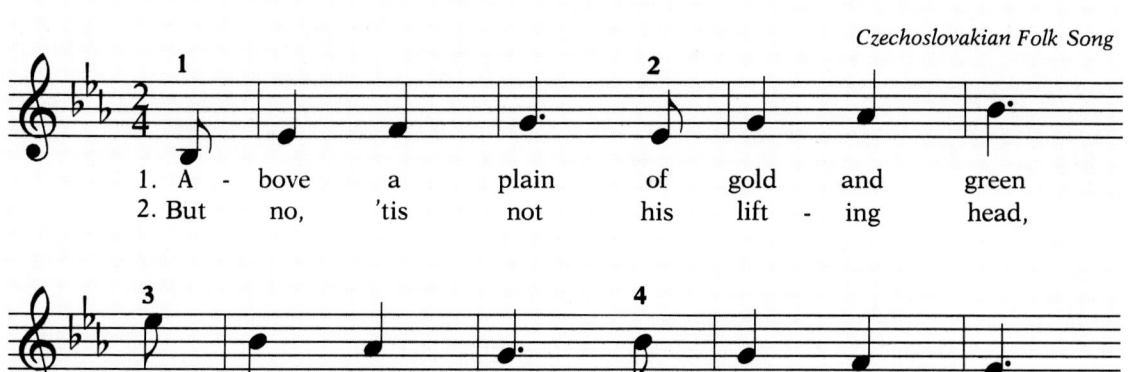
1. A - bove a plain of gold and green
2. But no, 'tis not his lift - ing head,

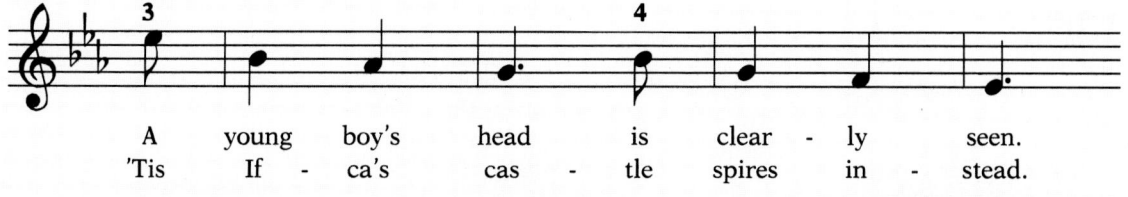
A young boy's head is clear - ly seen.
'Tis If - ca's cas - tle spires in - stead.

Refrain

A - hu - ya, hu - ya, hu - ya - ya, Swift - ly flow - ing wa - ter,

A - hu - ya, hu - ya, hu - ya - ya, Swift - ly flow - ing wa - ter.

HAPPINESS Copyright © 1965, 1967 by Jeremy Music Inc. All Rights Reserved. Reprinted by permission.
Happiness originated in the play YOU'RE A GOOD MAN, CHARLIE BROWN, a musical entertainment based on the comic strip "PEANUTS" by Charles M. Schulz.

Lift Ev'ry Voice and Sing

Music by J. Rosamond Johnson
Words by J. W. Johnson

Lift ev'ry voice and sing,
Till earth and heaven ring,
Ring with the harmonies of liberty;
Let our rejoicing rise high as the lis'ning skies,
Let it resound loud as the rolling sea.
Sing a song full of the faith that the dark past has taught us,
Sing a song full of the hope that the present has brought us;
Facing the rising sun of our new day begun,
Let us march on till victory is won.

Limbo Like Me

LIMBO LIKE ME
New words and new music adaptation by Massie Patterson and Sammy Heyward. TRO—Copyright © 1963 Ludlow Music, Inc., New York, N.Y. Used by permission.

Mule Train

*Words and music by Johnny Lange,
Hy Heath and Fred Glickman*

Mule train, (clip-pi-ty - clop, clip-pi-ty - clop,) Mule train, (clip-pi-ty - clop, clip-pi-ty - clop,) Clip-pi-ty -

clop-pin' o - ver hill and plain.
clop-pin' 'long the moun - tain chain.
clop-pin' through the wind and rain.

Seems as how they nev - er stop,
Soon they're gon - na reach the top,
They'll keep go - in' till they drop,

Clip-pi-ty - clop, clip-pi-ty - clop, clip-pi-ty, clip-pi-ty, clip-pi-ty, clip-pi-ty, clip-pi-ty -

clop-pin' a - long
(clip-pi-ty-clop, clip-pi-ty-clop, clip-pi-ty-clop,)

There's a
There's some
There's a

Sandy McNab

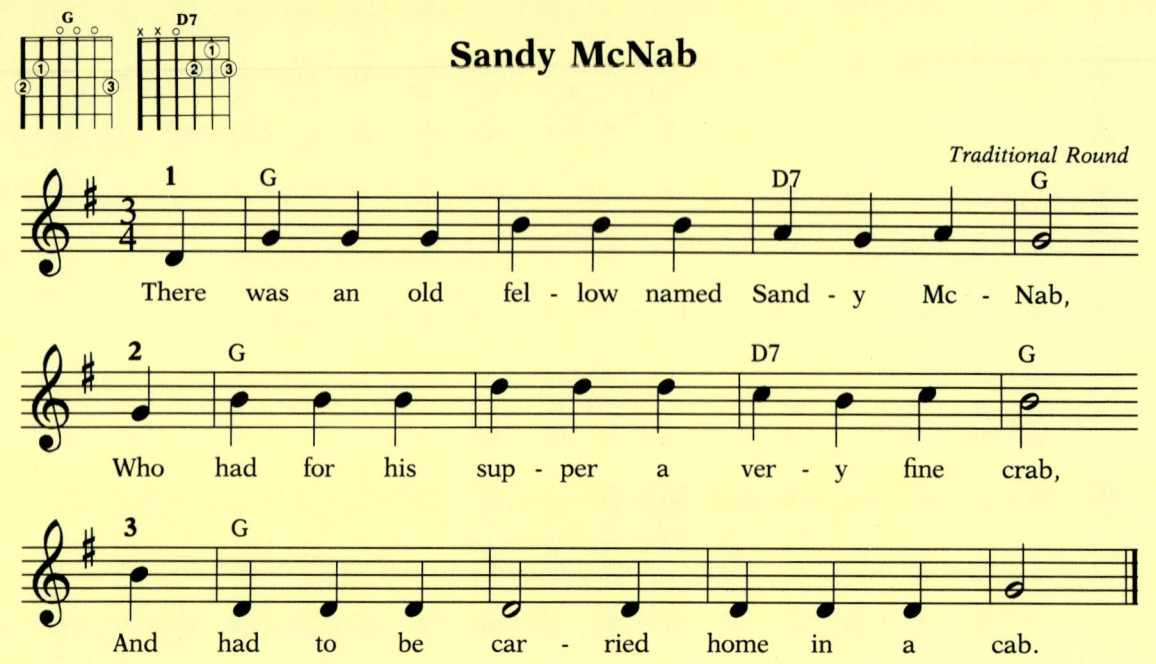

Sing a Rainbow

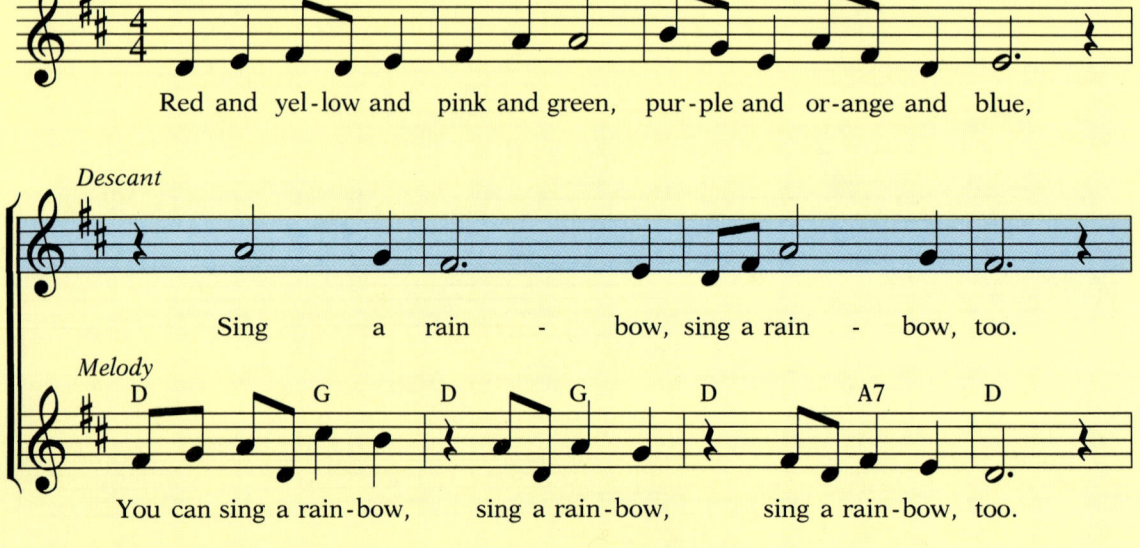

Arrangement Copyright © 1979 by Mary Val Marsh

The Turkish Revery

American Folk Song

1. "Cap-tain, cap-tain — What will you give me If I do sink the — Turk-ish Rev-er-y, If I sink her in the low-down,

2. "Gold and sil-ver — Shin-ing so bright, And my fair-est daugh-ter shall wed — you to-night, If you sink her in the low-down,

low-down, — low-down, If I sink her in the low-down lone-some low?"
low-down, — low-down, If you sink her in the low-down lone-some low!"

3. Then he bared his chest,
   And he swam in the tide,
   And he bored three holes in the old ship's side,
   And he sank her in the low-down, low-down, low-down,
   And he sank her in the low-down lonesome low.

4. Then he bared his chest,
   And he swam in the tide,
   He swam till he came to his own ship's side
   As she rolled in the low-down, low-down, low-down,
   As she rolled in the low-down lonesome low.

5. "Captain, captain,
   Take me on board!
   If you don't, you'll have to forfeit your word,
   For you promised in the low-down, low-down, low-down,
   For you promised in the low-down lonesome low."

6. "Sailor boy, sailor boy,
   Don't appeal to me,
   For you drowned sixty souls when you sank the *Revery*,
   When you sank her in the low-down, low-down, low-down,
   When you sank her in the low-down lonesome low."

7. "It it weren't for the love
   That I bear for your men,
   I'd sink you the same as I sank them!
   I'd sink you in the low-down, low-down, low-down,
   I'd sink you in the low-down lonesome low."

8. Then he bared his chest
   And down swam he.
   He swam till he came to the bottom of the sea,
   And he drowned in the low-down, low-down, low-down,
   And he drowned in the low-down lonesome low.

MORE CHORAL MUSIC

Singing in chorus is a very exciting musical experience. It provides the opportunity to blend your voice with others to produce beautiful music.

In this section, you will learn vocal techniques that will further develop your voice and your singing potential. You will learn songs written in different languages representing different musical styles and periods. Learning to sing these songs expressively, together with the other choral skills you learn, will prepare you to participate in joyous singing experiences for the rest of your life.

Preparation for Singing "Hanerot Halalu"

- Listen to the song, following the notation to find musical "road signs" (first and second endings and fermatas).
- Warm up your voice. Lightly sing the "Bim Bom's," as you hold one finger just under your nostrils to feel the warmth of the air. Concentrate on trying to hum the "m's" at the end of each syllable.
- Sing the pitches in the D minor scale. Then sing one of the three pitches in the tune-up.

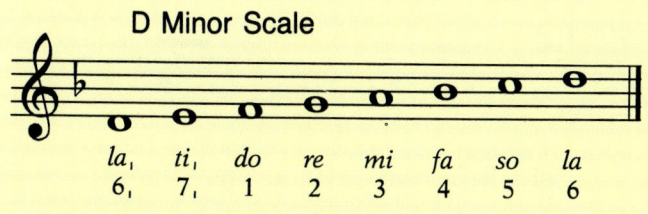

- Read the pitches in the pattern below. Notice that this pattern appears many times in the song.

Hanerot Halalu
A Song for Hanukah

Words and music by Baruch J. Cohon
Arranged by Blanche Chass

280

Preparation for Singing
"The Lion and the Unicorn"

This song is based on a children's poem written about 1800. It is about a fight between a lion and a unicorn.

- What does each animal actually represent?

- Warm up your voice before you sing. Practice the rhythm of the first phrase on page 284, saying "t's" instead of the words. You can feel your stomach muscles work as you do this.

- Clap the following rhythm patterns as you say the words.

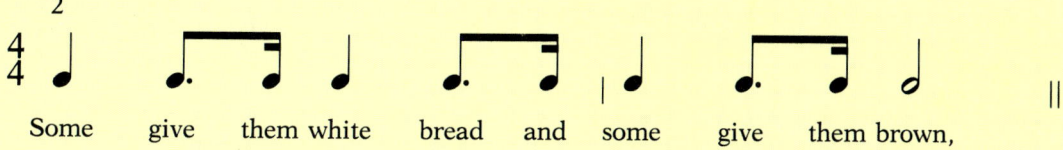

- Sing the following scale-wise melodic patterns for practice.

The Lion and the Unicorn

Preparation for Singing
"Sing a Song of Merry Christmas"

This Christmas song is an adaptation of "Kanon" on page 34. In this version, the three-part round is followed by a final homophonic section (melody with accompaniment).

- Warm up your voice while establishing the tonality of F major. Keep your voice light and bright.

- Read these five patterns.

- Look for these patterns in the song.

Sing a Song of Merry Christmas

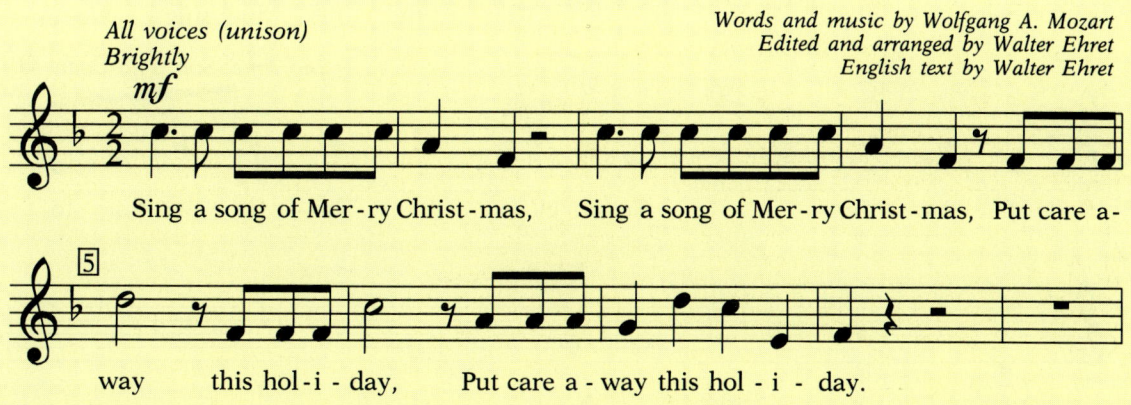

Preparation for Singing "Jubilate Deo"

The Latin text of this sixteenth-century canon means "Rejoice in the Lord, Alleluia!"

- Practice singing pure vowel sounds using these echo patterns.

Jubilate Deo
Rejoice in the Lord, Alleluia!

Music by Michael Praetorius
Text from Psalm 65
Edited by Doreen Rao

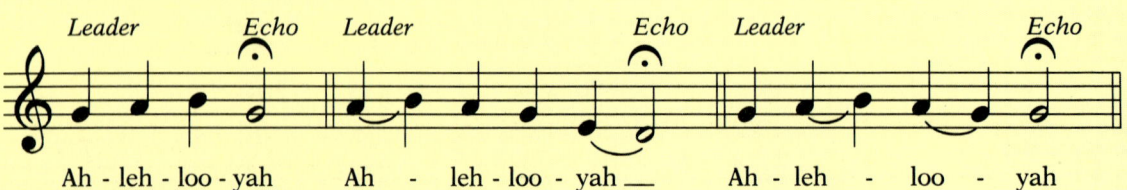

*Stress underscored syllables

JUBILATE DEO
from (Psalm 65) Music by Michael Praetorius, arr. by Doreen Rao. Copyright © 1986 by Boosey & Hawkes, Inc.
Reprinted by permission of Boosey & Hawkes, Inc.

Preparation for Singing "An Evening Falls"

The blue notes and syncopation tell you that this song is in blues style.

- Listen and decide if this style of music is appropriate for the words.

Singing the long phrases in "An Evening Falls" requires good breath support. Keep your shoulders relaxed and down as you do this breathing exercise.

inhale   exhale sss . . . 1 2 3 4 5 6 7 8 (9 10 11 12)

- Establish the tonality of F major by singing up and down its scale and continuing down to middle C.

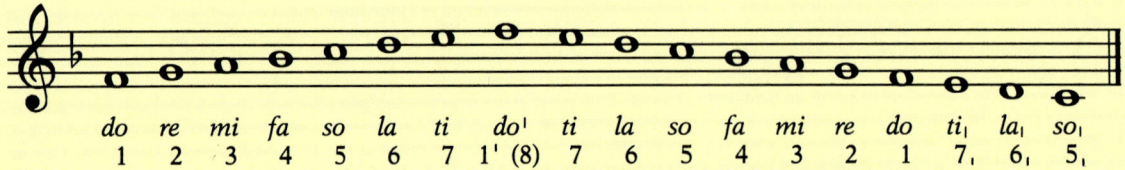

do re mi fa so la ti do¹ ti la so fa mi re do ti₁ la₁ so₁
1 2 3 4 5 6 7 1'(8) 7 6 5 4 3 2 1 7₁ 6₁ 5₁

- Sing these melodic patterns. Then find them in the song.

| 1 | | | 2 | | | 3 | | | 4 | | |
fa re do mi do so₁ re ti₁ so₁ so mi do
4 2 1 3 1 5₁ 2 7₁ 5₁ 5 3 1

When you sing, vowels carry the tone. Sing the vowel sound for as long as possible. Add the consonant at the last second.

wai - n, a - ll, ne - d, re - st, ri - ng, ea - ch, fee - t, hi - ll

AN EVENING FALLS
Music by Leroy Carr.
Accompaniment by Gordon Binkerd.
Copyright © 1978 by Boosey & Hawkes, Inc.
Reprinted by permission of Boosey & Hawkes, Inc.

PLAYING THE RECORDER

● Play B.   ● Play A.    ● Play G.

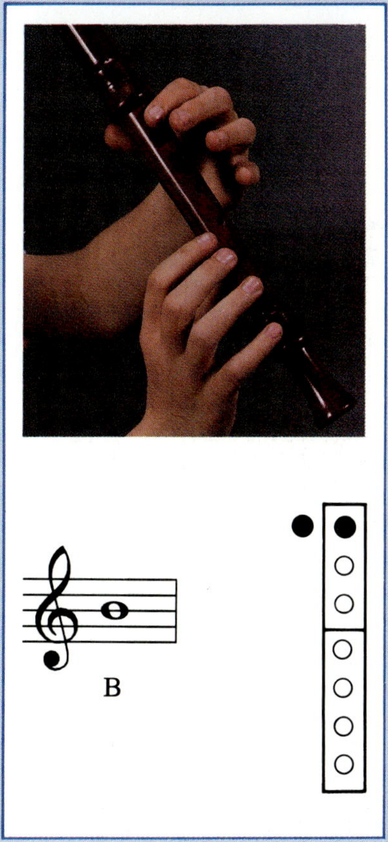

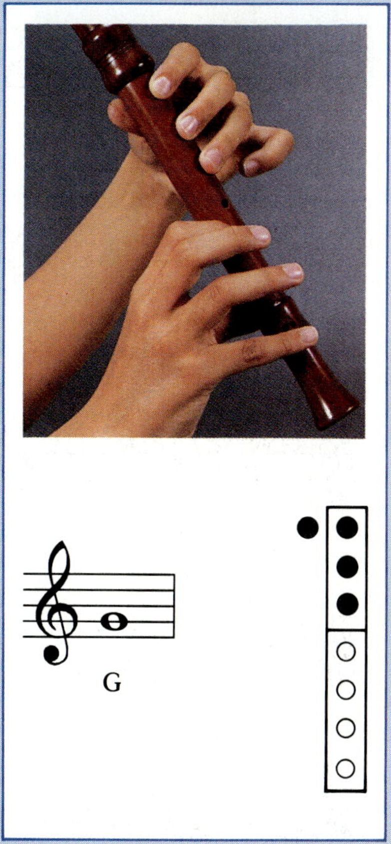

● Play each pitch as a long tone. Use a steady breath. Make the sound

SMOOTH

not

WAVY.

● Measure the length of your note. How long can you hold a good sound?

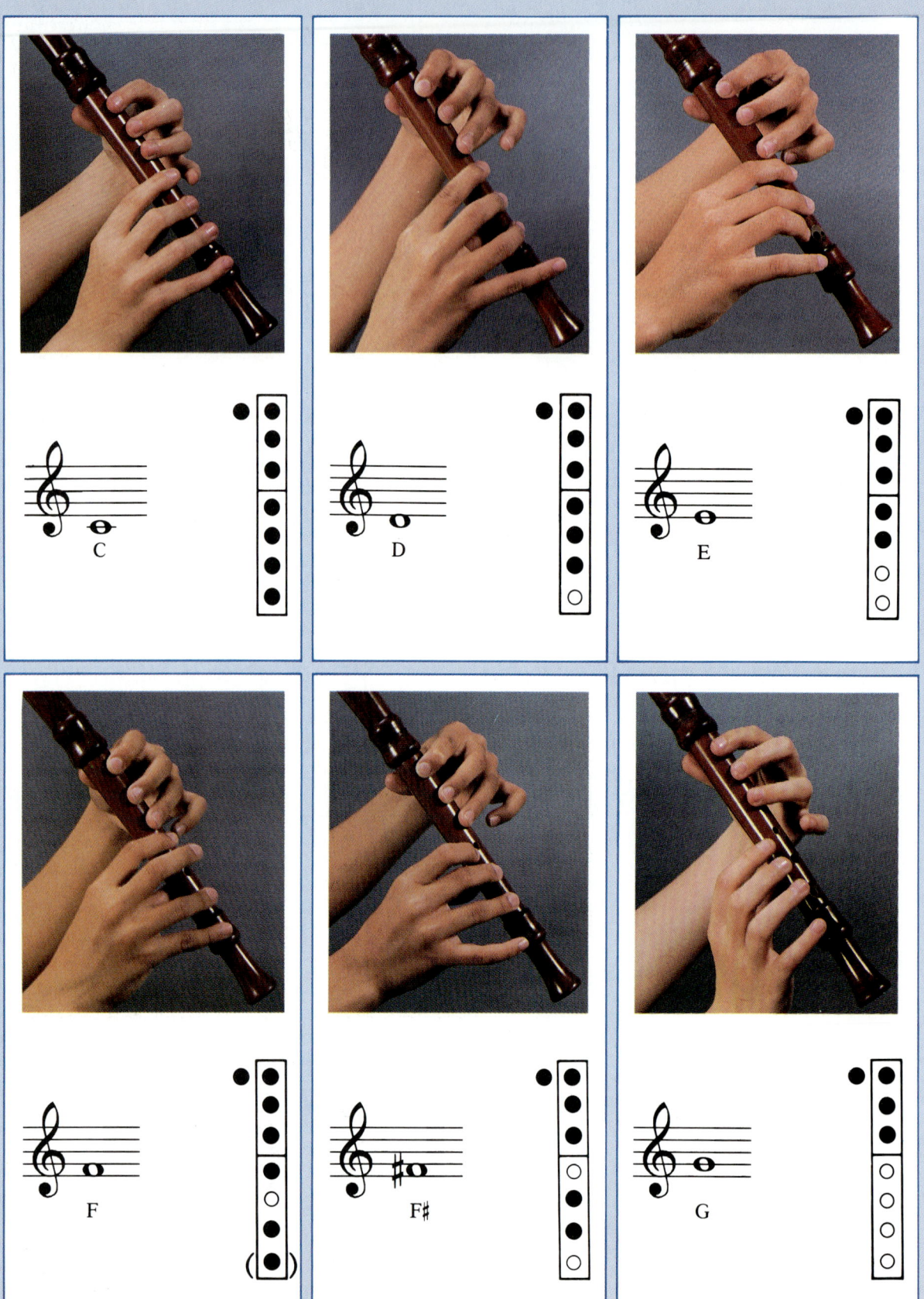

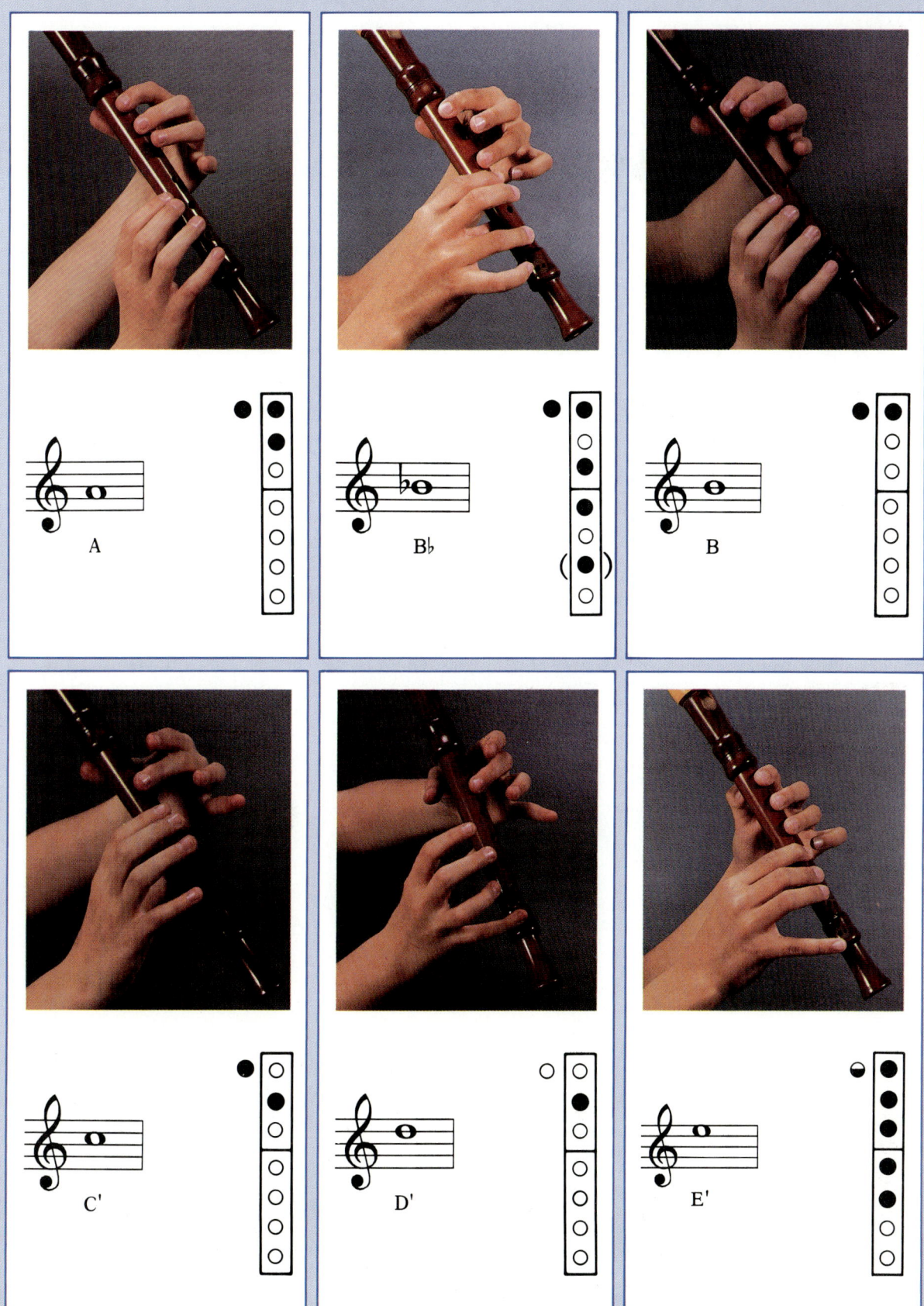

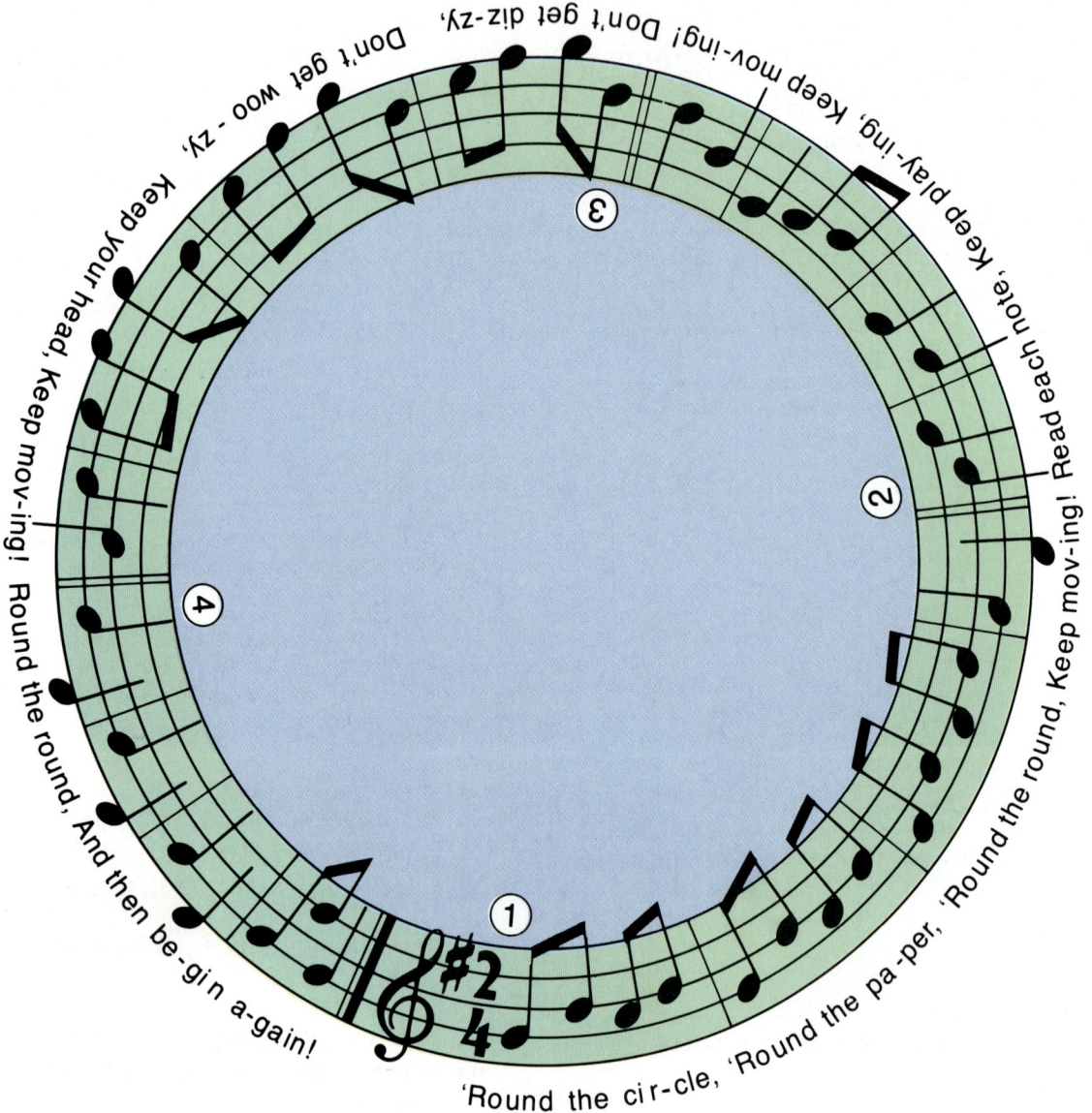

A Round Round
Created by Dorothy Gail Elliott

- Play this round. Start at ①. Follow the music around the circle. If you get dizzy, try playing the round backward.

- Play this round with three classmates.

GLOSSARY OF TERMS

accent a stress or emphasis on any given musical tone or chord, **126**

accompaniment a musical background for the melody, **56**

alto the lowest female voice, also called contralto; second highest part in choral or part music, **94**

ascending moving upward on a musical scale, **119**

atonal having no recognizable tonal center or key, **137**

ballad a song that tells a story, **150**

bar measure, **147**

bar line a vertical line on the staff marking off a measure, **41**

baroque period the period from 1600 to 1750, characterized by elaborate ornamentation in art, building design, and music, **15**

bass the lowest male voice; the lowest range of pitches of an instrument; the lowest part of a musical composition, **94**

bass clef (𝄢) same as F clef; a symbol placed on the fourth line of the staff, indicating that a note on that line is F below middle C, **114**

bluegrass a type of country music played by a band typically consisting of fiddle, mandolin, guitar, banjo, and bass, **215**

blue notes tones that are lowered one half step, most commonly the third, fifth, and seventh tones of the scale, **146**

blues a style of music that began in America in the early twentieth century, with roots in black American spirituals and work songs, **146**

brass family musical wind instruments made of brass or other metal, including trumpet, horn, trombone, and tuba, **226**

calypso a style of music from the West Indies, usually lively, rhythmic, and humorous, **222**

cambiata the stage when boys' voices first begin to change and they can sing some slightly lower pitches than before, **95**

canon a composition in which the melody is introduced and then imitated one or more times, **34**

chant a song or vocal expression that is repeated over and over usually in a rhythmic way, **224**

chorale a hymn with a plain melody and stately rhythm, usually sung in unison; also, an organized group of singers, **100**

chorale prelude a composition for organ based on the melody of a chorale and used as an introduction to the chorale, **101**

chord three or more tones produced at the same time, **23**

chromatic containing pitches not belonging to a given key; proceeding by consecutive half steps, **130**

chromatic scale a scale made up of all half steps, **132**

coda ending section, **20**

common time (C) another term for $\frac{4}{4}$ meter, **96**

concertino the smaller of the two groups of musicians used in baroque *concerto grosso* style, **15**

concerto a large work for solo instruments and orchestra usually written in three movements, 69

concerto grosso a style of composition developed during the baroque period (1600–1750), in which two groups of musicians, one small (*concertino*) and one large (*ripieno*), were used to alternate in an echo effect, 15

counter-melody a second melody; another way to create polyphony, 101

country music American music born in the rural South, with its roots in English and Scottish folk music, 215

cut time (₵) another term for $\frac{2}{2}$ meter, 190

damper pedal one of the three pedals on a piano, which holds felt bars (dampers) away from the strings so that they continue to vibrate, 59

descant a different melody, higher in pitch, sung with the main melody, 37

descending moving downward, 119

D. S. (*dal segno***)** repeat from the sign 𝄋, 120

duration the length of a tone, 12

dynamic markings words or symbols that show how loud or soft music is to be played or sung, 11

dynamics varying and contrasting degrees of intensity or loudness, 11

eighth note (♪), 10

eighth rest (𝄾), 35

episode the section of a fugue in which the main melody is not heard, 20

fermata (𝄐) a symbol placed over a note to show that it is to be held longer than its normal duration, 14

flat (♭) a symbol indicating that a tone is to be lowered a half step, 127

folk song a song that emerged from the culture of a group of people, usually of unknown authorship, 6

form the aspect of music having to do with the structure and design of a composition, 66

forte (*f*) loud, 11

fugue a composition in which three or more voices enter at different times and imitate the main melody in different ways according to a set pattern, 20

glissando a special effect created by sliding the fingers up or down the keys of a piano, 59

half note (♩), 10

half rest (𝄼), 35

half step a difference in pitch between any two adjacent keys on a keyboard instrument; for example, the distance between C and C♯ and between E and E♭, 118

harmony the sounding of two or more tones at the same time, 19

hemiola a pattern in $\frac{6}{8}$ meter in which two sets of three beats alternate with three sets of two beats, 220

homophony texture created when melody and harmony are used at the same time, 83

jazz music with roots in black American spirituals, blues, and ragtime, borrowing rhythms from Africa and Latin America and melodies from Europe, 158

ledger lines lines drawn above and/or below a staff to show pitches that are higher and/or lower than those on the staff, 12

legato smoothly connected in style, **37**

major scale the arrangement of whole and half steps in the following pattern: whole, whole, half, whole, whole, whole, half, **63**

measure the segment of music contained between two bar lines, **84**

melodic sequence a pattern within a melody that is repeated on different pitch levels, **68**

melody a series of pitches moving upward, downward, or staying the same; the tune, **14**

meter the grouping of beats and accents within a measure, as shown by the meter signature, **96**

meter signature the symbol on the staff at the beginning of a song that shows how beats are grouped and the kind of note that equals one beat, **84**

mezzo forte (*mf*) medium loud, **11**

mezzo piano (*mp*) medium soft, **11**

minor scale the arrangement of whole and half steps in the following pattern: whole, half, whole, whole, half, whole, whole, **63**

monophony texture created when melody is used alone, **83**

motif a short musical idea; a short rhythmic or melodic pattern, **32**

movement a part or self-contained section of a larger composition, such as a symphony, sonata, or concerto, **69**

musical notation way of writing music, **12**

nationalistic a style of music in which composers use folk music, typical dance rhythms, or literature of their country to express pride in that country, **60**

Neo-Classic style a type of music in which styles of music from the past are used in modern ways, **139**

note one of the symbols used to express the relative time value of tones, **10**

octave the distance between two pitches having the same name and located twelve half steps apart, **137**

opera a drama with costumes and scenery, in which all or most of the text is sung, **49**

oratorio a religious story told by soloists, chorus, and orchestra, but not acted on a stage, **82**

ostinato a repeated melodic or rhythmic pattern, **41**

overture a musical introduction to a larger work, such as an opera, **49**

percussion family musical instruments that are struck to produce a sound, including drums, cymbal, xylophone, tambourine, and piano, **226**

piano (*p*) soft, **11**

pitch the highness or lowness of a tone, **12**

polonaise a stately Polish court dance in $\frac{3}{4}$ time; also, the music for this dance, **60**

polyphony texture created when two or more melodies are used at the same time, **83**

polytonal music music in which two or more different scales, each with its own tonal center, are used at the same time, **136**

prelude music designed as an introduction to another work; a short self-contained piece, **21**

quarter note (♩), **10**

quarter rest (𝄽), **35**

ragtime a style of music in which the melody is strongly syncopated while the accompaniment keeps a steady beat, **156**

refrain a section of a song which repeats at the end of each stanza or verse, **72**

relative minor a minor key having the same key signature as the major key three half steps higher; for example, A minor is the relative minor of C major, **129**

Renaissance period a period of European history (1430–1600) characterized by interest in classical literature and art, **22**

rest a symbol indicating silence, **35**

rhythm the organization of musical tones with regard to their duration as distinct from their pitches, **10**

ripieno the larger of the two groups of musicians used in the baroque *concerto grosso* style, **15**

rondo a musical form in which the first section (A) is repeated after each contrasting section, **91**

round a song in which the voices sing the same melody but begin at different times, **11, 16**

scale an ascending or descending series of pitches arranged in order by a specified scheme of whole and half steps, **63**

scale-wise moving up or down the scale step by step, **114**

sharp (♯) a symbol indicating that a tone is to be raised a half step, **132, 199**

sixteenth note (♪), **85**

skip a distance in pitch of more than one step higher or lower, **38, 62**

soft pedal one of three pedals on a piano, which moves the hammer sideways so that not all the strings are struck when a key is played, **59**

soprano the highest female voice, classified as dramatic, lyric, or coloratura, according to tone quality and range, **94**

sostenuto pedal one of three pedals on a piano, which sustains only the notes which are being played at the moment the pedal is pushed down, **59**

spirituals one of the best-known types of black American music, which originated in the South before the Civil War, **144**

staccato detached or disconnected in style, **37**

staff set of five lines and four spaces on which music is written to show the pitches of the notes, **12**

step a distance in pitch of one note higher or lower, **38, 62**

string family one of the four groups of instruments in the orchestra, composed of violin, viola, cello, bass, and harp, **226**

subject the main melody in a fugue, **20**

suite an instrumental composition consisting of a succession of short pieces, **112**

symphonic poem an orchestral work that tells a story or creates a mood, **71**

symphonic suite an orchestral piece containing a series of movements, which are often arrangements of music from folk dances, ballets, operas, plays, or movies, **133**

symphony an orchestral work usually in three or four contrasting movements, **32**

syncopation a rhythm pattern that has unexpected sounds and silences, **41, 144**

synthesizer an electronic instrument that can imitate the sound of almost any existing instrument, **25**

tempo markings words that indicate how fast or slow a musical composition is to be played, **205**

tenor the highest male voice; in choral or part music, the part above the bass; the name given to one member of certain types of instruments, such as the tenor recorder, **94**

texture the way melody and harmony combine to create layers of sound, **8**

theme melody upon which a composition is based, **64**

threnody a song or poem of mourning, **183**

tie a curved line that combines the durations of the connected notes, **10**

tonal center the pitch around which the melody of a piece seems to center; often the last pitch, **119**

tonal music music that focuses the sound around one tonal center, **137**

tone a sound having pitch, **23**

tone color the unique sound of each instrument, **15**

tone row a prearranged series of tones not in a major or minor key, **137**

treble clef (𝄞) same as G clef; indicates that the pitch G is located on the second line above middle C, **114**

twelve-bar blues progression a chord pattern used in the style of American folk music called "blues," **147**

twelve-tone music a style of music based on a tone row that includes all twelve tones of the chromatic scale, **137**

unison two or more instruments or voices playing or singing the same pitches at the same time, **154**

voice vocal or instrumental part of a composition, **20**

voice range how high or low a person can sing, **94**

whole note (𝅝), **10**

whole rest (𝄻), **35**

whole step a distance equal to two half steps, **118**

whole-tone scale a kind of scale that uses only whole steps and does not sound either major or minor, **134**

woodwind family musical instruments that are played by blowing air through them, including flute, oboe, clarinet, and saxophone, **226**

CLASSIFIED INDEX

Folk Songs

African
A Ram Sam Sam, **250**
Benue, **105**
Ibo, **105**
Samanfo, **104**

African American
Dry Bones, **40**
Ev'ry Time I Feel the Spirit, **144**
Gospel Train, The, **247**
Old Ark, The, **242**
Rock-a-My-Soul, **6**
This Train, **145**
Who's That Yonder, **240**

American. See also *African American*
Autumn, **37**
City Blues, The, **148**
Cotton Eye Joe, **246**
Dinah, **241**
I Spurred My Horse, **243**
Joe Turner Blues, **146**
Lonesome Valley, **10**
Mama Don't 'Low, **230**
Perry Merry Dictum Dominee, **245**
Turkish Revery, The, **272**

Australian
Kookaburra, **249**

Bahamian
John B. Sails, **234**

Canadian
Huron Carol, The, **86**
Land of the Silver Birch, **244**

Czechoslovakian
Ifca's Castle, **265**

Dutch
We Gather Together, **75**

English
Come, Follow, **16**
God Rest You Merry, Gentlemen, **252**
Greensleeves, **9**
Lovely Joan, **14**
Oh, How Lovely Is the Evening, **134, 249**
Oliver Cromwell, **124**
Scarborough Fair, **202**
Sing Together, **250**
Summer Is A-Comin' In, **181**

Finnish
Harvest Time, **259**

Greek
Gerakina, **218**

Hungarian
Sing It All Together, **62**

Israeli
Do-Di-Li, **91**
Hava Nagila, **258**
Toembaï, **84**

Jamaican
Matilda, **228**

Traditional
Row, Row, Row Your Boat, **197**
Sandy McNab, **270**

Welsh
Deck the Halls, **96**

Holidays and Special Days

December
Carol of the Drum, **254**
Deck the Halls, **96**
Do-Di-Li, **92**
Do You Hear What I Hear? **89**
God Rest You Merry, Gentlemen, **252**
Hanerot Halalu, **280**

Hark! The Herald Angels Sing, **253**
Huron Carol, The, **86**
Rockin' Around the Christmas Tree, **256**
Sing a Song of Merry Christmas, **289**
Time for Acceptance and Love, **80**

Patriotic
America, **154**
America, the Beautiful, **152**

Thanksgiving
We Gather Together, **75**

Musicals
Song Sleuth
Find the Words, **171**
Harmony Sandwich, **170**
Listen to the Rhythm, **168**
On a Melody, **169**

We Can Do It If We Try, **172**
Write a Song, **166**

Why the Sun and Moon Live in the Sky
Ibo, **105**
Samanfo, **104**

Nature, Seasons, Out-of-Doors
Autumn, **37**
Autumn Canon, **251**
Harvest Time, **259**
Land of the Silver Birch, **244**
Orion, **110**
Tumbling Tumbleweeds, **131**

Poems
Enter This Deserted House, **46**
Music, **209**
Night, **109**

LISTENING SELECTIONS

"America" (version 2), performed by the Mormon Tabernacle Choir, **155**

Atmospheres by György Ligeti, **212**

"The Ballad of Billy the Kid" by Billy Joel, **150**

"Blue Monk" by Thelonious Monk, **160**

"Bonnie Prince Charlie/Road to Lisdunvarna/Lark in the Morning" by Mike Cross, **27**

Brandenburg Concerto No. 2, Third Movement, by Johann Sebastian Bach, **15**

Concerto in A Minor, First Movement, by Edvard Grieg, **69**

Concierto de Aranjuez, First Movement, by Joaquín Rodrigo, **219**

"Copacabana" from *Saudades do Brasil* by Darius Milhaud, **232**

Fantasia on "Greensleeves" by Ralph Vaughan Williams, **14**

Finlandia by Jean Sibelius, **71**

"Flight of the Bumblebee" by Nicolai Rimsky-Korsakov, **132**

🎵 *The Flying Dutchman* Overture by Richard Wagner, **49**

🎵 "Freddie Freeloader" by Miles Davis, **159**

🎵 Fugue in G Minor ("The Little") by Johann Sebastian Bach, **21**

🎵 "Gargoyles" by Otto Luening, **233**

🎵 "Greensleeves" performed on harpsichord by Igor Kipnis, **23**

🎵 "The Gunners Dream" from *The Final Cut* by Pink Floyd, **182**

🎵 "Hallelujah" from *Messiah* by George Frederick Handel, **83**

🎵 "Hickory Hollow," performed by Banks and Shane, **215**

🎵 "Jesu, Joy of Man's Desiring" (chorale), from Cantata No. 147 by Johann Sebastian Bach, **100**

🎵 "Jesu, Joy of Man's Desiring" (chorale prelude), from Cantata No. 147 by Johann Sebastian Bach, **101**

🎵 "Lovely Joan," **14**

🎵 "Mama Don't 'Low" performed by Banks and Shane, **231**

🎵 *Maple Leaf Rag* by Scott Joplin, **156**

🎵 "Mars" from *The Planets* by Gustav Holst, **112**

🎵 *The Moldau* by Bedřich Smetana, **64**

🎵 "Play of the Waves" from *La Mer* by Claude Debussy, **135**

🎵 Polonaise in A Flat Major by Frédéric Chopin, **60**

🎵 Prelude for Piano, No. 2 by George Gershwin, **158**

🎵 "Putnam's Camp, Redding, Connecticut" from *Three Places in New England* by Charles Ives, **136**

🎵 "Rocky Top" performed by Banks and Shane, **215**

🎵 "Roll Over Beethoven," by Electric Light Orchestra, **33**

🎵 "Russian Dance" from *Petrushka* by Igor Stravinsky, **123**

🎵 "The Sauce," performed by Lee Ritenour, **225**

🎵 "Shadowdance" by Shadowfax, **213**

🎵 "Staywithit" by Barbara Staton, **203**

🎵 Symphony No. 5, First Movement, by Ludwig van Beethoven, **32**

🎵 Symphony No. 94 ("Surprise" Symphony), Second Movement, by Franz Joseph Haydn, **229**

🎵 *Symphony of Psalms*, First Movement, by Igor Stravinsky, **138**

🎵 "Tarantella" from *The Fantastic Toyshop (La Boutique Fantasque)* by Rossini-Respighi, **198**

🎵 Three Pieces from *Eight Fragments* by Anton Webern, **137**

🎵 *Threnody for the Victims of Hiroshima* by Krzysztof Penderecki, **183**

🎵 *When Lilacs Last in the Dooryard*

🎵 *Young Person's Guide to the Orchestra* ("Variations and Fugue on a Theme of Purcell") by Benjamin Britten, **227**

ALPHABETICAL SONG INDEX

A
America, **154**
America, the Beautiful, **152**
A Ram Sam Sam, **250**
Autumn, **37**
Autumn Canon, **251**

C
Camptown Races, **248**
Carol of the Drum, **254**
Catch a Falling Star, **114**
City Blues, The, **148**
Come, Follow, **16**
Consider Yourself, **194**
Cotton Eye Joe, **246**

D
Deck the Halls, **96**
Dinah, **241**
Do-Di-Li, **91**
Dona Nobis Pacem, **257**
Do You Hear What I Hear? **89**
Dry Bones, **40**

E
Earthsounds, **276**
Evening Falls, An, **295**
Ev'ry Time I Feel the Spirit, **144**

F
Find the Words, **171**
Follow Me, **17, 260**

G
Gerakina, **218**
Ghost Ship, The, **42**
Give My Regards to Broadway, **190**
God Rest You Merry, Gentlemen, **252**
Gospel Train, The, **247**
Greensleeves, **9**
Guantanamera, **262**

H
Hanerot Halalu, **280**
Happiness, **264**
Hark! The Herald Angels Sing, **253**
Harmony Sandwich, **170**
Harvest Time, **259**
Hava Nagila, **258**
Hello! My Baby, **157**
Horseman, The, **128**
Huron Carol, The, **86**

I
Ibo, **105**
I Can See Clearly Now, **210**
Ifca's Castle, **263**
I Shall Sing, **126**
Island in the Sun, **222**
I Spurred My Horse, **243**

J
Joe Turner Blues, **146**
John B. Sails, **234**
Jubilate Deo, **292**

K
Kanon, **34**
Kookaburra, **249**

L
Land of the Silver Birch, **244**
Lean on Me, **120**
Let Love Come Near, **56**
Lift Ev'ry Voice and Sing, **266**
Limbo Like Me, **267**
Lion and the Unicorn, The, **284**
Listen to the Rhythm, **168**
Lonesome Valley, **10**
Lovely Joan, **14**

M

Mama Don't 'Low, **230**
Matilda, **228**
Mule Train, **268**

O

Oh, How Lovely Is the Evening, **249**
Oh, How Lovely Is the Evening (Whole-Tone Version), **134**
Old Ark, The, **242**
Oliver Cromwell, **124**
On a Melody, **169**
One Brick at a Time, **176**
Orion, **110**
Over the Sea to Skye, **200**

P

Perry Merry Dictum Dominee, **245**
Promised Land, **186**

R

Rock-a-My-Soul, **6**
Rockin' Around the Christmas Tree, **256**
Rocky Top, **214**
Row, Row, Row Your Boat, **197**

S

Samanfo, **104**
Sandy McNab, **270**
Scarborough Fair, **202**
Sing a Rainbow, **270**

Sing a Song of Merry Christmas, **289**
Sing It All Together, **62**
Sing Together, **250**
So Long, **150**
Song of Peace, **70**
Summer Is A-Comin' In, **181**

T

Take Me Home, Country Roads, **216**
That's What Friends Are For, **2**
Thing, The, **38**
This Train, **145**
Time for Acceptance and Love, **80**
Toembaï, **84**
Tumbling Tumbleweeds, **131**
Turkish Revery, The, **272**
Tzena, Tzena, **18**

V

Viva, Viva La Musica, **13**

W

We Are Family, **72**
We Can Do It If We Try, **172**
We Gather Together, **75**
Who's That Yonder? **240**
Write a Song, **166**

Y

You've Got a Friend, **274**

(Photo credits continued from page v)

MONKMEYER PRESS: 7. THE MUSEUM OF MODERN ART: Acquired through the Lillie P. Bliss Bequest, 117. NEW YORK PUBLIC LIBRARY, PICTURE COLLECTION: 1TCR. OMNI-PHOTO COMMUNICATIONS: © Elihu Blotnick, 3BR; © S. Rotner, 73L. PEABODY MUSEUM, HARVARD UNIVERISTY: photographed by Hillel Burger (T858-2), 87T, (T919-1), 87B. PHOTOGRAPHERS ASPEN: © Nicholas DeVore III, 232. PHOTO RESEARCHERS: © Inger Abrahmsen/Rapho Division, 55TR; © Archiv, 15, 20, 22, 32; © Fred Baldwin, 54–5TC; © Wesley Bocxe, 155; © Louis Goldman, 79TR; © Richard Hutchings, 3BL; © Bonny Jaques, 55C; © George E. Jones III, 137L; © Angelina Lax, 190TL; © Jeff Lepore, 108–9B; © Fred Lyon, 63; © Will McIntrye, 74BR; © Lawrence Migdale, 74BL; © R. Rowan, 30TL; © Anne Sager, 174–5B; © Gerry Souter, 137R. © GEORGE PICKOW: 26TR. QUESTAR MARITIME COLLECTION: 48. © DAVID RENTAS: 31C, courtesy, New York Philharmonic. RETNA, LTD: © John Bellissimo, 8B; © Andy Freeberg, 225; © Gilles Larrain, 159L; © Stephen Morley, 182; © David Redfern, 159R, 160; © Rocky Widner, 79TL. © HENRY RIES: 1C. © VICTORIA BELLER SMITH: 24T, 47, 66, 67, 95, 122T, 184, 185, 204, 236, 237. SMITH GALLERY, NY: 201. SOVFOTO/TASS: 133T. STAR FILE PHOTOS: © John Lee, 26TL,BL,C,BR. Courtesy, STEINWAY & SONS: 58 both. STOCK BOSTON: © Patrice Flesch, 230. THE STOCK MARKET: © Mark E. Gibson, 175TR; © Brownie Harris, 24B; © Marcia Keegan, 145; © Jeff Perkell, 142–3B; © PROCTOR, vii, viii–ix; © Richard Steedman, 149TL. STOCKPHOTOS: © Will Curwen, x-1B. © MARTHA SWOPE: 123BR, 139R, 176, 193 all, 194. TAURUS PHOTOS: © Pam Hasegawa, 96. REGINALD WICKHAM: 30–1B. WOODFIN CAMP & ASSOCIATES: © Craig Aurness, 152; © Chuck Fishman, 143LC; © Robert Frerck, 208TR; © Stephanie Maze, 220; © Bill Weems, 174–5TC; © Adam Woodfitt, 203R; © Mike Yamashita, 109RC.

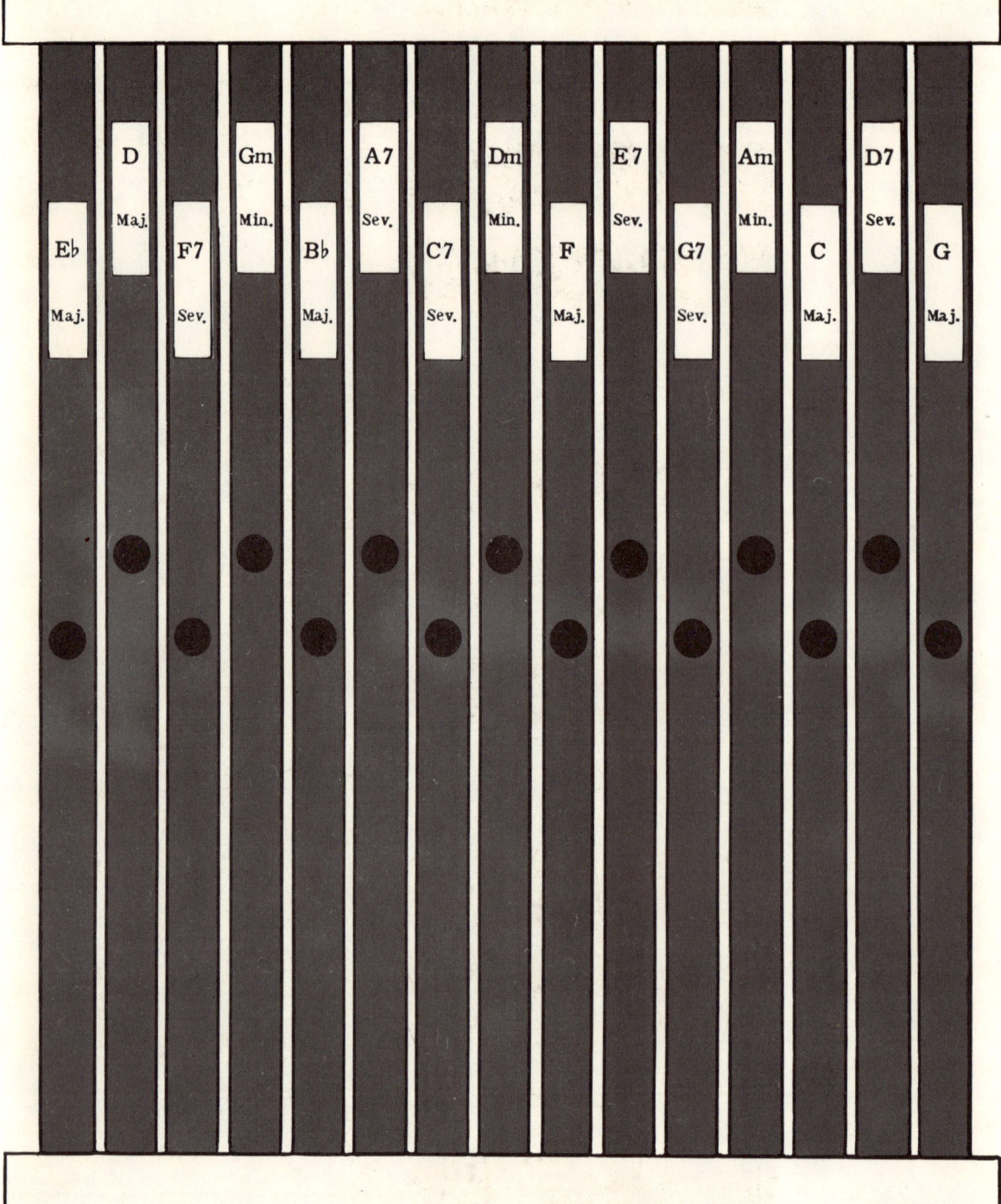